VISUALIZATION
The uses of imagery in the health professions

VISUALIZATION
The uses of imagery in the health professions

Errol R. Korn

Karen Johnson

The Dorsey Professional Series

DOW JONES-IRWIN
Homewood, Illinois 60430

ISBN 0-87094-403-7

Library of Congress Catalog Card No. 82-73617

Printed in the United States of America

1 2 3 4 5 6 7 8 9 0 K 0 9 8 7 6 5 4 3

This book is dedicated to the staff of Bay General
Community Hospital, Chula Vista, California, and, in
particular, the administration, for giving us the
opportunity to implement these techniques.
Acknowledgment is also given to the staff of the
Pain Rehabilitation Unit of Bay General Community
Hospital for eagerly learning these techniques and
applying them with great enthusiasm and success.

Preface

Medicine and medical care are at the present time undergoing a type of revolution. Although the technical and scientific aspects of medical care have grown beyond most people's expectations and have led to tremendous advances in conquering heretofore significant problems, the public has become increasingly sophisticated and assertive and thus less satisfied with the quality of medical care. These technical advances, in turn, have led to unreasonable expectations.

As medicine has grown more scientific, it has become less humanistic. In some scientific fields, however, the reverse is true. The physicists have shown us that as we become more and more scientific, we eventually get to a point at which the traditional scientific paradigm fails to give satisfactory answers. At that point, there seems to be a more unifying and actually more humanistic explanation. We believe that some of these principles can be applied to medical care and thereby allow the integration of scientific paradigms with humanistic philosophy.

It has been known for many years that we use only part of our mind's capacity. We also know that much of what transpires in the mind takes place at levels beyond our conscious awareness. Scientific evidence has demonstrated that much of what we previously thought of as uncontrollable is controllable if we learn the proper method of exercising this control. These techniques have been available for thousands of years.

In order to understand and utilize these methods, a new paradigm of health care must be devised. A basic feature of this paradigm is that mind-body dualism is a conceptual fallacy. In this new model, the mind and body are intricately interconnected, and changes in any part of either body affect every part of both. When we expand our belief system to include that concept, then we realize that there are no diseases that are purely physical, just as there are no diseases that are purely mental. Therefore, mental processes can change even the most grossly physical aspects of disease. In this book, we present the scientific and practical evidence that this can be accomplished and describe techniques that can lead to these changes.

Although this book emphasizes techniques that can be used by the health care professional, it is intended to stimulate an even higher purpose. By incorporating these principles into one's own life, anyone can learn to effect the changes which he or she wishes to effect. Additionally, by incorporating these changes as a way of life, the dynamics will be set in motion that effect changes in all those with whom one associates. We all know of the people in every profession, no more adequately trained than most, who consistently obtain better results both in the profession and in their own lives. Rather than ignoring the subtle qualities that lead to this success, by incorporating the known techniques into one's own life, this success is within the reach of all. Actually, we are all born with the capacity to integrate these functions within our lifestyle and to obtain the benefits derived from them.

There is mounting evidence in the scientific community that there is a sense of order within a human being, and the tendency is to move from disorder to order. This is manifested in humans by the natural tendency to expel offending matter such as bacteria and toxins. It implies that our nature is one of moving toward health and of eschewing disease. Our tendency is to interfere with this natural behavior that leads to most, if not all, of our diseases and also leads to interference with the natural order of healing. What we try to make clear in this book is that not only can we learn to stop interfering with this natural process towards order, but we can actually learn how to direct the activity of the mind in intervening in any function to lead to realization of a desired goal.

The book is divided into two sections. In Section I the general concepts are presented. They are supported by scientific and experiential data and allow the reader to understand and apply them to specific problems. Included are a derivation of a new model of health and an explanation of mind-brain functioning. In Section II, the practical uses of visualization are outlined. Attention is given to the scientific interests of the various health care professions and applications of visualization in counteracting the stress response. Specific disorders are discussed from a multispecialty interest with particular emphasis on pain.

We trust that this book will mark the beginning of a new understanding of one's profession. But even more, we hope that this book will lead to a new understanding of one's own life.

Errol R. Korn
Karen Johnson

Contents

SECTION II
Specific applications

Section I

General concepts

Chapter 1

The mind and the body

As we all know, the human being is an extremely complex organism. We are composed of many interconnected organ systems, each composed of large numbers of cells. These systems form a hierarchy of organization, which begins with the particle physicist. Young[1] has placed these levels of organization in perspective by noting that the human being is composed of 10^{27} proton-electron pairs. The first level of these pairs is atoms, with 20 proton-electron pairs per atom. The next level is that of the molecule. There are approximately 2×10^7 atoms per molecule. Some molecules (e.g., DNA) may have a very high degree of organization. The next level, that of the cell, is so complex it is still not understood.[1] The human being, on the multicellular level of organization, is composed of approximately 10^{14} cells. This is the highest level of complexity, but it still functions as a unit in such a way that every cell is coordinated in a hierarchy millions of times more complex than any state that has ever existed on earth.[1]

It seems unreasonable to believe that this complexity, i.e., the human being, functions in a completely random manner without any sort of control mechanism. It will be demonstrated that there is indeed a control mechanism which is quite exquisite. We will call it mind-brain.

For our purposes, we will use mind-brain as one functional entity because any discussion as to the identity or nonidentity of mind and brain

3

is beyond the scope of this book. However, we believe that consciousness and mind functions are not merely epiphenomena of brain activity, but are realities that transcend the anatomical structure called brain. For those who are more interested in this matter, we would suggest Barbara Brown's book, *Supermind*[2] and *Toward a Science of Consciousness* by Kenneth R. Pelletier.[3]

The brain and the nervous system

In spite of the controversy with respect to the associations between mind and brain, there is little doubt that the brain is responsible for many of the functions of the mind. Because we will propose that the mind-brain is at the apex of the hierarchy of mind-body functioning, and that the mind-brain exercises this control through the nervous and endocrine systems, it is important to have some idea as to the functions of the various parts of the brain and nervous system.

For our purposes, the approach used by Pelletier[3] is most appropriate; that is, a description of the brain from the lower (older) to higher (newer) levels. The brain contains 10^{10} neurons, approximately the same number of neurons as there are stars in the Milky Way.[4] These neurons are interconnected in a vast web, with each neuron exercising intricate inter-communication with great numbers of other neurons, and in turn being influenced by countless others. Some idea as to the complexity of this structure can be imagined by conceptualizing a telephone switchboard. With this idea, it is not difficult to understand how one part of the brain can affect another part or that the brain is the ultimate of feedback systems. Almost every part of the brain may act in positive or negative feedback with almost every other part of the brain, thereby affecting and delicately coordinating the limits of function.

The lowest portions of the brain, the subcortical areas, are primarily involved with regulating the functions necessary to the maintenance of life. The digestive, cardiovascular, respiratory, urinary, and vascular systems are the primary concern of the subcortical areas. Information is conveyed to the subcortical areas from the viscera by means of afferent neurons, and motor responses are transmitted back to the viscera by efferent neurons. These neurons reside within nerves that are components of the autonomic nervous system.

The *medulla oblongata,* myelencephalon, or "marrow" brain, is the first portion of the subcortex and the first portion of what is called the brain stem. Anatomically, this is located just proximal to the spinal cord and is somewhat larger in diameter than that structure. The nuclei of many cranial nerves are located in this area, including the hypoglossal nucleus (taste); the nucleus ambiguus (the motor nucleus of two cranial nerves, the glossopharyngeal and vagus); the motor nucleus of the vagus; the sensory nucleus of the vagus; and the cochlear nucleus (hearing). Because the vagus nerve provides motor and sensory function to the heart, lungs, digestive tract, and renal areas, the medulla is important as a center involving these vital functions. Syndromes involving the vagus nerve can lead to death, gut irregularities, cardiac arrhythmias, and difficulties with regulation of respiration. Also located in the medulla are the respiratory center, the cardiovascular reflexes, which are necessary for maintenance of blood pressure, and the emetic center.

The structure in the brain stem immediately superior or proximal to the medulla is the *pons*. Like the medulla, the pons also serves as a conduit for ascending and descending nerve tracts connecting the lower part of the body and spinal cord with the higher brain centers. Certain brain stem nuclei are located in the pons, and recent evidence supports the concept of the pons as a major component in the regulation of sleep.

The *cerebellum* is located posterior to the pons and the medulla and, although separate from the brain stem, lies at about the same level as that structure. The cerebellum is primarily involved with regulation of position and movement, and with muscular coordination. The pons and cerebellum together are known as the *metencephalon* ("after" brain).

As we move from an inferior to a superior position, we move from older to newer centers. This appears to be a teleological manifestation since, in the early evolution of mammalian life, the regulation of the vital life functions was most important for survival. As mammals became more complicated, the more complex functions developed. Superiorly, the next area encountered is the midbrain, or mesencephalon. This small area, which is involved with eye movement and partial regulation of voluntary muscle activity, is located between the pons and the cerebral hemispheres.

Proximally, the next area encountered is the *diencephalon,* which includes the thalamus, geniculate bodies, epithalamus, subthalamus, metathalamus, and hypothalamus.

The nerves responsible for conveying the sensations of pain, temperature, touch, and position and vibration sense all pass through the thalamic area. The *thalamus* seems to play a critical role in some types of sensation and represents the highest stages of sensory pathway projection in the subcortical areas. The cortical pathways originate in the thalamus. There is a syndrome called the *thalamic syndrome,* which is present in some people with strokes involving the thalamic area. This causes intense pain, considered by some to be the most severe pain experienced by humans, and one for which there is little treatment. There is some evidence that the thalamus also plays a mediating role in somatic skeletal muscle functions. Thalamic areas also constitute part of the arousal or reticular activating system described below.

The *hypothalamus* is a structure which has generated considerable interest in the past few decades. Parts of the hypothalamus secrete hormones (hypothalamic releasing factors) which govern the release of pituitary hormones. It is by this route that the hypothalamus (brain tissue) actually regulates endocrinological function by means of an intricate feedback mechanism. The hypothalamus also has the following attributes: (1) it is subject to regulatory influences from most other parts of the brain, including the higher structures; (2) it plays a role in temperature regulation and hunger; (3) it may be the location of a so-called pleasure center; (4) it may be involved in sleep regulation and food intake; and (5) it receives neural fibers from the higher centers such as the cerebral cortex and the limbic system, thereby being functionally associated with these areas and regulated by them to some degree.

The *basal ganglia* consist of gray matter located deep inside the cerebral hemispheres. With the cerebral cortex and cerebral white matter, they constitute the telencephalon (end brain). They consist of the corpus striatum, caudate nucleus, lenticular nucleus, globus pallidus, and amygdaloid nucleus. These nuclei are involved with regulation and integration of motor function.

The basal ganglia, along with associated parts of the cerebral cortex and midbrain, form the extrapyramidal system. This system is concerned with regulation of various types of movements, autonomic integration, and posture. Chemical neurotransmitters such as dopamine and acetylcholine are concentrated in this area of the brain, and disorders of synthesis or release of these compounds can result in parkinsonism, chorea, and athetosis.

An evolutionarily newer system, more functional than anatomical, is the *limbic system*. The limbic system is composed of portions of the cerebral cortex (frontal and temporal), hippocampus, cingulate gyrus, parts of the basal ganglia, and parts of the diencephalon (hypothalamic nuclei and thalamus). The limbic system has been called the visceral brain. Emotional states are reflected in, or corrolated with, electrophysiological activity in the limbic system.[5] The limbic system seems to be involved with the regulation and experience of emotion, consciousness, and behavior.

The newest portion of the brain, from an evolutionary standpoint, is the *cerebral cortex*. This structure consists of a thin layer of gray tissue covering the cerebral hemispheres. The surface area of the cortex is greatly increased because of the convolutions of the cerebral hemispheres. Portions of the cerebral cortices exercise control over the previously described lower areas of the brain. The central sulcus divides the frontal lobe anteriorly from the parietal lobe. The posterior central gyrus (parietal lobe) is the projection area for sensory modalities such as touch, pain, and temperature. Anterior to the central sulcus is the anterior central gyrus (frontal lobe), which is the primary motor projection cortex, controlling the voluntary muscle movements of the body. The visual cortex is located on the posterior surface of the brain, in the occipital lobe.

As noted previously, the temporal lobe, closely connected with the limbic system, is also the primary auditory and olfactory receptive area.

In addition to the primary motor cortex, the frontal lobe contains areas such as Broca's area, which is responsible for speech regulation. Most of the frontal lobe, however, has been associated with higher intellectual and psychic functions. These areas were called association areas but are now more commonly called uncommitted cortex.

In the evolution of mammals, the brain change which is the most marked is an increase in cortical tissue of the uncommitted type, i.e., not involved with primary or secondary motor or sensory functions.[6] These areas are most likely involved with the modulation and regulation of all of the brain functions and, we believe, are the areas anatomically responsible for the ability of thought and mental processes to change body physiology. It is interesting to note that there is a mammalian species on this planet that has more uncommitted cortex per unit weight than *Homo sapiens*—the cetaceans (dolphins and whales).

The *reticular activating system* (RAS) is composed of the reticular formation as well as portions of the subthalamus, hypothalamus, and thalamus. Initial studies demonstrated that this system was essential for initiating and maintaining awakeness and alertness. It thereby has an arousal function, activating the cerebral cortex to become receptive to ascending impulses transmitted from the somatic musculature and viscera. Its descending function may be similar but in the opposite direction. This suggests that the RAS may mediate those impulses from the periphery that will reach the higher centers in such a manner as to produce awareness of these stimuli. It also suggests that the RAS may determine which motor impulses from the higher centers actualize when reaching their target areas. Pelletier suggests that the RAS serves the

> . . . function of selecting and screening stimuli from the autonomic nervous system prior to their registration in the cortical, or more conscious, areas of the brain. Stimuli barred from conscious consideration and nevertheless registered—subliminally, are out of conscious awareness—where they may and do affect an individual's behavior.[7]

Pelletier notes that "the model suggests a continuum of consciousness, and defines the RAS as mediating conscious awareness along that con-

tinuum.''[7] The RAS mediates "conflicting information between the cortical and subcortical areas of the brain . . . (by) selecting which
information will be attended to and dominate the individual's perceptions.''[8] Although much is left to be accomplished in this area, considerable evidence already exists to implicate the RAS as the mediator
between neurological and psychological processes. If a neuroanatomic
structure or group of structures corresponding to the link between mind
and body is ever found, the RAS may serve this purpose.

The brain is extremely complex, both anatomically and functionally,
and what is known about the brain is only a very small part of what there
is to know. Almost every portion of the brain, either directly or with only
a few intermediary steps, is connected to every other part of the brain.
Therefore, it is apparent that any part of the brain can communicate with
and thereby modify functions of any other part of the brain. This ability is
in keeping with the functioning of the body generally, and the brain
specifically, as feedback systems. Feedback systems require precise control and modulation of alterations of function in any direction. The neuroanatomy of the brain serves as a perfect structural example for a
complex feedback system and demonstrates the interconnectedness between the body, autonomic and somatic, and the brain stem areas responsible for the direction of such a feedback system. The neuroanatomy of
the brain also demonstrates the anatomical pathways whereby the higher
brain centers can become aware of these functions and thereby assert
direction over them.

> Modern physics has rendered a model of the brain as a highly
> sensitive, poised system wherein the discharge of any one neuron
> contributes directly and indirectly to the excitation and inhibition of
> millions of other neurons within the very brief time of 20 millisec-
> onds.[9]

Although we do not have substantiated proof at this time as to how the
brain actually functions in this integrative manner, several theories have
been formulated, which will be discussed in Chapter 4.

Hemispheric function

All parts of the brain have multipotential. However, just as some parts
of the brain find it easier than others to differentiate into areas of specific
function (speech, motor, sensory, and so forth), each cerebral hemisphere
finds itself evolving functions that are characteristic of that hemisphere.

It has been known for a long time that the left cerebral hemisphere
exercises influence over the right side of the body, and vice versa.
However, it was not known until the work of Sperry et al[10] that each

cerebral hemisphere performs some functions uniquely related to that hemisphere.

In most people, the left hemisphere is considered the dominant hemisphere. This is true for right-handed people and for most left-handed people as well. The left hemisphere also houses the speech center in most Western people. There is some evidence, however, that the speech center for more spatial languages, such as Eastern languages, may have some right hemisphere coordination.

Sperry's observations were based upon studies performed in patients undergoing a commissurotomy. This procedure involved a severing of the corpus callosum, the structure connecting the two cerebral hemispheres. The procedure was performed in the 1960s to prevent the spread of seizures from one hemisphere to the other in people with severe, uncontrollable epilepsy.

Studies on these people led Sperry and his associates to conclude that each side of the brain acted differently and independently. In general, it was determined that the dominant hemisphere functions in a linear, logical, analytical, and verbal manner; whereas the nondominant hemisphere was more generalized, holistic, spatial, and intuitive. The differences are primarily in the mode or method of processing information.

Although there is still much controversy over the degree of specialization, and exactly which functions reside in each hemisphere, certain functions can be considered in the domain of each specifically. The left hemisphere operates cognitively and evaluates information in a logical, rational, sequential manner. It is involved with speech and words. In contrast, the right hemisphere is synchronous, intuitive, and synthetic. It deals with imagery and symbols rather than verbal modalities, is emotional in nature, and seems to predominate in such functions as dreaming, hypnosis, meditation, religious experiences, and drug-induced experiences.[11]

For example, if one were to experience a train with the left hemisphere, one would commence with the locomotive and sequentially examine each car until the caboose had been examined. This same information processed by the right hemisphere would involve a total view of the train as a whole functioning unit. The left hemisphere perceives each individual tree, while the right hemisphere perceives the forest as a whole.

The differences in the specialization of the hemispheres is probably not neuroanatomical in basis. It seems reasonable that each of these two basically different modes of processing information is important to our functioning and survival. It is optimal to perceive some things in a spatial, rational, left hemispheric fashion and others in a right hemispheric fashion. For most situations, a combination of both is important. As each of us develops through infancy and childhood, the right hemisphere begins to function primarily in its modes and the left hemisphere in its specific modes. The left hemisphere thereby deals more with analysis and reasoning, while the right hemisphere becomes more analogous to raw experience itself.[12]

These two different methods of functioning and processing information, plus the inherent, albeit suppressed, ability of each hemisphere to perform functions that the opposite hemisphere does more easily, gives us the flexibility which is so important in our ability to function as optimally as we do.

Many functions initially attributed to one hemisphere seem to be the property of both hemispheres. Creativity resides in both hemispheres, although some functions of the creative process, such as illumination, are probably right hemispheric functions. Music can be a function of either hemisphere. It seems as though professional musicians process music with the left hemisphere, whereas those untrained in music seem to appreciate more the holistic qualities of music using the right hemisphere.[13]

Recently, it has become fashionable to talk of utilizing the right hemisphere to a greater degree and to preach methods of training that area. Some of this is overreaction to our system and culture, which places more value on left hemispheric functions. Our schools are organized to teach predominantly in a left hemispheric manner. Many of the functions of day-to-day life are dependent upon left hemispheric functions. Therefore much of the value of the right hemisphere has been suppressed in our culture. Since many people tend to operate primarily in a left or right hemispheric mode, people who are basically right hemispheric tend to find many things difficult in our society. Much of what we will be discussing in this book will be based on increasing right hemispheric function. However, we wish to make it clear that we feel that neither the right hemisphere nor the left hemisphere should become predominant. Optimal functioning of the individual should mean optimal functioning and integration of both hemispheres, allowing us to use both in any situation. Thus we have a choice of which hemisphere is most optimal for the processing of, and reaction to, the information at hand. Therefore people who are predominantly left hemispheric in function might develop more right hemispheric abilities and then begin to integrate them more. The converse of this applies to people who are predominantly right hemispheric. As we will emphasize throughout this book, optimal health, functioning, and life in general depend not upon striving for one of two polar opposites, but rather upon maintaining a balance between the two. Very often we are able to experience something only by learning to experience its opposite: Without pain, for example, none of us would know the experience of pleasure. Those of us who spend our lives in fruitless search for elimination of pain never experience the fullness of pleasure and bliss that our life has to offer. Life, like brain functioning, should be a balance.

The mind-body connection and voluntary control of internal states

In the sixth century B.C. Socrates stated, "There is no illness of the body apart from the mind."[14] However, for the past 200 to 300 hundred years, we have been subject to a philosophy of dualism. We have treated the mind and body as separate entities. Even though brain and mind may not be identical, brain is a predominant part of mind. In our previous discussion of neuroanatomy, it is apparent that the mind-brain complex does have a significant amount of interconnection and intercommunication with the various parts of the body. From this alone, one would tend to doubt the concept of dualism.

The classical positions on the mind-body problem are well reviewed by Robert Holt.[15] The basic positions are those of *monism* and *dualism*. Monism is a belief in one fundamental reality. There are three forms of monism. (1) *Idealism:* The basic principle is that only the mind is real. This is a reductionistic viewpoint. (2) *Materialism:* Only matter is real. This, likewise, is reductionistic. (3) *Double aspect/identity:* Both mind and matter are but different aspects of one reality.

Dualism doctrines contend that there are two fundamentally different realms of reality. There are three subtypes of dualism. (1) *Metaphysical parallelism:* the belief that the two differing realms of reality are independent but are perfectly correlated and synchronized. (2) *Epiphenomenolism:* the belief that mental events are just epiphenomena of physical events. (3) *Interactionism:* the belief that there is a complex interaction between the mental and physical; i.e., that mental events can influence physical events and physical events can influence mental events.

The work of the past 10 years tends to favor the point that there is a complex interconnectedness between the mental and physical phenomena. Whether these are two fundamentally different realms of reality, or whether they are just different aspects of a complex total reality, is beyond the scope of this book. However, we believe there is little doubt that they are inescapably intertwined, and the more we learn to utilize this interconnectedness, the more we begin to take command over our own destiny.

The *autonomic nervous sytem* (ANS) supplies innervation to smooth muscles and glands throughout the body. It includes the endocrine system, viscera (heart, lungs, gastrointestinal tract, urinary tract), and blood vessels. Sensation is carried from these areas to the central nervous sytem, and motor impulses are conveyed in the opposite fashion. For many years it has been taught that the functions of the autonomic nervous system are autonomic or automatic. This presupposes that its functions are carried out below the level of conscious awareness; it was therefore assumed that autonomic functions were always uncontrollable by conscious mental activity. Neuroanatomically, a vast array of nerve fibers connect the autonomic centers in the lower areas of the brain to the cerebral cortex, where mental processes would have access to the ANS.

We have known for years of our conscious ability to direct certain autonomic functions. Almost all of us have had the experience of a purely mental process (thinking of our favorite food) causing activation or stimulation of an autonomic process (secretion of gastric acid). Likewise, by just thinking of a terrifying event, we can elevate our blood pressure, heart rate, and respiratory rate. All of these physiological phenomena, however, are considered to be bad. It seems as though we can direct undesirable phenomena but are unable to direct desirable phenomena. We will demonstrate, however, that anything we can learn to change in one direction, we can learn to change in the other. It seems that in our development, we easily learn to affect phenomena in a detrimental way rather than a beneficial way. Elmer and Alyce Green, two pioneer researchers in voluntary control of autonomic states, comment that

> every change in a physiological state is accompanied by an appropriate change in the mental-emotional state, conscious or unconscious; and conversely, every change in the mental-emotional state, conscious or unconscious, is accompanied by an appropriate change in the physiological state.[16]

For years, mystics have been teaching and practicing techniques designed to direct and control one's own internal functions. Scientists were reluctant to accept these statements and methods because of the limitations in measurability. In science, we tend not even to consider a phenomenon if we cannot measure it. In many cases, however, the inability to measure is due to our technology; i.e., the lack of proper tools for measurement rather than inherent untruths in the phenomenon itself. If we cannot evaluate a problem with complete objectivity due to lack of precision tools, we should not ignore it. While our scientists and investigators use the best tools available, one of the greatest scientists, Albert Einstein, used no external tool at all for many of his discoveries. His equipment consisted of his own mind in what were termed thought experiments.

The proper implication of objectivity is that one should always measure the errors of one's measurement, and resist the temptation to abandon measurement itself if complete accuracy is not possible.[17] In the past few decades, tools have become available to measure many autonomic functions precisely. The claim of voluntary control of internal states has been well documented. We will continue to use the term *voluntary control of internal states,* although Pelletier calls this "harmonious integration of voluntary and autonomic functions."[3] The investigations that have led to the demonstration of this control have developed into a discipline called biofeedback. Biofeedback demonstrates scientifically that human beings can develop conscious control over their internal states, and it provides the criteria and techniques that make this control possible.

In reality, the human being is a biofeedback or cybernetic system. Cybernetics may be defined as self-regulation and control achieved through sensing devices which measure the position of a vehicle with the condition of an environment and which, on this basis, make suitable adjustments to correct or regulate the vehicle or the environment.[18] The hierarchy of the nervous system, with the brain at its apex, is the means by which this regulation takes place. However, most of this occurs at unconscious levels, i.e., at the levels beyond those that we are aware of consciously. Our view of the unconscious is quite different from that of Sigmund Freud and more consistent with that of the eminent psychiatrist/hypnotherapist Milton Erickson. Rather than a bubbling cauldron of unresolved fears, conflicts, distorted perceptions, and guilt-initiated emotions, the unconscious is the control system by which all of our mind-body functions are conceptualized and integrated, and it is that part of the mind's structure that can receive our conscious desires and translate them into the myriad of actions necessary for the realization of those desires.

We are unable to localize the conscious and unconscious processes in the brain. However, Eccles feels that the convention of localization is that "conscious processes [are in] the cerebral cortex, and unconscious processes in the subcortical or diencephalic areas of the brain."[19] More likely, unconscious processes will be found to occur throughout the entire brain, according to the holographic principles outlines in Chapter 4. In addition, although we tend to accept the cerebral cortex as being the mediator of conscious processes, we believe that the evidence accumulated by biofeedback shows that conscious processes can even be in distinct subcortical areas, or if conscious processes are strictly the domain of the cerebral cortex, the interconnections between the cortex and subcortical areas can become so attuned that we become consciously aware of even the most autonomic of subcortical and brain stem functions. There is increasing evidence that the brain is the center of consciousness but that the entire nervous system of the body is responsible for various aspects of conscious awareness.[20]

By becoming consciously aware of changes in body functions, we can begin to direct and regulate these changes in purposeful fashion. The first important principle in developing these skills is becoming *aware* of the specific physiologic function to be controlled. At some level of our consciousness, we certainly must be aware of every physiologic function. If we were not aware of these functions at some level, we would not be able to control them with the precision that we do. However, as mentioned above, this control takes place at unconscious domains. Establishing control consciously necessitates becoming aware of the physiology at conscious levels. This can be accomplished without the need for any external devices. The purpose of this section is to demonstrate that we can perform control under circumstances which allow precise scientific measurement and documentation. This is what we feel to be the primary value of the technology of biofeedback; i.e., its ability to provide scientific documentation of the phenomena under discussion.

The physiologic changes that take place within the body are extremely subtle. For many reasons, not the least of which is our living in an environment providing a surplus of sensory information, we become less and less attuned to the subtle sensory information provided by our own bodies. We are only aware of the physiology of our bodies when we develop gross alterations of that physiology, such as in disease. However, we are usually unaware of the moment-by-moment subtle variations that take place within our biocybernetic systems.

In order to direct the physiology of our bodies we must first learn to become aware of the desired physiological parameter at a level many times more subtle than our usual awareness. The biofeedback device enables us to do this in a manner closely akin to that of the home stereo system. In the stereo system movement of the needle in a record groove generates a very small amount of electrical current. The very weak signal is then fed through a device which is able to amplify the signal. By amplifying, or increasing its intensity, the signal can then be fed back to the listener by means of loudspeakers. The initial current was much too small to power loudspeakers, whereas the amplified current has sufficient power to enable this feedback to take place at a conscious level, in this case the auditory realm. The biofeedback device picks up a signal of some sort from the human being and feeds it back to that same human being. Essentially, the only limitation is the ability to measure a physiologic change. By suitable means, virtually any physiologic change can be amplified and then fed back to the individual to allow this regulation to take place.

We have had biofeedback measuring devices for many years. Some of those in common clinical practice are the electrocardiogram (EKG), sphygmomanometer (blood pressure), electroencephalogram (EEG), electromyogram (EMG), and thermometer. Once the physiological signal has been measured and amplified, it can then be fed back to the individual by any one of a number of methods. The usual modes are visual (colored lights, meters) or auditory. At this point, the individual learns to change the parameter being measured. Every physiologic change is accompanied by a change in a person's emotional state,[3] and most likely every change in emotional state is accompanied by a change in physiologic state. By using methods similar to those that we will be describing later, the individual can change his or her emotional state to the degree that physiologic changes can be measured in the desired direction. In biofeedback we are not really controlling physiologic functions but are actually controlling the "existentialist," or body-feeling, state.[21]

The Greens[21] have developed their own theory as to how this mechanism takes place. Sensory perception of events taking place outside of the body causes an emotional and mental response. Similar responses can be elicited by direct perception of internal events. This direct perception can take place as one becomes aware of the physiologic response either directly or by means of the biofeedback device. In any event, the emotional and mental response, they feel, leads to a response in the limbic system, which then causes a response in the hypothalamus and pituitary which, in turn, leads to some physiologic response. The physiologic response can set up a perpetuating cycle by being directly perceived by the individual or by being perceived, as mentioned above, by the biofeedback device and then initiating the same or another emotional and mental response that is mediated by the same previous structures within the brain. This seems to be an accurate scheme of how these systems actually function.

Precisely which functions of the internal system can be controlled voluntarily? Most of the workers in biofeedback feel that any physiologic function can be controlled as long as it meets the criterion of being able to be measured specifically. Remember, as long as a function can be measured specifically, it can be amplified and fed back to the subject.

Much of the work of the past decade in biofeedback has been adequately summarized in the text by Basmajian.[22] We will cite here only part of the information necessary to validate the previous statements.

Control of heart rate by means of electrocardiographic biofeedback has been successful in patients with cardiac arrhythmias such as sinus tachycardia, paroxysmal atrial tachycardia, Wolff-Parkinson-White syndrome, and atrial fibrillation.[23] Patients with premature ventricular contractions have been taught to control and lessen the prevalence of these abnormal rhythms for as long as five years.[24] By control of the sensorimotor rhythm, patients have learned to decrease the frequency of epileptic seizure activity. As long as a decade ago, Basmajian was able to demonstrate that people could learn to control the discharge of a single motor unit; i.e., the discharge of a single anterior horn cell.[25]

By purely mental processes, people have been able to control hypertension. These mental processes have included both biofeedback and other methods of changes in states of consciousness to be discussed in Chapter 3.[26]

People have also been able to learn to direct gastrointestinal function. The lower esophageal sphincter, dysfunction of which leads to esophagitis and other esophageal problems, has been controlled substantially in at least one study.[27] Additionally, patients with fecal incontinance due to either surgery or congenital defects were able to become continent.[28] Control over vomiting by using only mental processes has been accomplished.[29] By purely mental processes people have been able to learn to direct cerebral blood flow.[30,31] Patients with diarrhea, by using such a simple biofeedback device as a stethoscope and by becoming aware of their bowel sounds, were able to alleviate their problem.[32]

Biofeedback technology has provided us with precise measurements of the ability of average individuals to learn control and direction over their internal processes. As will be demonstrated later, the biofeedback device is not necessary in learning this control. However, it has been extremely important in documenting scientifically the fact that these controls do take place. The biofeedback literature is becoming quite voluminous, and in the future it should provide scientific documentation of the controls for all types of functioning. As tools become more sophisticated, and as we are able to measure many different changes simultaneously and provide appropriate feedback, the effectiveness of biofeedback will be virtually unlimited.

Technology now allows us to substantiate some of the incredible control that people have developed over their internal processes. This control has been postulated by mystics for thousands of years; therefore, it was only natural that studies be attempted on practitioners of various mystical arts to determine the degree of control that these highly trained people could manifest. In general, much has been validated, but some of the more dramatic claims have yet to be substantiated or disproved.

Some of the most accurately documented studies were performed by the Greens on the yogi Swami Rama. As will be shown later, learning control of hand temperature generalizes to control of the autonomic nervous system by controlling vascular reactivity. Clinically, it is only necessary for one to learn some element of hand-warming of a general nature. Swami Rama was able to increase the temperature of the hypothenar side of the right palm, while simultaneously decreasing the temperature of the thenar side of the same hand.[33] This indicates an incredible degree of autonomic control, since both sides of the hand receive separate innervation. In an even more incredible task, Swami Rama was able to place his heart into a cardiac arrhythmia (atrial flutter) for more than 16 seconds. At that time, his average ventricular response was 306 per minute.[34] People who have experienced such an arrhythmia, or who have worked with people experiencing this problem, know how difficult a situation it can be. Certainly, it would be unusual to manifest no untoward outward response, as Swami Rama did. Additionally, under direct observation he was able to create and remove cystlike structures within the muscle tissue.[35]

The Greens also performed studies on Yogiraja Vaidyaraga, in which they demonstrated a marked lowering of the metabolic rate.[36] He was placed in an airtight box containing about 60 cubic feet of air. He stayed in the box for a period of 7½ hours. In 1½ hours, a candle, which was lighted inside the box, went out due to lack of oxygen. His initial heart rate was 80 per minute, and his respiratory rate was four per minute. At the end of the 7½ hours, his heart rate increased only 10 beats per minute, and his respiratory rate increased only to six. The electroencephalogram showed almost steady alpha rhythms.

Anand,[37] in his studies on Shri Ramananda Yogi, demonstrated a significant decrease in oxygen consumption during the period of time the yogi was enclosed in an airtight, sealed metal box. Physiological studies on yogis preceded even the modern biofeedback era. Bagchi and Wenger studied yogis in a publication appearing in 1959.[38] They observed that, by voluntary control, the yogis were able to decrease their respiratory rate to four to six per minute, increase the galvanic skin resistance (GSR) to greater than 70 percent, develop a predominance of alpha waves on the EEG, and decrease their heart rate to approximately 24 per minute.

In general, people trained in spiritual disciplines, as well as the average individual, can develop control over autonomic physiologic processes. As summarized above, a substantial accumulation of literature has scientifically documented these phenomena. It is the purpose of the later chapters in this book to demonstrate how this control can be facilitated. If all of these phenomena seem incredible, people working with them for some time have developed a certain understanding for the control of mind over body. Although it is not the purpose of this book to theorize on such potentialities, they should be mentioned. One of the foremost researchers in biofeedback and self-regulation, Barbara Brown, in her latest publication, *Supermind,*[2] has developed several theories as to the exquisiteness of mind functioning and its direction over the processes of the body. Some of these concepts are:

1. Human beings have an innate biological awareness of their physical state, down to the level of the single cell.
2. Human beings can control the direction and flow of nerve impulses throughout the body.
3. The human mind can intervene in and direct any physiological function.
4. Disease originates in intellectual processes. Stress has its effects on

health because the rational mind confronts situations with which it cannot cope.
5. Human beings have an unconscious sense of order in which they anticipate the sequence of natural events and move from chaos toward unity.
6. Will is an independent function of mind.

The placebo response

Any discussion of the effects of mind-body connections would be incomplete without a discussion of the placebo and the placebo response. A placebo may be defined as "any treatment or aspect of treatment that does not have a significant action on the patient's symptoms or disease."[39] We most commonly think of a placebo as a sugar pill, but the placebo response can be elicited by mechanical procedures, such as operations or therapies of various sorts, and also by the attitudes of the people (family, therapist, and so forth) interacting with the patient. The scientific community has used the placebo response as part of its scientific investigation, i.e., the double-blind study, whereby the active therapy was compared to the inactive or placebo therapy. Unfortunately, we have always studied the responders of the active group.

A high percentage of people respond to the placebo, and we feel that these are the people who should be studied so that we can maximize the placebo reaction in everything we do. The medical literature in any field will show that one third to two thirds of subjects taking the placebo therapy respond both subjectively and objectively. Although responders to the active therapy frequently are significant statistically when compared to placebo, if we look at the statistics we find great numbers of people responding to placebos. Benson, in a review of the studies of the placebo response in patients with angina pectoris,[39] compiled 13 studies with 1,187 patients over the past four decades and demonstrated subjective improvement in 82.4 percent ±9.7 percent. Not only was there subjective improvement, but objective changes also existed.

The placebo effect works solely by mental processes due to the patient's expectations of effectiveness. As will be demonstrated later, expectation is the primary factor governing the actual outcome of events, not only in therapy but in virtually everything related to our lives. Remember also that we tend to think of the placebo response as being beneficial. The placebo effect can also be detrimental to us when our expectations are that a negative effect will happen (nocebo).

We believe the placebo response is directed by the individual's innate ability to direct physiological functions by means of thought processes. In most of us, however, this response takes place at purely unconscious levels. The fact that it happens with such frequency, albeit unconscious, testifies to its innate survival abilities and power. We believe that by making these methods conscious, and thereby more directed and focused, their effectiveness can be increased even more.

References

1. A. M. Young, "The Social State, Laboratory of the Self," in *Consciousness and Reality,* ed. C. Muses and A. M. Young (New York: Avon Books, 1968), pp. 151–164.

2. B. Brown, *Supermind* (New York: Harper & Row, 1980).

3. K. R. Pelletier, *Mind as Healer, Mind as Slayer* (New York: Dell, 1977).

4. D. L. Wilson, "Brain Mechanisms, Consciousness and Introspection," in *Expanding Dimensions of Consciousness,* ed. A. A. Sugerman and R. E. Tartar (New York: Springer, 1978).

5. E. Green and A. Green, "General and Specific Applications of Thermal Feedback," in *Biofeedback: Principles and Practice for Clinicians,* ed. J. V. Basmajian (Baltimore: Williams and Wilkins, 1979), pp. 163–169.

6. C. Furst, *Origins of the Mind* (Englewood Cliffs, N.J.: Prentice-Hall, 1979), p. 116.

7. K. R. Pelletier, *Toward a Science of Consciousness* (New York: Dell, 1978), pp. 78–80.

8. Ibid.

9. Ibid., p. 138.

10. R. W. Sperry, M. S. Gazzaniga, and J. E. Bogen, "Intrahemispheric Relationships: The Neocortical Commissures: Syndromes of Hemisphere Disconnection," *Handbook of Clinical Neurology,* vol. 4, ed. P. J. Vinken and G. W. Bruyn (Amsterdam: North Holland, 1969).

11. R. G. Ley, "Cerebral Asymmetries, Emotional Experience and Imagery: Implications for Psychotherapy," in *The Potential of Fantasy and Imagination,* ed. A. A. Sheikh and J. T. Shaffer (New York: Brandon House, 1979), pp. 41–65.

12. Pelletier, *Science of Consciousness,* p. 95.

13. T. G. Bever and R. J. Chiarello, "Cerebral Dominance in Musicians and Nonmusicians," *Science* 185 (1974), pp. 537–39.

14. Pelletier, *Mind as Healer, Mind as Slayer,* p. 156.

15. R. R. Holt, "On the Nature of Generality of Mental Imagery, in *The Nature and Function of Imagery,* ed. P. W. Sheehan (New York: Academic Press, 1972).

16. E. E. Green, A. M. Green, and E. D. Walters, "Voluntary Control of Internal States: Psychological and Physiological," *J Transpers Psychol* 2, part 1 (1970), pp. 1–26.

17. Ibid., p. 9.

18. A. M. Young, "Consciousness and Cosmology" in *Consciousness and Reality*, ed. C. Muses and A. M. Young (New York: Avon Books, 1974), pp. 151–64.

19. J. C. Eccles, "Conscious Experience and Memory," in *Brain and Conscious Experience*, ed. J. C. Eccles (New York: Springer-Verlag, 1966), pp. 314–44.

20. Furst, *Origins of the Mind*, p. 22.

21. E. Green and A. Green, *Beyond Biofeedback* (New York: Delacorte Press, 1977), pp. 125, 158.

22. J. V. Basmajian, *Biofeedback: Principles and Practice for Clinicians* (Baltimore: Williams and Wilkins, 1979).

23. B. T. Engel, "Behavioral Applications in the Treatment of Patients with Cardiovascular Disorders," in *Biofeedback: Principles and Practice for Clinicians*, ed. J. V. Basmajian (Baltimore: Williams and Wilkins, 1979), pp. 170–79.

24. T. Weiss and B. T. Engel, "Operant Conditioning of Heart Rate in Patients with Premature Ventricular Contractions," *Psychosom Med* 33 (1971), pp. 301–21.

25. S. L. Wolf, "Anatomical and Physiological Basis for Biofeedback," in *Biofeedback: Principles and Practice for Clinicians*, ed. J. V. Basmajian (Baltimore: Williams and Wilkins, 1979), pp. 5–30.

26. A. P. Shapiro, G. E. Schwartz, D. C. E. Fergusen et al., "Behavioral Methods in the Treatment of Hypertension," *Ann Int Med* 86 (1977), pp. 626–36.

27. M. M. Schuster, "Operant Conditioning in Gastrointestinal Dysfunctions," *Hosp Prac*, September 1974, pp. 135–43.

28. B. T. Engel, P. Nikoomanesh, and M. M. Schuster, "Operant Conditioning of Rectosphincteric Responses in the Treatment of Fecal Incontinence, *New Engl J Med* 290 (1974), pp. 646–49.

29. J. D. White and D. Taylor, "Noxious Conditioning as a Treatment for Rumination," *Ment Retard* 5 (1967), pp. 30–33.

30. R. Jevning and A. F. Wilson, "Behavioral increase of cerebral blood flow," paper presented at the annual meeting of the American Physiological Association, 1978.

31. R. Mathew, "Biofeedback Control of Skin Temperature and Cerebral Blood Flow in Migraine," *Headache* 20 (1980), pp. 19–28.

32. S. Furman, "Intestinal Biofeedback in Functional Diarrhea: Preliminary Report," *J Behav Ther Exp Psych* 4 (1970), pp. 317–21.

33. Green, et al., *Beyond Biofeedback*, p. 197.

34. Ibid., p. 204.

35. Ibid., p. 210.

36. Ibid., p. 266.

37. B. K. Anand, "Studies on Shri Ramananda Yogi during His Stay in an Airtight Box," *Indian J Med Res* 49 (1961), pp. 82–89.

38. B. K. Bagchi and M. A. Wenger, "Electrophysiological Correlates of Some Yogi Exercises," in *Electroencephalography, Clinical Neurophysiology and Epilepsy. First International Congress of Neurological Sciences,* vol. 3, ed. L. Van Bagaert and J. Radermecker (London: Pergamon, 1959).

39. H. Benson and D. P. McCallie, "Angina Pectoris and the Placebo Effect," *New Engl J Med* 300 (1979), pp. 1424–29.

Chapter 2

Stress and health

Chapter 1 outlined the intricate interconnectedness of the mind and the body. References were cited demonstrating that changes in physiological functions lead to changes in mental functions and that changes in the emotional state result in physiological changes. Further demonstrated was the fact that mental processes can lead to the appropriate control and direction of body physiology. The practical applications of these methods for specific goals will be explored in later chapters. This chapter will focus on the interrelationships of the psyche and soma in causation of disease and, conversely, in maintenance of health. The concepts of stress and the stress response, which are major factors in disease formation, will also be discussed.

Estimates are that 50 percent to 70 percent of all of our diseases are stress-related,[1] and evidence will be presented to demonstrate that this is probably a very conservative estimate. Many people join us in the belief that all disease is stress-related and psychosomatic in the true sense of the word; i.e., a medically undesirable physiological response to psychological stress.[2] Indeed, a foremost researcher into mental processes and psychic control of somatic functions feels that disease has its origin in intellectual processes and that stress affects health because our rational mind confronts situations with which it cannot cope.[3] If we believe that the psyche and soma are interrelated in this way, then by learning the mental processes outlined in this book, we can begin to initiate a positive program toward optimal health.

Concepts of health maintenance

Most of us in this country have equated health with the mere absence of disease, which has actually meant the absence of *demonstrable* disease. In the past few years many people have come to the realization that optimal health, or wellness, involves more than this. As medicine became more scientific, of necessity, individual parts of the human being were studied. Common sense will show that this is an artificial situation (but also a necessary one for scientific discovery), which has resulted in the advances of modern medicine. However, we tended to regard these findings as absolute, forgetting that they were products of artificial conditions in a laboratory environment. Any change in a system, no matter how small, affects the functioning of that entire system. To understand this functioning in a truly optimal way requires us to become holistic.

Holism is a philosophical concept that perceives the whole as more than the sum of its parts, a concept particularly applicable to the human being. No matter from which level the human being is examined, the gross level (organs), microscopic (individual tissues), cellular, or biochemical, the individual is still more than the simple addition of all of these component parts, no matter how fine or subtle the level from which they are scientifically studied. Not only are we more than our hearts, lungs, kidneys, and liver combined, we are also more than the sum total of all of our biochemical reactions. Even the molecular biologist would be unable to explain all human functioning by studying these special areas only. The qualities that make us more than the sum of our individual parts are difficult to define and demonstrate scientifically. We may call these qualities mind, consciousness, spirit, or will, or some combination of these. The human being is something more than the individual parts, and you can label this "something more" with any name you wish. If terms such as spirit or will are uncomfortable, then substitute for this a neutral term such as *one,* or a letter such as *a*.

The mind-body dualism proposed by the French philosopher Rene Descartes in the 17th century and effectively carried in the mainstream of medical thinking until the present time, is no longer tenable. The mind and body must interact and, in fact, the human being is even more than the combination of mind and body, especially if one equates mind with brain.

There exists a vast body of circumstantial and anecdotal evidence that the individual's psychological functioning is important to his or her physical functioning. Vaillant demonstrated this scientifically by biennially following a group of 204 men over four decades.[4] Of those with the best mental health, as judged by many factors, only two developed a chronic illness or were dead by age 53, whereas of those with the worst mental health, 18 developed chronic illness or were dead by age 53. This was significant even when such risk factors as obesity, tobacco, and alcohol were eliminated.

One of the most refreshing outcomes of this new realization of wellness is that each individual must play an active role in the treatment of disease and in the creation of health. This active role consists of more than just presenting oneself at the doctor's office for an annual checkup or receiving immunizations as a child. It consists of optimally nourishing the interrelated parts of the human being: body, mind, and spirit, the latter referring to that as yet scientifically undefinable essence that makes us a living human being, something more than a human being who is dead. The dead still have brain and body, but not the life force that makes us what we are. With respect to the mind and spirit, we must actively engage in processes which lead to full development of those functions. These methods will be referred to in more detail in Chapter 3.

With respect to nourishment of the body, this includes the concepts of what we take into our body, such as foods and poisons, and also what we do with our body, i.e., activity and rest. The importance of this was aptly demonstrated by Lester Breslow in a 1975 study of 11,000 adults.[5] Factors associated with a longer life were three meals a day, especially breakfast; moderate exercise; seven to eight hours of sleep per night; absence of cigarette smoking; absence of obesity; and no more than moderate alcohol use. For those with less than three of these factors, the average life expectancy of a 35-year-old male was 67, whereas if a person had all or all but one of these factors, the average life expectancy was 11 years longer. For many people the degree of responsibility shown for our health consists of a desire to turn the body in to the physician and return for it the following week, trusting that it will be fixed, as an automobile would be serviced. This attitude is inappropriate, and although most of us intellectually agree with the inaccuracy of this description, unconsciously we act as though we believe it entirely.

Another concept inherent in health maintenance and optimal wellness is the power of belief systems. *Belief systems* are essentially self-fulfilling prophecies. We experience our world through our deeply rooted unconscious beliefs, and these beliefs act as sort of a screen or filtering system. We all know very well that what we observe and experience is open to interpretation. Many people can experience the same event and all of them will describe it differently, these differences being determined primarily by the individual's beliefs. Essentially, belief systems act as filters

through which only a certain percentage of what is potentially observable
is being actually observed and assimilated. Belief systems are self-rein-
forcing, i.e., what is expected will be observed, and what is observed
confirms the expectations.[6] The repeated cycle of expectation—observation confirming expectation, and confirmation reinforcing expectation—
can, over a long period of time, lead to considerable rigidity. If we really
believe that we cannot change physiological functioning with thought
processes, then in reality we cannot. However, if we can learn to change
the belief system even a small fraction, the amount of increase in observable experiences changes exponentially, opening up vast new horizons of
experiential phenomena. Conversely, increasing rigidity of our belief
systems, which is usual in most people, may lead to disease because each
time an individual confronts a challenge to a held belief or attitude, he also
experiences personal stress.[7]

Another important factor in these "new" concepts of health maintenance is that symptoms and diseases are not necessarily bad. Unfortunately, we have accepted the message promulgated by the media and the
drug manufacturers that we are never supposed to feel pain or illness. In
most of us, however, these are messages to stop and take stock of our life,
including our actions and beliefs. Remember that we learn to experience
everything in a relativistic manner. For example, we know pleasure only
because we have previously experienced pain. If we were to have nothing
but pleasure, we would evolve into the essentially nonfeeling characters
portrayed by Huxley in *Brave New World*. That is not to say we should
not strive toward those things we see as beneficial, such as elimination of
a disease process or a change in an uncomfortable symptom, but we
should realize that the presence of a disease or symptom may be our clue
that assessing the situation and commencing those changes appropriate to
growth will lead toward our beneficial evolution. Symptoms may be an
indication of the individual's attempt to undergo a self-healing process.[8]
These concepts consider illness to be regenerative rather than degenerative. This is in accord with Brown's idea that in the human being there is a
sense of order and a tendency to move from chaos to unity.[3] This is also
compatible with the work of Nobel Prize winner Ilya Prigogene, in which
he speculates that many systems, possibly including the human system,
manifest negentropy; that is, movement from relative disorganization to
higher degrees of organization. Many researchers in the field of psychology and psychiatry have noted that people demonstrating addictive behaviors are, in fact, attempting to restore some degree of order to their
lives. The use of addictive drugs and alcohol initially provides some
satisfaction of those needs for order; however, the persistent use or abuse
of those substances eventually negates the minimal positive effects initially received. Many of us lack the responsibility to take positive action

in regard to wellness, yet we take action that interferes with the innate drive we all have toward homeostasis.

Stress and the stress response

When most of us discuss stress, we are actually talking about the *stress response*. Selye defines this as the nonspecific response of the body to any demand.[9] Any situation which causes us to change, or adapt, is capable of eliciting the stress response. These situations can be either internal or external in origin, and can take the form of situations, thoughts, diseases, and so forth. In any given individual, almost anything conceivable can elicit the stress response. That which elicits the stress response is called a *stressor*.

The stress response is a total body response mediated by the nervous system, particularly the sympathetic branch of the autonomic nervous sytem, and the endocrine system. As mentioned in Chapter 1, the hypothalamus regulates these adaptive systems of the body. Originally, the stress response was called the fight or flight response, a response enabling the organism to accumulate rapidly all of its resources to respond to the stressor. Since, in the initial stages of our evolution, these stressors tended to be manifested by an enemy, we responded by fight or flight.

The psychological responses produced are exactly those which we would tend to deduce as being best for the fight or flight response. Although the functions of the autonomic nervous system are now known to be much more complex than the simple sympathetic versus parasympathetic that medicine had heretofore considered, most of the simple sympathetic effects are those found in the stress response. The endocrine system leads to a secretion of adrenal cortical (cortisone type) and adrenal medullary (adrenaline type) hormones, as well as thyroid hormone. These lead to such physiological phenomena as acceleration of the heart rate, dilatation of the pupils, inhibition of gastrointestinal peristalsis and secretion, inhibition of bladder emptying, constriction of gastrointestinal and urinary sphincters, diversion of blood flow into the muscles, increase in blood pressure, increase in respiratory rate, and increase in metabolic rate.

The mere fact that we have such a highly organized total body response teleologically implies a need for this response, and we can note the value of this response in assuring survival of the species. Certainly, those individuals with a well-developed stress response would be more apt to survive immediate dangers to life and limb. Those of us alive today are the descendants of those progenitors with the most highly developed stress response.

In addition to its necessity for survival as a species, a certain level of stress is necessary for our survival as individuals. In each of us, the optimal level of stress, called eustress, differs. Each one of us has an optimal stress level. To keep stress from becoming distress, we must have not only the right amount but the right kind for the right duration.[9] However, as we will see below, stress is also responsible for many, if not most, of our diseases. This has become a double-edged sword, not because of the innate difficulties in the stress response itself, but rather due to our differing methods of perceiving and responding to stress.

Stress is neither inherently good nor bad. It is beneficial when it enables us to survive a potentially harmful situation, or when, in the context of eustress, it provides the baseline level of stress necessary for our functioning. It becomes harmful when it exceeds the eustress level and becomes distress, and particularly when it becomes repeated or prolonged. According to Selye, the first stage of the stress response is the alarm stage. At that point, the products of the stress response build and lead to a generalized hyperarousal state. When the stressful situation has ended, we then return to the baseline, or eustress state. If the stress is prolonged, we eventually reach a point in which we can no longer maintain the response. This leads to the stage of exhaustion, which, in a relatively short time, can become irreversible, leading to death.

Some of the problems that we have with stress can be more readily understood from an anthropological basis. *Homo sapiens* has been on this planet for at least a million years; therefore, it is not necessary to speculate that the stress response we have may be genetically evolved from other species. In that million years our stress response developed in situations totally different from that experienced since the industrial revolution, and especially during the past half century. Due to the sheer increase in the amount of sensory input we experience, the amount of stressful situations that we encounter are vastly greater than our prehistoric ancestors faced. However, many of the stresses our ancestors acquired were in life-death situations; now they clearly are not such, but we respond to them as though they are. Essentially, we respond to dollar situations with million-dollar weapons, or we respond to waiting in the slow line in the supermarket as though a 20-ton dinosaur were contemplating us as the blue plate special.

Also, many of the stressors we experience elicit a stress response which in us is subliminal; i.e., the products of the stress response are not of sufficient intensity that we are even aware of it consciously. However, unconsciously they still take their toll. It seems as though the stressors our ancestors faced may have been fewer in number, but more maximal in their elicitation of the products of the stress response. Our ancestors were keenly aware that the stress response was elicited, were able to manifest appropriate action against the cause of the stress response, and, we believe, practiced some method of rest. This rest is different from that which most of us experience and will be discussed in further detail later.

Stress and disease

As previously noted, stress is in some way responsible for 50 percent to 100 percent of all of our diseases, and certainly for the great majority of nonspecific symptoms unrelated to specific disease processes such as anxiety, apprehension, palpitations, headaches, other nonspecific pain, irritability, and unhappiness. Earlier in this chapter we alluded to the relationship between psyche and soma in producing symptoms and disease. This does not mean that diseases are imagined or in the head but that, although they are in the body, they are initiated by mental processes. Leigh and Reiser[10] describe what they call a nonlinear field-systems model of psychosomatic disease. This takes into account the fact that any disease process, in a truly holistic manner, is a result of multiple interrelated factors and very rarely, if ever, is the result of a single factor. The factors to be considered are constitutional, genetic, sociocultural, interpersonal, intrapersonal, and environmental.

Some of the problems in relating to the concept of stress leading to diseases can be observed from the point of view of ignoring the meanings of the signals of stress. Simeons describes this as a conflict between the older, diencephalic portions of the brain which govern such basic instincts as hunger, sleep, and fear, and its cortical elaborations, emotions such as pity, guilt, hope, and so forth. The diencephalon continues to react to threats in the old way (as manifestations of basic instincts), but the cortex misinterprets these signals and thereby leads to an interpretation as an abnormality. For example, fright (diencephalic experience) may lead to an inability to sleep and to an increase in heart rate, both of which are normal responses to fright. If the cortex interprets this abnormally, the inability to sleep may be interpreted as an abnormality such as insomnia and the elevated heart rate as heart disease.

> When these once normal and virtually important reactions . . . do not reach his conscious awareness, he interprets them as something abnormal and regards them as afflictions. He speaks of indigestion when apprehensiveness kills his appetite, and insomnia when fright keeps him awake at night. . . . It is man's civilization which prevents him from realizing that such bodily reactions may be merely the normal results of diencephalic alarm and the mobilization of

those marvelous flight mechanisms to which he owes his existence as a species.[11]

When the individual's belief system interprets these normal responses as abnormal, they serve as a feedback mechanism, thereby increasing abnormal responses. Eventually, after long periods of time, these processes can be set and actually lead to development of physically manifested diseases such as hypertension. Essentially, an accumulating cycle of minute stress symptoms that is ignored rather than halted appears to be the means by which psychosomatic disease becomes established.[12] It appears that it is not stress per se that is the problem, but rather our cortical misrepresentation of stress-associated symptoms, as well as the prolonged, unremitting types of stress that we experience in our modern society. In our evolution it appears that the sources of stress were very clear and well-defined, and had temporal boundaries such as a beginning and an end. Now we have sources of stress that are not well-defined, either spatially or temporally, i.e., we really do not know where they are or what they are, and certainly have no immediate prospect as to their becoming resolved. Additionally, multiple sources of stress exist at the same time. This all may lead to progressive elevation of our stress threshold, making us even less aware as time progresses of the fact that we are experiencing a stress response at all. However, just because we are unaware of experiencing stress does not negate its effectiveness in producing dysfunction and disease.

Pelletier[13] discusses a model of the psychogenesis of diseases in which stressful situations that are difficult to resolve, for many of the reasons stated above, lead to a perception in the individual of overwhelming stress. At that point, numerous coping mechanisms may be evolved; however, the choice of which coping mechanism is actually utilized is an unconscious choice. This choice may be that of a psychosomatic disorder which serves to release the subject from the stress factors. Because this coping mechanism is effective, it leads to a tendency to utilize it in any like situations in the future.

We feel that all diseases are stress-related because stress and its associated influence on the mind-body axis tends to leave us, for multiple reasons, in a situation that is vulnerable to the development of a disease. The specific disease cannot be predicted; however, the probability of developing significant disease certainly can be. Even such seemingly uncontrollable diseases as infections probably do have a psychosomatic influence, as noted by Stein and associates.[14] They review studies showing the relationships of these processes to susceptibility to infections and neoplasms by means of changes in both humoral and cell-mediated immune responses. Solomon[15] reviews a host of studies, outlined below, demonstrating the relationship between stress and emotional factors with the development of infectious disease and other immune abnormalities. Studies in mice involving stress restraint caused increased susceptibility to *herpes simplex virus infections*. In another study, exposure of mice to both *Coxsackie B* virus and stress caused disease, whereas neither alone would cause disease.

Evidence of the association of stress with increased susceptibility to viral-induced tumors and immune globulin production were also cited. Electrical stimulation of the lateral hypothalamus in rats produced alterations of immune gamma globulin. As noted previously, the hypothalamus is the mediator of the stress response in the central nervous system. Mechanical destruction of the dorsal hypothalamus produced suppression of certain antibodies leading to prolonged retention of antigens in the blood. Stress in mice led to decreased synthesis of interferon. All of these show that psychosocial processes, predominantly stress, lead to changes in the immune system which, in turn, can lead to various diseases.

Holmes and Rahe[16] developed the Social Readjustment Rating Scale based on 394 subjects, and this led to the development of the ratio illustrated in Table 2-1. They substantiated the predictability of this scale in subsequent studies. Those with a total score of greater than 300 in the previous year had about a 90 percent chance of developing a significant illness or health change. Even with scores as low as 150, there was a 50 percent chance of developing these similar changes. Many of these life changes would be regarded as beneficial to a great number of people. However, as mentioned above, the body reacts with stress to anything that causes a change or adaptation. Therefore, each one of these is associated with some amount of stress. It appears as though certain amounts of stress, which can be predicted by the Holmes and Rahe scale, can predict the development of disease. Also, if the specific disease is not predicted, almost any disease can become manifest. The life changes predict the propensity to develop an illness, not the specific illness developed. We believe that this scale and its subsequent validation is the most pertinent evidence in the literature regarding association of stress and disease in the human being. The diseases can range from those which are thought to be primarily psychologic to those which are thought to be psychosomatic, to those which have been previously thought to be purely physical, such as infectious diseases.

Other associations between stress-related factors and disease are demonstrated by the association of personality types and coronary artery disease, as described by Friedman and Rosenman.[17] There seems to be an increased incidence in coronary artery disease in patients they labeled as type A, people who are essentially time urgent, competitive people with easily aroused hostility. These are contrasted to the type B personality who can relax without guilt because of the absence of time urgency and who seems to understand his or her own strengths and weaknesses. This

Table 2-1
Social readjustment rating scale

Event	Mean value
Death of spouse	100
Divorce	73
Separation	65
Jail term	63
Death of close family member	63
Personal injury or illness	53
Marriage	50
Fired from job	47
Reconciliation	45
Retirement	45
Change of health of family member	44
Pregnancy	40
Difference in frequency of sexual relationships	39
New family member	39
Business readjustment	39
Change in financial state	38
Death of a close friend	37
Change in line of work	36
Change in number of arguments with spouse	35
Mortgage greater than $40,000	31
Foreclosed mortgage or loan	30
Change in work responsibility	29
Son or daughter leaving home	29
In-Law trouble	29
Outstanding achievement	28
Wife beginning or ending work	26
Beginning or ending school	26
Change in living conditions	25
Revision in personal habits	24
Trouble with boss	23
Change in work hours or conditions	20
Change in residence	20
Change in school	20
Change in recreation	19
Change in church activities	19
Change in social activities	18
Mortgage or loan less than $10,000	17
Change of sleep habits	16
Change in number of family get-togethers	15
Change in eating habits	15
Vacation	13
Christmas	12
Minor violations of the law	11

Source: T. H. Holmes, and T. H. Rahe, The social readjustment rating scale. *J Psychosom Res* 11:213–218, 1967.

demonstrates another documented relationship between stress, as manifested by the type A personality, and disease, which will be reviewed later.

Another dramatic example of the relationship between stress and harmful phenomena is that of sudden death. Engel[18] reviews numerous publications relevant to sudden death as a result of psychological influence. These all seem to involve events that are impossible to ignore, leading to an overwhelming response of either excitation or giving up. Whatever the subjective emotional experience, it leads to invocation of the stress response of such a magnitude as to cause lethal events, cardiac or otherwise. Some of the situations described are the impact of death of a person close to the individual, acute grief, threat of loss of a close friend, mourning or anniversary thereof, individual loss of stature or self-esteem, personal danger or threat, implied danger or threat, a condition existing after a danger or threat is over, or even reunions, triumphs, or happy endings.

We have presented documented evidence of the relationship of stress and emotional factors to the development of disease, as well as the necessity of stress and the stress response in our survival both as a species and as individuals. The presence of this so-called double-edged sword leads one to search for a way of keeping the inherent benefits of the stress response while minimizing the harmful effects. Evidence has accumulated over the past decade that we have within us the ability to accomplish this.

Management of the adverse effects of the stress response

The stress response as a double-edged sword, on one hand, provides us with a means of survival and, on the other, leads to most if not all of our diseases. Combating the adverse effects of stress has become a major preoccupation within many segments of our society. Unfortunately, the direction that stress management has taken has frequently led to harmful results. We have erroneously been led to believe that we should never experience stress and its resultant symptoms. When we experience these symptoms, rather than learning from them, we have been taught to ignore them. When they reach the intensity whereby they can no longer be ignored, then we are led to the panacea, tranquilizers.

Blackwell,[19] in a 1975 review of the use of tranquilizers, stated that in 1972, 144 million prescriptions were written for psychotropic drugs. Half of these were accounted for by two minor tranquilizers, Librium and Valium. At that time, Valium had shown an increase of about 7 million prescriptions per year, and in 1973, 20 percent of all adults in the United States had taken a psychotropic drug within the previous 12 months. If these statistics sound rather alarming, it would be our prediction that statistics accumulated this year would be even more so. Because these products do nothing to change the basic nature of stress and the stress response, they likewise do nothing to alter the detrimental effects of stress. Their addiction potential poses grave dangers, and they negate the basic value of the stress response as a survival learning mechanism.

It is our belief that in evolutionary development we have had the appropriate tools for minimizing and possibly negating the harmful effects of the stress response. One of the major methods for accomplishing this, if not *the* major method, is adequate rest. However, what truly was rest and relaxation thousands of years ago was totally different from that which we consider rest and relaxation now. For many people, relaxation means sitting or lying on the couch in front of the television set, munching on salt-covered potato chips, and consuming significant quantities of alcoholic beverages. In addition, many people consider rest and relaxation wasted time, and therefore, when we do approach some state of relaxation, we may actually be increasing our stress response. In fact, Pelletier reports that we have very naive attitudes toward relaxation, and the physiological and psychological characteristics of stress are the responses actually produced in much of our relaxation activities.[20]

The stress response is a highly integrated, total body response with specific and general survival qualities. The human organism is an intricate system of cybernetic feedback controls. In order to maintain the precision of these controls, there need to be regulatory factors to alter the course of any parameter in any direction. If there is a factor that can enable the blood glucose concentration to decrease (insulin), there must be a substance or factor that will enable the blood glucose to increase (glucagon). For most processes in the body there exists an equal and opposite. We contend that, if the equal and opposite has not been discovered yet, sometime in the future it will be. Therefore, to counteract the harmful effects of this necessary stress response, the body should have an equal and opposite. Is this true?

In the late 1960s and early 1970s, Herbert Benson and his associates initiated studies which led to the 1975 publication *The Relaxation Response*.[21] This response was initially termed a hypometabolic response because it was associated with a decrease in metabolism as measured by oxygen consumption. In fact, the decrease in oxygen consumption was so profound that in three minutes it exceeded by more than twofold the decrease in oxygen consumption produced by sleep in five hours. Other measurements demonstrated the relaxation response to lead to a decrease in respiratory rate, a decrease in heart rate, production of predominant alpha rhythm as measured by the electroencephalograph, and a decrease in blood pressure. These physiological parameters are predominantly the antitheses of those parameters noted in the stress response.

Benson's initial studies were performed on practitioners in the transcendental meditation (TM) technique. Later, Benson developed his relaxation response technique which, essentially, is transcendental meditation with the substitution of the word *one* for the Sanskrit word or mantra used in TM. The physiological changes in the relaxation response were essentially equivalent to those of practitioners of TM. From this, Benson postulated that there were four basic requirements for a technique to elicit the changes characteristic of the relaxation response: (1) a quiet environment; (2) repetition of a mental device, such as the word *one* or a Sanskrit mantra; (3) a passive or receptive attitude, and (4) a comfortable position. Benson noted that these characteristics were not just products of his relaxation response or TM, but were also found in the practices of many disciplines such as yoga, Sufism, Christian mysticism, Hebrew mysticism, Buddhism, Taoism, shamanism, and even in secular literature and music.

Fortunately, it is not necessary to elicit this response every time we experience the stress response. It seems as though 10 to 20 minutes of practice once or twice a day is adequate.

The anatomic source of this response or the response's initiation is still to be determined. It appears as though the hypothalamus, which is responsible for the initiation and organization of the stress response, may also be the site of the relaxation response. Walter R. Hess, a Nobel laureate physiologist, was able to produce a response similar to the relaxation response by stimulating a part of the cat hypothalamus. Hess called this the "trophotrophic response."[22] The area of the hypothalamus stimulated was separate from the area which, when stimulated, would cause the fight or flight response.

The methods by which the relaxation response and similar methods may lead to a change in the way we respond to stress was postulated by Pelletier.[23] He noted that when stress-producing stimuli, such as noise or heat, were administered to yogis in meditation, their electroencephalographic pattern remained unchanged: They continued with a prominent alpha rhythm and did not exhibit blocking of alpha as most of us would. However, even more importantly, when the yogis were not in meditation, the usually noted habituation response was not present; i.e., each subsequent stimulus produced the same intensity of response. (In habituation, each subsequent stimulus produces less of a response.) It appeared as though each stimulus seemed to be responded to in the same way with the same intensity every time it was presented, leading to the conclusion that practitioners of the relaxation response would experience stresses as a series of discrete short-term stresses[24] and thereby bring their general stress level back to the baseline, no matter how many stresses were experienced. Most of us, when exposed to numerous stressors over a period of time, experience a gradual elevation in the stress threshold, or basal level, until we reach a point at which the body can no longer adapt. At that point we experience illness.

Most of the remaining chapters of this book will describe methods and techniques for dealing with certain specific problems in the medical and allied health professions. There is an even greater purpose to these methods: They can be used in a general fashion to alleviate the harmful effects of the stress response and to promote general wellness. We will be emphasizing that the most important aspect of these methods is their general effectiveness. Frequently, the use of the general method is all that is necessary in producing desired specific effects. The power and effectiveness of these methods lies at least as much in their general actualizing nature as in their specificity.

References

1. K. R. Pelletier, *Toward a Science of Consciousness* (New York: Dell, 1978), p. 185.

2. E. Green and A. Green, "General and Specific Applications of Thermal Feedback," in *Biofeedback: Principles and Practice for Clinicians,* ed. J. V. Basmajian (Baltimore: Williams and Wilkins, 1979).

3. B. Brown, *Supermind* (New York: Harper & Row, 1980).

4. G. E. Vaillant, "Natural History of Male Psychological Health, *New Engl J Med* 23 (1979), p. 1249.

5. K. R. Pelletier, *Mind as Healer, Mind as Slayer* (New York: Dell, 1977), p. 310.

6. Ibid., p. 26.

7. Ibid., pp. 106–107.

8. Ibid., p. 27.

9. H. Selye, "On Stress," in *Mind Styles, Life Styles,* ed. N. Lande (Los Angeles: Price, Stern, Sloan, 1976), pp. 19–26.

10. H. Leigh and M. F. Reiser, "Major Trends in Psychosomatic Medicine," *Ann Int Med* 87 (1977), pp. 233–39.

11. A. T. W. Simeons, *Man's Presumptuous Brain: An Evolutionary Interpretation of Psychosomatic Disease* (New York: E. P. Dutton, 1961).

12. Pelletier, *Science of Consciousness,* p. 193.

13. Pelletier, *Mind as Healer, Mind as Slayer,* p. 15.

14. M. Stein, R. C. Schiavi and N. Camerino, "Influence of Brain and Behavior on the Immune System," *Science* 191 (1976), pp. 435–40.

15. G. F. Solomon, "Emotions, Stress, the Central Nervous System and Immunity," *Ann NY Acad Sci* 1611 no. 2 (1969), pp. 335–43.

16. T. H. Holmes and T. H. Rahe, "The Social Readjustment Rating Scale," *J Psychosom Res* 11 (1967), pp. 213–18.

17. M. Friedman and R. H. Rosenman, *Type A Behavior and Your Heart* (New York: Alfred A. Knopf, 1974).

18. G. L. Engel, "Sudden and Rapid Death During Psychological Stress," *Ann Int Med* 74 (1971), pp. 771–82.

19. B. Blackwell, "Minor Tranquilizers: Use, Misuse or Overuse?" *Psychosomatics* 16 (1975), pp. 28–31.

20. Pelletier, *Mind as Healer, Mind as Slayer*, p. 23.

21. H. Benson, *The Relaxation Response* (New York: Morrow, 1975).

22. Benson, *The Relaxation Response*, p. 68.

23. Pelletier, *Science of Consciousness*, p. 152.

24. K. R. Pelletier, "A Conversation with Ken Pelletier," *Med Self-Care* 5 (1978), pp. 3–9.

Chapter 3

Altered states of consciousness

Imagery plays a predominant role in governing our receiving information, comparing it to previous experience and initiating behavioral actions in response to that information no matter what our state of awareness (see Chapter 4). However, as powerful as imagery is in our everyday life in the waking state, there is ample evidence that the use of imagery becomes much more powerful in other states of consciousness. Also, experiences of these different states of consciousness accrue benefits in themselves in addition to the beneficial effects of imagery. This chapter is devoted to a discussion of states of consciousness (SC) and altered states of consciousness (ASC).

Information about SC and ASC is largely experiential and theoretical. Scientific instruments sensitive enough to measure discrete states of consciousness with precision do not exist. We can measure various physiological functions; however, similarities in these functions do not necessarily mean identity in the states studied but may merely be indicative of similarities. Experiential and intuitive data are important in permitting some understanding of these phenomena, and they do have validity. However, variations in individual experiences and in verbalizing those experiences may lead to considerable discrepancies. Three volumes that summarize much of what is known and theorized about the fields of SC and ASC have been published recently.[1-3] We will summarize much of that information and present a simplified scheme of our own for understanding these phenomena.

John Locke defines consciousness as "the perception of what passes in a man's own mind."[4] Consciousness may therefore be described as the phenomenon of being aware of one's own mental processes and one's own existence. Precise definitions of *conscious* and *consciousness* are to be found in treatises on philosophy and mysticism. For our purposes, consciousness can be equated with awareness; thus, a state of consciousness indicates a state of awareness. This is not to say that consciousness may not have meanings in a much broader and universal sense, but these are not necessary for the purpose of our work.

We will define SC as a distinct physiological and psychological condition of awareness. This is fairly similar to Tart's definition of a discrete state of consciousness as a ". . . unique, dynamic pattern or configuration of psychological structures . . . an active system of psychological subsystems."[5] Although we have hinted at the discreteness of SC, we feel that individual SC are more a part of a continuum, and the differences will be not in discreteness from state to state but in a gradual overlap of characteristics. For the sake of identification and teaching, however, it is more practical to consider these as discrete states. There may be variations within each state, and if these variations do not change the overall characteristics of the system, they comprise what Tart calls subsystems. For example, we all have a fairly good idea of what the waking state is; we also know that our awareness, perceptions, feelings, and physiological processes differ from time to time when we are still in a waking state. These differences are due to dissimilarities in the subsystem of the waking state. Nevertheless, there are enough characteristics of waking present so that we know that we are still in the waking state, even when we are experiencing different subgroups.

Tart outlines the following subsystems:[5]

1. *Extroceptors*. Sense organs for perceiving the external world.
2. *Interoceptors*. Mechanisms and sensing devices for perceiving internal sensations.
3. *Input processing*. The ability to perceive only that input which is important to us.
4. *Memory*.
5. *Sense of identity*. The "I" quality that becomes attached to certain other bits of information that we receive, thus personalizing them.
6. *Emotions*.
7. *Evaluation and decision making*. Cognitive processes, rules, and methods we have learned for handling information.

8. *Space/time sense*. The feeling for flow of space and time, based on our psychological structures and biological structures rather than clocked time.
9. *Motor output*. Internal motor states such as gland activity, and external motor states such as skeletal muscle activity.

Tart notes that the subsystems that compose a state of consciousness are actually psychological structures, each one differing slightly from the others in the way they process information. These structures interact to form a system, and this interaction acts to stabilize the system by the methods mentioned above.[6]

We remain in discrete SC as long as they remain stable. When alternate SC become more stable, or when the one we are experiencing becomes less, we proceed into the new SC. Tart defines four methods of stabilizing SC:[5] (1) loading, (2) negative feedback, (3) positive feedback, and (4) limiting.

Loading stabilization refers to keeping the system experiencing and performing activities of an appropriate or desired nature so that most of the energy is used in these activities; therefore, there is not sufficient energy left over to disrupt the system. An example of this is the usual day-to-day patterns of our lives at home, at school, or at our occupations, all of which begin to develop a form of regularity and familiarity. To these we keep adding other tasks which increase that regularity and familiarity so that we become more bound to them. This is reminiscent of the way we become increasingly trapped within our belief systems, as mentioned in Chapter 2.

Negative feedback stabilization consists of continuous correction of anything causing deviation from the norm. Corrections are put into operation when a subsystem senses that the actions of another subsystem strays beyond the limits necessary for stabilization of the SC. Tart gives the example of "anxiety that results when thoughts stray into certain areas that are taboo for the thinker."[7]

Positive feedback stabilization consists of detecting acceptable activities and rewarding them, such as the experience of pleasure when we have acceptable thoughts or have performed an acceptable activity.

Limiting stabilization is the ability of the system to limit any destabilizing influences of any subsystem. An example of this may be the individual's ability to overcome some effects of drugs when these effects would act as destabilizing activities.

Tart defines the *normal state of consciousness* (NSC) of a person as "the one in which he spends the major part of his waking hours."[8] He notes that this state "is culturally relative and represents only a fraction of the potentialities open to the human being."[6]

Rather than NSC, we prefer to use the term *usual state of conscious-*

ness (USC). Most people would agree that the usual state of consciousness that we experience is *waking*. We would like to add to this two states that have been labeled by many as ASC—sleeping and dreaming. These may actually be intermediary states, because they do have some of the characteristics of ASC. However, since we experience dreaming and sleeping, like waking, on a rather regular basis, we prefer to include them with USC.

Altered states of consciousness _____

Ludwig defines ASC as a "mental state induced by various psychological, physiological or pharmacological maneuvers or agents, which can be recognized subjectively by the individual himself . . . as representing a sufficient deviation in subjective experience of psychological function from certain general norms for that individual during alert, waking consciousness."[9] Using Tart's systems approach to SC, mentioned above, a person would "experience a qualitative shift in his pattern of mental functioning . . . *some quality or qualities of his mental processes are different.*"[6] An ASC can be induced if we apply disrupting forces to the existing SC, thereby interfering or withdrawing attention from the stabilizing forces and then apply patterning forces.[10] The patterning forces act to bring together various psychological structures into subsystems and to organize them to form a new system, which then must develop stabilization forces of its own. The greater the stabilization of the new SC or ASC, the more it will persist. Because an ASC is usually somewhat disorganized initially, the SC usually returns to the baseline state. However, with this approach it is obvious how ASC can become more prominent and persist for longer periods of time; i.e., by fortifying both the patterning forces and the new stabilizing systems. This is important because of the value of some ASC in maintaining wellness and promoting growth and realization of one's full potential either alone or with the addition of imagery.

As Tart notes, an ASC involves a radical reorganization of structures such as taking an automobile apart and using its part to build an airplane.[8] A transitional state exists after the disintegration of an SC and before it is reorganized into an ASC. In this transitional state there is much vulnerability, and the organization can easily go back in the direction of the previous SC. The disruption of the stabilizing forces of a baseline SC can be either direct, by such means as state-altering drugs or trauma to the central nervous system, or indirect, by such means as sensory deprivation or sensory overload. More gentle methods can be used to induce desired ASC in a way that these ASC can become progressively more stabilized and more useful.

We define ASC simply as any SC different from USC, that is, any state or states differing from sleeping, waking, or dreaming. This is not much different from Fromm's definition of ASC as those that differ frmm the waking state.[11] We agree in part with Benson's description of altered states of consciousness as those we "do not commonly experience" and that "usually . . . [do] . . . not occur spontaneously. . . ."[12] Budzynski notes that ASC are highly variable from moment to moment.[13] We basically agree with this view but feel that stabilization of these states can occur, making them more easily attainable and useful for further endeavors.

In the following section, we will discuss various ASC. It is important to reiterate that ASC, like any SC, may not be discrete states, but may be a continuum. As mentioned by Zinberg: [14]

> Are alternate states of consciousness discrete states, to use Tart's word, or are the differences among *altered states of consciousness* merely differences of degree, as Singer insists? Just where does deep contemplation in a usual *state of consciousness* become a meditative, alternate state of consciousness? Is losing myself in a vivid daydream in the usual state (though on the edge of it) compatible to the extreme loss of self-consciousness experienced in giving oneself up to a line of speculative thought while on a "trip"? Obviously, there must be connections; it is, after all, the same mind, brain, body, persona in operation in both the usual and the changed state of consciousness.

Table 3-1 lists various ASC from several sources. The purpose of the table is to demonstrate that many labels are given to various ASC, and that there is a considerable overlap. More important, however, is that there seems to be evidence that none of these terms describe states themselves. Rather, the names actually describe either the method used to produce or induce the state, or the characteristics of the state. Table 3-1 lists which of these parameters, in our opinion, are predominant for each state mentioned. This is important because we will make a case that many on these states bear similar characteristics and that, therefore, the methods used to produce these states can be somewhat interchangeable in leading to the benefits of the various states. Not only do we believe that many of these states are beneficial to the individual, but also that in times of great need these states appear spontaneously to enable us to respond to the situations in an optimal fashion.

Not all of the states mentioned describe a specific state. Some, like meditation, can actually be produced by many different methods, such as the various meditative practices; even a meditative state produced by a single practice most likely consists of many different states, particularly in the evolution of the individual practicing the techniques. This may be understood by referring to Brown's description of Tantric Mahamudra

Table 3-1
Altered states of consciousness

	References	Describes method	Describes character- istics
Meditation	7,11,13,15,16	X	
Hypnosis/trance	7,11,13,15,16	X	
Drugs/psychedelic	7,11,13,15,16	X	
Sensory deprivation	11,13,16	X	
Sensory overload	13	X	
Religious practices	11,12,13	X	
Ecstacy	11,15		X
Dervishes	16	X	
Stress (severe/prolonged)	13	X	
Dreams	7,11,15,16	X	
Daydreams	11,16		X
Psychotic	11		X
Fugue	11		X
Dissociation	11,15		X
Hypnagogic	7,11,15		X
Creative	11,15		X
Transcendental	15	X	
Extrasensory awareness	15		X
Biofeedback	11	X	
Progressive relaxation	17	X	
Autogenic training	12,18	X	
Relaxation response	12	X	
EEG states (alpha, theta)	19		X

meditation.[20] This type of meditation is organized in such a way that the objective is to disrupt the subsystems of the USC that lead to changes subjectively at each level. The first group of exercises begins to aid awareness of inner experience, and they are designed to eliminate the internal chatter. This leads to the next stage, that of perception without thought. This, in turn, is followed by a world without perception, and later progresses to a world without self. Other forms and systems of meditation produce states with even more subdivisions and changes.

Our definition of ASC encompasses all of those states not included in USC, and we include in these USC waking, sleeping, and dreaming. For our purposes, dreaming may be considered as a transitional state, a usual state because we experience it on a regular basis, but an altered state because it has many of the characteristics and benefits of ASC. Many of the ASC listed in Table 3-1 are not conducive to our purposes—to enable the individual to realize his or her full potential and to take control of body-mind processes. We feel that in order to accomplish these goals, an ASC must have certain characteristics. These characteristics are similar to those outlined by Marsh[21] when describing daydreaming, i.e., inward focusing of attention; continued awareness of the background structure, although the foreground structure may be different; unreal, coherent, but improbable attributes, albeit not bizarre; and a flow slower than ordinary states of consciousness. To these characteristics we would like to add the necessity that the state be controllable by the individual and inherently safe. This could eliminate from consideration such factors as drug-induced or drug withdrawal states, because they both lack inherent safety and controllability. Likewise, we feel that sensory overload is not necessarily a safe condition, whereas sensory isolation probably is. In this scheme, dreams would be transitional since they can be controlled, but with a considerable degree of effort, sometimes more effort than in some of the other states. Certain states such as psychotic and hallucinatory states and psychomotor seizures are not goals that we would have people strive for. We would also eliminate from consideration unconscious or semiconscious states produced by such methods as brain trauma, anoxia, and general anesthesia.

Fromm[11] describes an ego-psychological theory of ASC which identifies the characteristics of ASC in a different way from that mentioned above. An understanding of some of the characteristics essential for our purposes may be gained by referring to Table 3-2. We are primarily interested in those states in which the attention is focused or expansive. The ego activity can be either active or receptive for the particular purposes involved. Activity refers to the ability of the individual to make a choice, whereas in receptivity this activity is relinquished freely. Both of these differ from passivity, in which autonomy is lost.

We are interested in SC which involve relaxation and turning of consciousness inward. The states are active rather than passive and are of a calm or relaxed nature. In states with these characteristics, it appears as though we relinquish some of the control functions of the left hemisphere and allow the right cerebral hemispheric function to predominate.[22] Csikszentmihalyi[23] has stated succinctly the characteristics needed to produce a conscious change to the ASC that we are interested in: (1) awareness and action merging in concentration that is sustained and not distracted, (2) focusing of attention on a limited area dispassionately, (3) development of hyperawareness of those feeling states related to the activity, (4) development of skills adequate for the demand of the activity, and (5) development of clear perception of those necessary cues and environmental responses. These would then lead to the development of an ASC which, according to Tart, is "a different way of (1) perceiving reality, and (2) different 'logics' for understanding it and interacting with it."[24]

Table 3-2
Characteristics of ASC based on Fromm's ego-psychological theory[6]

State	Attention	Ego
Normal waking	N	a
Waking/entranced	F	a
Free association	UF	r
Daydream	UF	r
Dream	HA	a/r
Psychedelic drugs	HA	r
Hypnosis	F	r>a
Autohypnosis	F	a/r
Biofeedback	F	a/r
Transcendental meditation	F	a/r
Concentrated meditation	F	a
Satipatthana meditation	E	r
Vipassana meditation	E	a

Note:

   a = Active
   r = Receptive
   N = Normal
   F = Focused
   UF = Unfocused
   E = Expansive
   HA = Hyperaroused with narrow attention

Physiology and similarities of ASC

In the previous section we delineated some of the characteristics of ASC and some of the names given to them. We have mentioned that these names describe not a state but either the method of producing the state or certain characteristics thereof, as noted in Table 3-1. Table 3-2 delineated some differences in certain of these states, based on the action of one's ego and attention. In this section we will discuss the physiological measurements made in various ASC and use them to delineate the similarities. We believe that the similarities are greater than many writers have heretofore elucidated and that many of these processes are capable of leading to states which can produce similar desired responses. Many of the differences are semantic rather than real and have resulted in considerable confusion, both in the scientific literature and with the consumer of health care. Unfortunately, an additional incentive to keep many of these disciplines separate is pecuniary. If one can advertise something as unique, then only those trained in such uniqueness are capable of administering therapy or instruction. To be sure, there are some real differences, as pointed out by Luthe and Blumberger.[25] These relate to the mode of instruction, whether it be through others or self; topographic, that is, related to specific and continuous body areas, or nontopographic; directed versus nondirected; symptomatic versus nonspecific; and verbal versus nonverbal. However, there are many devices similar to most, such as a mental device, passivity, relaxation, quietness of the environment and, in many, the necessity of a trained instructor.

In this section we will be basically comparing some of the major methods of inducing ASC. These include meditation (transcendental meditation, Zen meditation, yogic meditation), autogenic training, progressive relaxation, hypnosis, and biofeedback.

Transcendental meditation (TM) is a type of meditation based on yogic scriptures as taught by Maharishi Mahesh Yogi and his followers. This requires trained instruction and four major components: (1) a quiet environment, (2) a repeated mental device, (3) a passive attitude, and (4) a comfortable position.[12] In TM, the mental device is a secret Sanskrit word called a mantrum. Benson,[12] utilizing these four requirements, developed what he calls the relaxation response (RR). The difference between RR and TM is that the mental device is the English word *one*.

Zen meditation is a type of meditation practiced by followers of the specific discipline of Zen Buddhism. Likewise, yogic meditations are followed by practitioners of various yogic disciplines. There are many variants of yogic and Zen meditations, but scientific studies are limited to just a few of these.

Autogenic training (AT) is a discipline originated by Shultz in the early part of the century and more recently popularized by Luthe.[18] Although there are many later variations for the advanced student, the initial trainee is instructed in the standard exercises of (1) heaviness, (2) warmth, (3) heart regulation, (4) self-regulation of breathing, (5) warmth in the solar plexus area and the upper mid-abdomen, and (6) forehead cooling. These and later exercises all follow a rather rigid and strict training regimen, and one is advised to master each stage before proceeding to the next.

Progressive relaxation (PR) was first taught as a separate discipline though the work of Jacobson in the fourth decade of this century.[17] Essentially, PR consists of alternately contracting and then releasing the contracted tension in the various muscle groups of the body in a sequential fashion.

Hypnosis has been recognized as a medical and scientifically valid therapeutic tool since the late 1950s and was in use prior to that time. Hypnosis has had its problems as being too mystical for the scientific and too regimented for the spiritual. There are many different theories as to what hypnosis actually is, and only one of these attributes hypnotic phenomena to ASC. We agree fully with the descriptions of Milton Erickson, however, that hypnosis does involve a trance state and altering

of one's state of consciousness. The problem with adequately categoriz-
ing hypnosis is that it can be a self-induced phenomenon, such as meditation, or can be induced with the guidance of others. Also, it can be goal-
directed, as when giving suggestions to overcome a habit or illness, or it
can be nongoal-directed, as when used for general relaxation. It is with
hypnosis that much of the argument as to similarities and differences take
place. For example, Kroger[26] feels that all of the disciplines mentioned
above are merely phenomena of hypnosis, whereas practitioners of the
above disciplines feel that hypnosis is a distinct phenomenon. Certainly,
if one uses the traditional hypnotic paradigm of a hypnotist hypnotizing a
subject, the practitioners may be correct. However, if one uses broader
definitions of hypnosis, then Kroger's statements may be correct. In fact,
Muses, who feels that trance and hypnosis are part of everyday life, states
that "there is really no such thing as an 'ordinary state of consciousness.'
Everyone to the degree governed by his or her acculturation, upbringing,
and value system development and entrenchment, is in a state of waking
trance to some degree. Acculturation is slow hypnosis, as is all conditioning and behavioristic manipulation."[27]

Some of the principles of biofeedback (BF) were mentioned in Chapter
2. Many have called biofeedback training, using the electroencephalogram (EEG), a specific state. Indeed, with feedback of the appropriate
EEG signal, one can learn to induce a predominance of EEG alpha
rhythms (8 to 12 Hz) in the occipital-temporal area.[28] Alpha has been
associated with a pleasant state of mind—relaxed, quiet, slow and tran-
quil—as contrasted with beta.[29] However, these subjective responses
are not unique to alpha biofeedback training and can also be seen with
TM,[12, 30,31] Zen meditation,[12] yogic meditation,[12,32] and autogenic training.[12] In fact, the EEG is probably the crudest biofeedback instrument
used, and it is hard to conceptualize that a few electrodes placed on the
scalp are able to measure the complexity of the functionings of the human
brain with its millions of neurons. As pointed out by Alford, "EEG
machines merely give a statistical average of the rhythmic firings of tens
of millions of neurons, giving little more information about actual brain-
mind processing than microphones placed on the surface of the Houston
Astrodome tell about the playing of football."[33]

The most complete physiological studies with respect to various altered states of consciousness have been performed on practitioners of
TM.[12,34,35] The results have been mentioned in the previous chapter as
being compatible with the relaxation response; i.e., decreased oxygen
consumption, decreased respiratory rate, decreased heart rate, predominance of alpha rhythm, and decreased blood pressure. Later studies have
also demonstrated a decrease in muscle tension,[30] decrease in blood
lactate (the substance thought to accumulate during anaerobic metabolism and anxiety states),[36,37] increased flow in the cerebral blood ves-

sels,[38] and increased galvanic skin response (GSR) which are thought to be compatible with a relaxed state.[30] In addition to predominance of alpha, TM has been shown to yield a synchronization in the anterior and posterior areas,[39] and increased coherence in the alpha and theta ranges.[40] These measurements would have more significance than the simple EEG, and they show a functioning of the brain as a unit rather than as isolated areas, each involved in its own particular subspecialization. Additionally, there was an increased alpha-to-delta ratio, interpreted as demonstrating increased wakefulness; and a decreased beta-to-alpha ratio, interpreted as demonstrating decreased activation.[31] In fact, the effect on metabolism was very profound. Oxygen consumption is a measure of metabolism, and in TM this parameter fell to 16 percent of baseline within a few minutes, whereas in the deepest of sleep the decrease is only 8 percent to 10 percent and takes several hours to achieve.[35] The fact that the oxygen consumption decreased and the carbon dioxide elimination decreased by the same amount indicates that there was no change in the O_2-to-CO_2 ratio. Additionally, carbon monoxide production was decreased by 30 percent, and the blood lactate was decreased.[41] These results imply that more of the body's metabolism is aerobic even in this hypometabolic state.

AT has also been shown to decrease the respiratory and heart rates, produce a predominance of alpha in the EEG, and decrease muscle tension.[12] These changes are quite similar to those found in TM. Likewise, Zen and yogic meditations result in similar changes in the above parameters.[12,32]

PR leads to decreases in the respiratory rate, heart rate, blood pressure, and muscle tension.[42] It also has been shown to result in alpha EEG predominance and increased GSR.[30]

The real problem develops when one attempts to study the physiology of hypnosis. Whereas with TM and the other disciplines the methods used are quite standardized, the methods of hypnosis induction are varied. In fact, some of the methods of hypnosis induction are quite similar, if not identical, to those used in AT and PR. Additionally, some of the hypnosis relaxation techniques have considerable similarity to many types of meditative practices. Although most of the other techniques mentioned are self-induced, we feel that with hypnosis the differences are in the methods and content of the hypnotic suggestion rather than in the mode of induction. We agree with Sheikh et al.[43] that there is great overlap between what is labeled hypnosis and what is labeled otherwise, such as guided imagery. We are in agreement with Wallace and Benson[44] that the physiologic changes of hypnosis actually reflect the milieu suggested by the hypnotist or, in the case of autohypnosis, established by the experiencer. Comments in the past that have tended to favor differences between hypnosis and other disciplines have had two methodologic errors.

First, both hypnosis and the discipline to be studied were not in the same protocol, but the latter was compared to previous studies on hypnosis. This makes little scientific sense. Second, the studies of hypnosis did not take into account differences in the subject matter of the hypnotic session. In our opinion, the landmark study overcoming these methodologic errors was performed in 1977 by Morse and associates.[30] They studied 48 patients divided into four groups: (1) practitioners of TM, (2) autohypnosis, (3) subjects trained in both TM and autohypnosis, and (4) subjects trained in neither. The subjects were then evaluated according to five states: (1) alert, waking—A, (2) meditation—M (TM or SM, simple word meditation), (3) hypnosis, relaxed type—HR, (4) hypnosis, task-performance type—HT, and (5) relaxation alone—R. The HR group corresponds to what we call nongoal-directed hypnosis, and the HT group to what we have called goal-oriented hypnosis. Parameters measured were (1) respiratory rate, (2) pulse rate, (3) blood pressure, (4) GSR, (5) EEG, and (6) muscle activity. In the GSR, all of the relaxed states (TM, SM, HR, HT, and R) scored significantly better than the A state. Of paramount importance was that there were no significant differences between either of the hypnosis states and either of the M states. The results of all but one of the objective measurements were similar to the GSR. There were similarities between R, H, and M on EEG alpha production and synchronization of slow alpha. Interestingly, muscle activity was the only measured objective parameter where TM participants scored higher. This may be due to limitations of the technique used for hypnosis, an eye-fixation method. Of interest was that the HT group showed physiologic responses more like the A group, and diametrically opposed to the HR group. This scientifically validates the previous hypothesis that the content of the hypnosis session profoundly affects the physiological parameters.

For nongoal-oriented hypnosis, the characteristics were similar to TM and those of the relaxation response. However, in goal-directed hypnosis, the parameters varied according to the scene and may very well have been like the waking state. Also, the physiologic responses of the two meditation groups, SM and TM, were quite similar. This study does not show that the states produced were the same, but rather that the physiologic responses produced by different meditative techniques were similar and were much like those in HR. While practice of a certain meditation technique or techniques may, within significant periods of time, lead to changes not measurable by our usual physiologic parameters, this does not negate the similarities, at least in early stages. Since most of the population will not practice a meditative method with the discipline and perseverance necessary to achieve these advanced states, the similarities are more important for most of us. Therefore, we believe that for attaining the benefits of any of these ASC, practice of any of the above methods is satisfactory as is the practice of many similar methods not as yet studied physiologically.

In another study, Walrath and Hamilton compared HR with TM. The parameters measured were heart rate, respiratory rate, and GSR. They noted no significant differences between the two practices on the parameters mentioned.[45] Shapiro and associates[46] reviewed the literature on behavioral methods in treatment of hypertension up to 1977. In all, there were five studies on PR, two on AT, two on hypnosis, one on Zen meditation, one on hatha-yoga, four on TM, one on RR, and three on multiple methods. From a cumulative standpoint, no significant difference was noted in the effectiveness of the various methods in decreasing systolic and diastolic pressures.

In 1969, Paul[47] compared PR and HR with respect to heart rate, respiratory rate, muscle tension, GSR, and reported anxiety. With the exception of GSR the results were similar for the two practices investigated, both of which demonstrated superiority in the parameters measured when compared to the control. Another study investigating hypnosis and relaxation[48] compared responses from the hypnotic susceptibility scales, subjective experiences, EEG, and EMG and likewise found no significant differences. Barmark and Gaunitz[49] presented a phenomenological comparison of HR and TM. The subjects studied were 23 practitioners of TM and 19 subjects who scored high on hypnotic susceptibility scales and were subsequently taught hypnosis. The phenomena tested were attention to environment, attention to body posture, attention to respiration, relaxation, body heaviness, experience of body temperature, differentiation between subject and object, experience of time, concentration, and imagery. In all of the phenomena tested there were no significant differences between the TM group and the HR group—with the exception of imagery, which tended to be more vivid in HR than in TM.

We have presented the above information in order to demonstrate basic similarities in the types of ASC mentioned when observed from physiological, experiential and/or phenomenological standpoints. Therefore we feel justified in reaching the conclusion that many of these techniques can lead to states bearing enough similarities to yield to the practitioner the beneficial effects described for any one of them. Likewise, there is a tremendous degree of overlap, such that practitioners of one art may actually be practicing another art, the confusion coming only from semantics. We disagree with Luthe's comment with respect to adding hypnosis to autogenic training, thereby achieving autogenic hypnosis: "The hypnotic element of eye fixation (sometimes in combination with monotonous auditory stimuli . . .) is added in order to promote a shift to the hypnotic state."[25] We feel that these two techniques lead to mutually similar, if not identical, states. As Kroger states, the practitioners of various arts of ASC "who are not familiar with modern and sophisticated techniques of hypnosis, which do not require an induction technique, would actually not believe they are using task-motivated instruction in the hypnotic manner. Likewise, those using various forms of meditation and ASC are seldom aware that they are resorting to self-hypnosis."[26]

The techniques may differ, but the results are quite similar. A technique that works for one individual may not for another, and therefore, many approaches and methods are necessary to achieve significant therapeutic effectiveness in the greatest number of people. If we realize that we are working with varying techniques and not varying results, then cooperation rather than competition will become the keynote—to the benefit of all consumers of medical care.

General (nonspecific) uses of ASC

It has been noted that elicitation of certain ASC, particularly RR and TM, develop physiologic changes that are the opposite of the stress response. It is our belief that this is our species' innate way of preventing the detrimental effects of the stress response. The evidence presented in the previous section of this chapter extrapolates these benefits to any method that is nongoal-directed, such as RH, AT, nongoal-directed BF, and other forms of meditation. Evidence that these ASC can also aid in promoting wellness, creativity, learning, self-actualization, pain relief, alteration of habits, and many other desirable effects will be mentioned in later chapters. Therefore, because ASC in and of themselves are beneficial and because they allow the processes of imagery to be more effective, we feel that instruction in ASC is the important initial step, prior to any specific training in imagery. Frequently, the daily practice of ASC alone is all an individual needs. Only after this instruction has been given and practiced by the individual do we believe that specific imagery instruction should be initiated.

There are many ways of inducing ASC, and some of our methods will be discussed in Chapter 5. These are by no means exclusive to us, and other methods can be equally satisfactory. However, in dealing with general and specific problems, learning to reproduce the experience of ASC is the first and most important step in our program, and it must be learned in order for any general or specific imagery to be effective. The relationship between ASC and imagery has been well established. ASC such as hypnosis have been shown to intensify the imagination.[50]

The responsivity to hypnosis has been demonstrated to be related to a person's ability to involve him or herself in fantasy and imagination.[51,52]

In fact, hypnotic suggestions usually result in subjective imagery formation.[43] Many studies have demonstrated a nonlinear relationship between the susceptibility of hypnosis and imagery.[53] As Richardson notes,[54] the multitude of sensory input that we experience is what actually prevents imagery from taking place and being perceived, and imagery is more likely to be elevated to conscious awareness when we are in a state in which we remain awake and with much of the internal stimuli subjugated; i.e., when we are experiencing an ASC.

References

1. N. E. Zinberg, ed., *Alternate States of Consciousness* (New York: Free Press, 1977).

2. C. T. Tart, ed., *Altered States of Consciousness* (New York: Anchor Books, 1972).

3. C. T. Tart, *States of Consciousness* (New York: E. P. Dutton, 1975).

4. C. Marsh, C. "A Framework for Describing Subjective States of Consciousness," in *Alternate States of Consciousness*, ed. N. E. Zinberg (New York: Free Press, 1977), p. 121.

5. C. T. Tart, "Putting the Pieces Together: A Conceptual Framework for Understanding Discrete States of Consciousness," in *Alternate States of Consciousness*, ed. N. E. Zinberg (New York: Free Press, 1977), pp. 158–219.

6. C. T. Tart, "The Basic Nature of Altered States of Consciousness: A Systems Approach," *J Transpers Psychol* 8 (1976), pp. 45–64.

7. Tart, "The Basic Nature of Altered States of Consciousness," p. 182.

8. Tart, *Altered States of Consciousness*, pp. 1–6.

9. A. M. Ludwig, "Altered States of Consciousness," *Arch Gen Psychiat* 15 (1966), pp. 225–34.

10. Ibid., p. 217.

11. E. Fromm, "An Ego-Psychological Theory of Altered States of Consciousness," *Int J Clin Exp Hyp* 25 (1977), pp. 372–87.

12. H. Benson, *The Relaxation Response* (New York: Morrow, 1975).

13. T. H. Budzynski, "Biofeedback and the Twilight States of Consciousness," in *Consciousness and Self-Regulation: Advances in Research*, ed. G. E. Schwartz and D. Shapiro (New York: Plenum Press, 1976), pp. 361–85.

14. N. E. Zinberg, "The Study of Consciousness States: Problems and Progress," *Alternate States of Consciousness* (New York: Free Press, 1977), p. 9.

15. K. H. Pribam, "Some Observations on the Organization of Studies of Mind, Brain, and Behavior," in *Alternate States of Consciousness*, ed. N. E. Zinberg (New York: Free Press, 1977), pp. 220–29.

16. A. M. Ludwig, "Altered States of Consciousness," in *Altered States of Consciousness*, ed. C. T. Tart (New York: Anchor Books, 1972), pp. 11–24.

17. E. Jacobson, ed., *Progressive Relaxation* (Chicago: University of Chicago Press, 1938).

18. W. Luthe, ed., *Autogenic Therapy*, vols. 1–5 (New York: Grune and Stratton, 1969).

19. E. Green and A. Green, *Beyond Biofeedback* (New York: Delacorte Press, 1977).

20. D. P. Brown, "A Model for the Levels of Concentrative Meditation," in *Int J Clin Exp Hyp* 25 (1977), pp. 236–73.

21. C. Marsh, "A Framework for Describing Subjective States of Consciousness, in *Alternate States of Consciousness*, ed. N. E. Zinberg (New York: Free Press, 1977), pp. 121–57.

22. R. G. Ley, "Cerebral Asymmetries, Emotional Experience, and Imagery: Implications for Psychotherapy," in *The Potential and Fantasy of Imagination*, ed. A. A. Sheikh and J. D. Shaffer (New York: Brandon House, 1979), pp. 41–65.

23. M. Csikszentmihalyi, "Flow: Studies of Enjoyment," United States Public Health Service Report No. RO1 H M 22–833–02 (Washington, D.C., 1974).

24. C. T. Tart, "Science and the Sources of Value," *Phoenix: New Directions for the Study of Man* 3 (1979), pp. 25–29.

25. W. Luthe and S. R. Blumberger, "Autogenic Training," in *The Psychosomatic Approach in Medical Practice*, eds. E. D. Wilkower and H. Warnes (New York: Harper & Row, 1977), pp. 146–63.

26. W. S. Kroger, *Clinical and Experimental Hypnosis* (Philadelphia: J. B. Lippincott, 1977), pp. 141–45.

27. C. M. Muses, introduction to *Consciousness and Reality*, ed. C. Muses and A. M. Young (New York: Avon Books, 1974), pp. 3–4.

28. J. Kamiya, "Operant Control of the EEG Alpha Rhythm and Some of Its Reported Effects on Consciousness," in *Altered States of Consciousness*, ed. C. T. Tart (New York: John Wiley & Sons, 1969).

29. K. Gardner, "Control of States of Consciousness: Attainment through External Feedback Augmenting Control of Psychophysiological Variables," *Arch Gen Psychiat* 25 (1971), pp. 436–41.

30. D. R. Morse, J. S. Margin and M. L. Furst et al., "A Physiological and Subjective Evaluation of Meditation, Hypnosis and Relaxation," *Psychosom Med* 5 (1977), pp. 304–24.

31. J. P. Banquet and M. Sailhan, "EEG Analysis of Spontaneous and Induced States of Consciousness," in *Scientific Research on the Transcendental Meditation Program*, vol. 1, ed. D. Orme-Johnson and J. T. Farrow (Livingstone Manor, N.Y.: Maharishi European Research University Press, 1977), pp. 165–72.

32. B. K. Bagchi and M. A. Wenger, "Electrophysiological Corrolates of Some Yogi Exercises," in *Electroencephalography, Clinical Neurophysiology, and Epilepsy*, vol. 3 of the First International Congress of Neurological Sciences, ed. L. Van Bagaert and J. Radermecker (London: Pergamon, 1959).

33. D. K. Alford, "The Effects of Literacy on Cognition and Being in the World," *Phoenix: New Directions for the Study of Man* 3 (1979), pp. 31–42.

34. D. Orme-Johnson and J. T. Farrow, *Scientific Research on the Transcendental Meditation Program*. Collected papers, vol. 1 (Livingstone Manor, N.Y.: Maharishi European Research University Press, 1977).

35. R. K. Wallace, "Physiological Effects of Transcendental Meditation," *Science* 167 (1970), pp. 1751–54.

36. R. Jevning, A. F. Wilson, W. R. Smith et al., "Redistribution of Blood Flow in Acute Hypometabolic Behavior," *Am J Physiol* 235 (1978), pp. R89–R92.

37. F. N. Pitts and J. N. McClure, "Lactate Metabolism in Anxiety Neurosis," *New Engl J Med* 277 (1967), pp. 1329–36.

38. R. Jevning and A. F. Wilson, "Behavioral Increase of Cerebral Blood Flow." Paper presented at annual meeting of American Physiological Association, 1978.

39. J. P. Banquet, "Spectral Analysis of the EEG in Meditation," *Electroencephalogr Clin Neurophysiol* 35 (1973), pp. 143–51.

40. P. H. Levine, J. R. Herbert, C. T. Haynes et al., "EEG Coherence during the Transcendental Meditation Technique" in *Scientific Research on the Transcendental Meditation Program*. Collected papers, vol. 1, ed. D. Orme-Johnson and J. T. Farrow (Livingstone Manor, N.Y.: Maharishi European Research University Press, 1977), pp. 187–207.

41. R. K. Wallace and M. D. Garrett, "Decreased Blood Lactate during Transcendental Meditation, *Fed Proceed* 30 (1971), p. 376.

42. T. Borkovec and D. Fowles, "A Controlled Investigation of the Effects of Progressive and Hypnotic Relaxation on Insomnia," *J Abnorm Psychol* 82 (1973), pp. 153–58.

43. A. A. Sheikh, P. Richardson and L. M. Moleski, "Psychosomatics and Mental Imagery: A Brief Review," in *The Potential of Fantasy and Imagination,* ed. A. A. Sheikh and J. T. Schaffer (New York: Brandon House, 1979), pp. 105–18.

44. R. K. Wallace and H. Benson, "The Physiology of Meditation," *Altered States of Awareness: Readings from Scientific American* (San Francisco: Freeman, 1972).

45. L. C. Walrath and D. W. Hamilton, "Autonomic Correlates of Meditation and Hypnosis," *Am J Clin Hyp* 17 (1975), pp. 190–96.

46. A. P. Shapiro, G. E. Schwarts, D. C. E. Fergusen et al., "Behavioral Methods in the Treatment of Hypertension," *Ann Int Med* 86 (1977), pp. 626–36.

47. G. L. Paul, "Physiological Effects of Relaxation Training and Hypnotic Suggestion," *J Abnorm Psychol* 74 (1969), pp. 425–537.

48. W. E. Edmonston, "The Effects of Neutral Hypnosis on Conditioned Responses: Implications for Hypnosis as Relaxation," in *Hypnosis: Developments in Research and New Perspectives,* ed. E. Fromm and R. E. Shor (New York: Aldine, 1979), pp. 415–55.

49. S. M. Barmark and S. C. B. Gaunitz, "Transcendental Meditation and Heterohypnosis as Altered States of Consciousness," *Int J Clin Exp Hyp* 27 (1979), pp. 227–39.

50. M. B. Arnold, "On the Mechanism of Suggestion and Hypnosis," *J Abnorm Soc Psychol* 41 (1946), pp. 107–28.

51. T. X. Barber and L. B. Glass, "Significant Factors in Hypnotic Behavior," *J Abnorm Soc Psychol* 64 (1962), pp. 222–28.

52. P. W. Sheehan, "Hypnosis and the Manifestations of Imagination," in *Hypnosis: Research Developments and Perspectives*, ed. E. Fromm and R. E. Shor (Chicago: Aldine-Atherton, 1972).

53. A. Richardson, Voluntary Control of the Memory Image," chap. 5 in *The Nature and Function of Imagery*. ed. P. W. Sheehan (New York: Academic Press, 1972).

54. A. Richardson, *Mental Imagery* (New York: Springer, 1969).

Chapter 4

Imagery

The soul . . . never thinks without a picture.
Aristotle

Imagery is the basis of our thought processes. There is evidence that we thought in images long before we ever had words, both ontogenetically and phylogenetically. The capacity to form language is innate within the human species. However, specific languages are human inventions, whereas imagery is our innate way of processing information. Many sources attest to the universality of imagery in our species.[2,3]

In the development of the individual, the earliest forms of cognition seem to be visual in nature.[4,5] Words developed later as a means of describing both external and internal realities, the latter less adequately. Both realities consist of images. Those who can describe the images with a greater degree of accuracy become authors. In fact, it has been stated that the greatness of Shakespeare lies in part in the tremendous range of vocabulary he employed, in his constant use of words evoking smell, touch, taste, sounds, or sights, which permitted him to reinvoke images with which we had lost touch.[6] Pictures or images represent patterns or symbols, and words are necessary to explain the meaning of these symbols[7] and are the best available tool for making our thoughts and ideas known to others.[8] Imagery creates a more immediate experience of a situation or memory rather than the distant experience conveyed by a verbal experience or memory.[9]

Primary process thinking is the mode of cognition in preverbal children, implying thinking in images.[10] In altered states of consciousness (ASC), primary process/visual information thinking also seems to predominate. Bugelski relates the word and image connection as a cyclical process; i.e., words arouse images leading to an emotional response that results in giving meaning to words.[11]

Definition and functions of imagery

When discussing imagery, most people tend to think of imagery in a visual mode because visual imagery tends to be our primary mode of processing external information. In many, it is also the primary mode of processing internal information because most of the valid research on imagery has been performed with visual imagery. However, for the therapeutic uses of imagery to be most effective, we should utilize as many of the five sensory modalities as possible, since we all process the external world with them: visual, auditory, kinesthetic (feeling), olfactory (smell), and gustatory (taste)[12] (see Chapter 5).

We basically agree with Gordon that an image is a sensory perception in the absence of the external object or stimulus which usually results in that perception (in Sheehan).[13] However, this differentiation of imagery as an internal event, from perception as an internal representation of an external event, can be very difficult. In the early part of the century, it was discovered that a physical stimulus could be confused with an imagination image without any recognition of this by the observer, a phenomenon known as the Perky effect.[14] We also know that in hallucinations, internally created images can seem to have an external locus. Hallucinations do not necessarily imply psychoses, as they can be seen as phenomena of other ASC such as hypnosis. Holt feels that the dual concept of perception versus mental image is artificial and should be replaced with the idea of imagery as a continuum. He defines imagery as a

> subjective phenomenon that may have any combination of external and internal influences. When the weight is clearly on the side of sensory input, the common terms percept or perceptual image will serve interchangeably; and when the weight is on the side of inner, central inputs, I shall speak of mental images. . . .[15]

Several models of imagery have been proposed. First is the *analog,* or *representational,* model which has been popularized phenomenologically and which attributes a role to imagery cognition.[16,17] A *propositional* model theorizes that images on a conscious level are epiphenomena or imagery processing, the latter taking place at an abstract level.[18] In this model the propositions (logical relationships between concepts[19]) are the informational units necessary to analyze the phenomena of imagery. These propositions are abstract representations rather than semantic. According to Phlyshyn[18], an image is an internally constructed perceptual description that can easily be reduced to the above mentioned propositions. A third model is that of *role playing,* or *imagining,* in which the person experiencing an image acts as if the object represented were already present or the presence were anticipated.[20,21] Hampson and Morris extrapolate these concepts to form a *cyclical model* of imagery in which the images are both created and used by the same system. They state that imaging, as perceiving, is a cyclical activity and that conscious experience has a part to play in controlling these cycles.[22] This conscious control is of paramount importance in the use of imagery in therapeutic and self-improvement situations in establishing direction and validity for imagery.

Our internal imagery world is just as real, emotionally and physiologically, as the external world. Evidence to support the previous statement will be presented later. Many authors have attributed numerous functions to internal imagery. We will define the *functions* of imagery as those activities which take place whether or not we are aware of them, whereas the *uses* of imagery need to be actively directed by us, at least in part, on a conscious level. Table 4–1 lists representative examples of those functions of imagery and their appropriate sources.

Table 4-1
Functions of imagery

Function	Reference
Primary process thinking, unconscious processes	3, 10
Cognition in children	23, 24
Carrier of effectively charged memories, ideas, impulses	5
Root of structure of language	7, 8
Information storage	22
Spacial information	23
Mediation of verbal learning	23
Structuring of meaningful order	23
Relation of past to present experience	23
Fixing of experiences for future use	23, 25
Preserving, elaborating, repeating, and intensifying of experiences	25
Expression of unconscious wishes	26
Psychic equivalent of an event	27

Universality of imagery

Imagery has appeared ubiquitously in early records of the human species throughout all cultures. In Doob's view, it therefore "must reflect a human ability that has survived from an early evolutionary stage."[28] Inferential anthropological evidence for early imagery is represented by cave paintings made 10,000 to 60,000 years B.C.[3,28] In fact, Samuels and Samuels have stated that primitive man's basic consciousness was visual.[3] Other inferential anthropologic evidence for the validation of imagery includes mnemonic devices and observations.[28] Most Eastern philosophies attribute great value to imagery, particularly in meditative states. Some Western philosophies are beginning to use imagery methods, and more esoteric Western philosophies have used them for a long time. Aristotle believed that thought was composed of images.[29] Hermetic philosophy taught that the physical world could be affected by imagery,[29] a point of view which has been increasingly accepted by that most exact of our sciences, physics. In fact, before Descartes, imagery was thought to be a physiological reality.[1]

Shamanistic practices utilized visualization to travel through the essence of an ill person to effect diagnoses and therapy. Similar processes have also been used by faith healers, Christian Scientists, and esoteric and mystical groups such as the Rosicrucians. In addition to the belief that imagery could affect physical entities, Hermetic philosophy believed that disease could be cured by the visualization of perfect health, a type of imagery that we call end-result imagery. As mentioned earlier, imagery appears throughout the literature and philosophies of the East, including the Vedic literature of India and tantric traditions, as well as in cabalism (Hebrew mysticism).[25] Jung's idea of the collective unconscious as the reservoir of thoughts and images of all mankind attests to the universality and ubiquity of imagery.[30]

Art is an external representation of imagery. Jung's concept of art included psychological art, which was drawn from experiences, and visionary art, which "derives its existence from the hinterland of man's mind." He felt that this was true symbolism, primordial in nature. There is a type of art found in all societies, no matter how primitive, that is called the mandala. This essentially consists of a central focus of attention with radiating spokes. It is respresented by such objects as the Aztec calendar and even by flowers. Jung felt that the mandala was a representation of deep inner experience, that it was a true expression of the collective unconscious and that, when it was objectified as an image on paper or canvas, the artist was expressing not just his or her inner feelings but the experiences of mankind. LaBarre provides added evidence that imagery appears in all known cultures and developmental levels.[31]

Can we all image? _____

In the previous section, we presented evidence for the ubiquitousness of imagery. However, when working with patients and clients, and when presenting workshops to professionals and the general public alike, we frequently meet people who feel they lack the ability to image. It is our belief that anyone has this ability. Generally, people do have individual differences in their abilities to image. "The average person," according to Horowitz, tends to fall somewhere in the spectrum from vivid to non-vivid in all image modalities."[32] We believe, however, that even a relatively nonvivid imager can learn to increase the vividness of his or her imagery. We also believe the statement by Samuels and Samuels that it is really not important that the image be as vivid as life, but rather that we be able to control the image even if we have a mind's eye image; i.e., a "strong sense of knowing what it looks like."[29]

"While the ability to generate and employ mental imagery varies across people," writes Marks, "the potential to do so is probably universal. Given appropriate and optimal conditions of training and performance, it is likely that all persons could utilize imagery—encoded information."[33] Many believe that once sensations have been experienced, they are retained somewhere within the system and that the ability to recall and reexperience the situation and its associated sensations are available to all of us, although we rarely take advantage of these possibilities.[34]

Imagery exists in all five modes of perception; therefore a person who is not able to visualize vividly may be able to hear or feel vividly. Maltz asserts that an image is more effective if the person "feels" as well as sees.[35] To that we would like to add the concept that an image is more successful if a person uses all five modalities of perception.

Many who feel they are unable to image have this feeling because they have only modest ability in the visual mode. These same people are apt to be unaware of the values of imagery in the other sensory modalities. We all experience visual imagery, however. We all dream, and in dreams, the predominant sensory modality is visual, yielding ample evidence that the inability to image is quite rare.[24] If, in fact, we all have the ability to image even when considering primarily the visual mode, what is it that prevents us from experiencing this universal phenomenon regularly? Richardson feels that much of this problem is related to the large amount of sensory phenomena that we are exposed to and experience in our daily civilized lives.[24] He also feels that imagery is more likely to become manifest when we "remain awake" and when "all external stimuli" are not "functionally operative." This is very similar to what we discussed in Chapter 3 with respect to altered states of consciousness enhancing the experience of imagery. Dolan and Sheikh feel that imagery may be inhibited when an individual has experienced widespread traumatic episodes in his or her past.[9] We would like to offer an even more simplistic explanation, which is also true for most systems of the body: Any system or ability that is not nurtured tends to atrophy. When we do not utilize the birthright of imagery experience, we eventually "forget" the experience entirely.

For those who have nonvivid manifestations of imagery, it is possible to increase this ability by practice. The techniques described in Chapter 5 and the remainder of the book will give examples of how to accomplish this. And for those who continue to feel they have the inability to image in the visual mode, we refer to Ahsen's window washer image.[25] In this, the patient/client is asked to imagine that the therapist is a window washer contracting to wash the windows in the client's residence. In order to quote a price, the window washer needs to know how many windows there are in the residence. Therefore the client is asked to provide this information. Almost immediately, the client's eyes will deviate to the side opposite the nondominant hemisphere, indicating the possibility of non-dominant hemisphere stimulation. At the point, even before the answer is given, interruption of the client will then yield the information that he or she was actually counting the windows. How can one count the windows without visualizing them, even if the image is not clear and tends to be a mind's eye image? This will demonstrate to even the most recalcitrant of subjects that imagery is not only possible, but that he or she uses it every day for the solution of many of life's problems.

Imagery: The eye and the brain

With respect to external visual stimuli, we know that the signal is received by the eye, focused by the lens onto the retina, and transmitted by means of the optic nerve to the visual cortex. The eye in this case serves as the receptor, or sense organ, and the brain is the final pathway. We know that this exists for all other types of sensations, such as the ear and brain for hearing, the peripheral sense organs and brain for kines-thetic sensation, the tongue and brain for taste, and the nose and brain for olfactory sensation. The only thing common to all of these modes of sensation is the brain. The question now must be: Do we see with our eyes?

Von Senden answered this question nicely in a report about surgery for congenital cataracts.[36] In the 1930s, operations were performed on people who were blind since birth because of cataracts. When these were per-formed on adults, they experienced very confusing sensations, without any sense of organization. Some reported blotches of colors, and most reported that all of their other senses were distorted. The outcome was that some refused to open their eyes, others experienced hysterical blindness, and some even committed suicide. Almost none of these people actually ever learned to see. However, when these same operations were performed on children, they experienced the same experiences as the adults, but they were able to react in a different way. Instead of the distortion of the other sensations by the visual sensations, these children were able to use their other senses to organize the new sensory input because these children were still in a learning phase.

Essentially, we see with our brain, our eyes being merely receptors. The organization the brain gives to this sensory input is, in a large part, a learned ability. We believe this occurs for all other forms of sensation as well.

"The objects we see *are* images, all made up of whirling, rapidly moving constituents, says Muses."[7] It is obvious that most of us do not perceive the world as objects in this manner, although the new physics tells us that Muses' statement is correct. The explanation of this seeming paradox lies in the fact that our brain organizes these patterns into recognizable images and that the organization is amazingly consistent from individual to individual and from society to society.

A corollary of this is that imagery, even in the visual mode, does not depend upon the possession of adequately functioning sense receptors (for example, eyes). In a comparative study of 91 blind and 91 sighted patients, Johnson noted that the blind demonstrated significantly greater creative imagery, which he defined as the "power of the imagination to break away from perceptual set to produce direct, personal, fantasy and symbolic analogies with simple or complex image patterns."[37] He concluded from this study that creative imagery did not depend on the presence of the visual sensory receptors.

The evidence seems to favor the localization of imagery within the nondominant hemisphere.[4,38,39] (Refer also to the discussion on hemispheric specialization in Chapter 1.) Imagery also seems to be related to hypnotizability, which itself may be a function of the right hemisphere.[40] In addition, it appears that imagery, particularly in altered states of consciousness, may actually help train individuals in the utilization of their spacial, nondominant hemisphere.[41]

We agree with Holt that "imagery is a legitimate and feasible as well as a topical subject of scientific inquiry."[15] Contrary to the view of rigid behaviorists, subjective internal phenomena can no longer be ignored in the light of scientific evidence. The subjective phenomena of imagery and ASC have been demonstrated to produce marked and physiological changes. For those who are interested in scales and tests of measurement of imagery, we refer the reader to Richardson's manuscript, "Mental Imagery."[24]

Types of imagery

In keeping with our species' usual tendency to categorize, differentiate, and classify, names have been given to certain types of imagery. This categorization is necessary from a scientific viewpoint and enables us to be somewhat more precise in our communication. However, it also tends to lead us to believe that the various categories are distinct and separate forms. We feel that imagery, like almost all of our other experiences, resides upon a continuum and no matter how precise we are in our classification, there still is considerable overlap. If we keep this in mind, we are less apt to be misled by categorizations. In fact, after this brief discourse on types of imagery, the remainder of the text pays little attention to the various so-called specific types.

Table 4-2 delineates the types of imagery as we have been able to determine from our own experience and from the literature. Various names are given to what we consider to be similar processes. We have divided the table into two categories. The first is basic types of imagery that delineate general groups, followed by specific types.

One of the most important differentiations is between spontaneous and induced imagery. We believe both are important. *Spontaneous images* are those which arise into one's consciousness without conscious effort.

Table 4-2
Types of imagery

Basic	
1A	Spontaneous (pure, unbidden)
1B	Induced (receptive, bidden)
2A	Concrete
2B	Abstract (symbolic)
3A	End-Result (specific)
3B	Process (specific)
3C	General
Specific	
4	After image
5	Daydream/fantasy
6	Dreams
7	Hypnagogic, hypnopompic
8	Hallucinogenic
9	Guided imagery
10	Memory imagery
11	Imagination imagery
12	Eidetic imagery

Samuels and Samuels feel that these images come from a part considerably deeper than the ego and that they not only appear to awareness as visualizations, but also as feelings and intuition.[30] They feel that these images relate to our fundamental needs and can bring to awareness those areas that need changes or resolutions. In future chapters we will be dealing with these spontaneous images. Of the types of imagery listed under specific images, daydreams, dreams, hypnagogic imagery, and hallucinations are predominantly spontaneous imagery. However, we must note that none of the types of imagery listed under specific imagery are wholly spontaneous or wholly induced. Much can be learned about oneself and one's particular problems and personality by paying attention to spontaneous images, particularly in ASC. Brown terms spontaneous images unbidden, and feels that they represent the unconscious and are associated with ego receptivity or ego passivity.[26]

Induced images are those which we create with some element of conscious or preconscious activity. These images can lead to changes in any aspect of oneself or environment and are the means by which we communicate with our mind. Samuels and Samuels feel that these images come from the ego and are useful for solving problems.[29] They are conditioned by habits and cultural factors and have bases in learned experiences. Brown[26] calls these bidden images, voluntary in nature, related to the preconscious, and associated with ego activity.

Much of the research in imagery fails to take into account differentiation between abstract and concrete imagery. Most of the work focuses on concrete images, leaving the abstract realm to words. We feel this is an unfortunate oversight and that much creativity resides in the abstractness of imagery. The more conscious an image is and the more consciously directed it happens to be, the more concrete it will appear. The closer the image is to the source of thought and the deeper levels of oneself, the more abstract it tends to be. The mandala tends to be a universal image of abstractness, and when looked upon by our conscious, rational, left hemisphere, it has very little impact other than being a pretty picture. However, when we override this part of the mind and begin to use the spacial processes of the right hemisphere, we begin to get in tune with the deeper meanings of its symbolism. Concrete images seem to be most important when used as induced images to program changes and goals into oneself; and abstract images are more potent than concrete images when they appear spontaneously. Because of the abstractness, these require much more time to become understandable, but once understood, they have considerably greater informational impact.

We use the terms *end-result* and *process images* to differentiate the therapeutic styles of imagery (see Chapter 5). *End-result* imagery, which was popularized by Maltz in *Psycho-Cybernetics*,[35] consists of a concrete image of the desired result as having already taken place. In therapeutic endeavors, this is the most important and powerful specific image. *Process* images are images of the actual or fantasized mechanism by which a desired effect could be achieved. A simple example of a process image would be the imagery of hand warming as a treatment for migraine headaches. End-result imagery is significantly more important than process imagery and should be taught first because, frequently, nothing further is needed. End-result and process images are examples of *specific* imagery.

General images are those which are not directed toward a specific goal but are utilized for overall achievement, such as relaxation, stress response reduction, ego strengthening, and actualization. Just as we feel end-result imagery is more important and should be taught prior to process imagery in most cases, we also feel that general imagery is much more important than specific imagery and, likewise, should be taught prior to the institution of any specific imagery instructions. Frequently, just the use of altered states of consciousness alone, with or without general imagery, is all that is needed to achieve a desired goal. An additional value of general imagery lies in its adaptability and applicability to many varied situations, whereas specific images are necessarily more limited. As in building a house, if the foundation is strong, what is built upon it can also be strong, whereas the converse is not true. With respect to imagery, if one is well-trained in the general principles, then one can apply this knowledge to many diverse situations.

An *after image* is the image obtained by closing the eyes after looking for a period of time at a bright object with a dark background, or vice versa. This image cannot be scanned with the eyes, and moves as the eyes move. The image may be positive in nature, but after a few seconds becomes negative; i.e., dark becomes light and vice versa, and colors appear as the reciprocal of their original color. Of all the forms of imagery, this type appears to be the least dependent upon levels of cerebral cortical activity and most dependent upon simple sensory stimulation.[24] This type of imagery is not utilized in a therapeutic situation as far as we are aware.

Daydreams and *fantasy* are types of imagery seen in mild ASC. A daydream tends to be primarily spontaneous, whereas fantasy has a significant element of induced qualities in it. These may be either concrete or abstract, and they do have some therapeutic value both in allowing a person to become more in touch with his or her own subconscious activity as well as in directing future changes. We feel that these differ from more potent therapeutic forms of imagery primarily in that the ASC is not profound and the degree of controllability is not as acute.

Dreams are phenomena that we all experience, involving imagery in all the senses but more specifically in visual modalities. We know from psychoanalytic work that dreams are primarily spontaneous, may be concrete or abstract, and do contain significant information about the individual. Dreams can also be induced, and when this phenomenon takes place, they become of even greater therapeutic importance.

Hypnagogic imagery is that which occurs in the state just prior to falling asleep, whereas *hypnopompic* is that imagery which occurs in the state just immediately after awakening. These states are universal phenomena and usually are associated with extremely vivid visual imagery. However, these states are short-lived as the individual either awakens or falls asleep. The imagery is primarily spontaneous and may be either concrete or abstract. Because of the spontaneity of the imagery, it may have some emotional impact; however, its short duration leaves this type of imagery with little to be desired as a therapeutic tool. The importance of these types of imagery is that they demonstrate to the individual that he or she does indeed possess the capacity to image.

Hallucinations are a very real-appearing form of imagery. These can appear in any or all of the five senses. Many of us tend to think of hallucinations as being associated with psychoses. However, several nonpsychotic state can manifest hallucinations. The characteristics of hallucinations are that they appear to be of external locus rather than internal and that they are assumed to be perceptions by the person experiencing them. Hallucinations can be seen with various drugs, hypnosis, and sensory deprivation. Richardson summarizes studies in which it appears that people with poor imagery in a nonhallucinogenic state tend to be more likely to hallucinate.[42]

Guided imagery is imagery of any of the other types suggested in part or whole to a subject by a guide. Much of the therapy discussed in later chapters can be classified under guided imagery.

Memory imagery consists of the bringing back to awareness of a past event. There are significant differences between this type of imagery and the eidetic image (see below). As Richardson notes, the memory image is unstable, often incomplete, and indefinitely localized.[24] A memory image may either be spontaneous or induced and usually is concrete. It is useful in therapeutic endeavors, both to create mutual places of safety and to discover information about oneself. Memory images can also be used to train the individual to develop and use imagery more successfully.

Some examples of imagery used for these purposes would be to image an early childhood room, a typical day in one's life, one's occupational surroundings, various vacation spots, a relationship with one's siblings or parents, and so forth. Since this is one type of imagery that is very useful therapeutically, we will reiterate an earlier comment that the controllability of the image is much more important than the vividness. It appears that the accuracy of the memories is greater the more vivid the image;[24] however, accuracy of the image is not always necessary from a therapeutic standpoint.

Imagination imagery consists of images which differ in qualitative or quantitative ways from those originally perceived. Imagination images can also be created totally but usually do have some elements recovered from memory. Imagination images can be spontaneous or induced and, because of their nature, do not necessarily have to be concrete but may have significant symbolic or abstract components. Imagination images can be used for general purposes or as end-result or process images. In fact, imagination images are the most common specific images used in our therapy. Some of the previously noted subdivisions, such as daydreams, fantasies, dreams, hypnagogic and hypnopompic images, hallucinations, and guided images, may be wholly or in part imagination images.

Eidetic imagery has been related to photographic memory and has been felt to be most frequent in young children, decreasing as the individual grows older. Richardson notes that the eidetic image is as vivid as a perception, can be scanned (that is, does not require a fixed gaze), is externally localized, and can persist for weeks to years. Although it does not necessarily enable the person to recall past events with greater accuracy, it does give the individual more confidence because of the greater vividness.[24] Barber and Wilson note that eidetic imagery tends to be more prevalent in non-Western culture where there appears to be a greater need for right hemispheric type of spacial abilities.[43]

Recently, Ahsen has given even more impact and meaning to eidetic imagery. He feels that eidetic images are accompanied by somatic events and a "feeling of meaning."[25] Eidetic images seem to be similar to the images invoked with electrical stimulation of the cerebral cortex. Eidetics seem to appear more slowly and cannot be arbitrarily changed but are subject to changes in a certain natural direction.[25] They differ from memory images in that the detail is greater and they are less easily changed at will. The eidetic image needs a considerable amount of attention to keep it in one's visual focus, and has much therapeutic value. Eidetic images can be spontaneous or induced and tend to be concrete in nature, although some abstraction is certainly not out of the realm of possibility with this type of image. Eidetic images can be either specific or general.

Imagery and the language of the brain

Earlier in this chapter we alluded to the universality of imagery and its role as the language of the brain. If you believe that thought processes can lead to changes in physiological as well as psychological functions, and that these thought processes are the result of mind-brain activity, the important question would be: How do we program in the appropriate thought processes? Just as with a computer, you need to use software that speaks the language of that computer. With the human biocomputer, one must use the appropriate language, and that language is imagery or patterns.

In addition to the supporting evidence already mentioned, we believe there are exciting new theoretical foundations for the use of imagery as the language of brain processes and phenomena. This evidence comes forth in the form of a theory developed by the eminent neuroscientist, Karl Pribram.[44,45]

Pribram's theory is called the holographic theory, based on his comparisons of the brain to the hologram. Holography, as with many discoveries of physics, demonstrated the validity of mathematical predictions (the mathematical principles of holography were discovered in 1947, but the actual production of the hologram was not realized until the 1960s). Our theories and mathematical abilities far precede the technological development necessary to substantiate these theories. That is why some of Einstein's predictions in the earlier part of this century are just now being proven and why we believe the predictions of this holographic theory of brain functioning will be proven in the near future as the technology progresses.

The discovery of the laser beam made possible the demonstration of the reality of holography. When the laser beam is split into two parts, one of which is reflected directly onto a photographic emulsion and the other off an object onto the photographic emulsion, the basic stuff for a hologram is produced. The two sources of light arrive at the photographic plate out of phase. This means that the crests and troughs of the wave form of light are not identically superimposed upon each other. To understand this phenomenon, one need only imagine a still lake with two pebbles dropped into the lake a distance apart, and then to imagine the intersection of the waves produced by each pebble. These intersections occur because the waves are out of phase. The waves would be in phase if the two stones entered the water simultaneously and in the same place, so that only one set of outwardly moving concentric waves could be seen. When the photographic plate is developed and exposed to ordinary light, no specific image is seen except for the possibility of a pattern. This pattern is actually the interference pattern of the light waves. All the information necessary to reproduce the image of the original object is recorded in this pattern. The necessary factor is the use of a laser of the original wave length. When this is beamed through the photographic plate, the original image is reproduced in full three-dimensional form. If the photographic plate is broken into small pieces, each piece, no matter how small, contains all the information of the entire object; and when the original laser beam is shone through this fragment, the entire image is reproduced, albeit with less clarity. In essence, every part of the hologram contains information necessary for the reproduction of the entire object, or, as William James stated nearly a century ago, it is "to see the world in a grain of sand."

The mathematics of holography is that of Fourier analysis, which is used to explain waves and involves transforming patterns into their component sine waves. As Pribram notes, "No matter how complicated a wave form is, you can break it down to its component sine waves. Seven, or at the most twelve . . . describe even a fairly complex pattern rather well."[44]

Some of the observed phenomena leading Pribram to his holographic theory was experimental evidence demonstrating that a tremendous amount of the brain can be damaged and memory will still exist. In fact, it appears that only 2 percent of the fibers are necessary for the memory system to function adequately. This would imply that memory is located throughout the brain rather than in one specific location. Already, the memory system bears a likeness to the principles of holography. All neurons branch, and when a nerve impulse goes through the neuron and it branches, it creates an electrical potential which, in turn, creates a wave front. Wave fronts also approach from other directions, and where these wave fronts intersect, an interference pattern is set up. This presumably could act like the interference pattern that produces holograms.

Numerous studies have shown that Fourier transforms are the most accurate way of explaining the function of several systems of the body, such as the auditory system (Helmholtz), the motor system (Bernstein), and the visual system (Campbell).[44] This theoretical and experimental information seems to favor the holographic concept of brain functioning.

Our interest in this method of brain functioning resides in its utilization of patterns that are more akin to images than the sequential type of thought process, which is more akin to words. We believe that the concrete images are certainly patterns, but we are even more interested in the primordial thought processes or patterns that are abstract and even those that go beyond abstract. We feel that these are subjective experiences of the more primordial patterns that mark the essence of brain function.

Practically, Fourier transforms have demonstrated their usefulness as the fastest way to analyze data. In a computer, data can be transformed to Fourier components, allowing cross-correlations to be done rapidly. In this manner the computer is simulating what neural holograms do in the brain.[44] As mentioned above, one does not have to analyze data linearly in a stepwise, sequential, left-hemispheric manner but can holistically correlate it in a spacial, pattern-like, right-hemispheric manner. In fact, Pribram himself alludes to correlation between the frequency domain of Fourier theorum and imagery by stating that the "amount of information . . . processing is fantastic! [The] brain can do this only if one stage of information processing is in the frequency domain, like a hologram. In such instances . . . [it is] best not to speak of information-processing, but of image-processing."[44]

This theory may now be applied to all forms of brain storage of information and initiation of motor responses. Pribram delineates the following relationship:

$$\text{Object} \xrightarrow{\quad * \quad} \text{Wave Storage} \xrightarrow{\quad * \quad} \text{Image}$$

In this diagram, the object is broken down into its component wave patterns by means of Fourier analysis and is stored. This storage mechanism is analogous to a hologram. The same mathematical transfer of functions that allows the equation to go from object to storage can allow the reciprocal encoding of information to the image stage. As Pribram states, "The storage of wave patterns is . . . reciprocally related to the imaging of objects! The wave functions are transforms of objects and then images."[46] For example, with respect to sensory motor system learning, an entire activity such as a tennis serve could be analyzed by means of Fourier transforms. Then, if the brain reciprocally transforms it hologram into a motor pattern, the entire movement sequence can be imitated. As Pribram notes, "The brain can instantly resonate to and thus 'recognize' wave forms. Once 'recognized,' the inverse transform allows them to be implemented in behavior."[44]

Another interesting phenomenon is that in this frequency domain, time and space cease to exist and everything happens at once, synchronously.[44] This means that we can instantly correlate past experience, no matter how far distant, with present situations.

Another interesting analogy is that our objective reality of sights, sounds, tastes, kinesthetic sensations, and visual impressions actually comes from the brain's mathematics, which, in essence, acts as a lens. This lens transforms the blurs or frequencies of energy patterns that we perceive into concrete phenomena.

In summary, we feel that there has been adequate scientific evidence that at least the visual, motor, and auditory realms function by means of Fourier holographic processes; i.e., the storage of sensory information and the initiation of motor processes based upon frequencies or patterns. We believe that these patterns are most akin to images in our ordinary perceptual sphere. The images may be concrete, in which case they represent use of the brain's lens to change a process from the frequency domain to the domain of usual reality. However, when these images are more abstract, they become more like the frequency domain itself. We feel that the use of the images is a more complete and rapid means of entering the frequency domain, where the brain actually works. This gives added support to the use of imagery as a means of relaying information to, and receiving information from, the brain.

General instructions

The remainder of this book will be devoted to the uses of imagery, those applications of imagery to personal growth and development that require some conscious activity on our part. We have listed the functions of imagery; i.e., those that take place even without our conscious awareness. The uses of imagery will be outlined here and more fully described in later chapters.

For most goals it is important to utilize our methods in a specific hierarchy:

1. Learn and practice ASC without specific imagery, possibly with the use of general images.
2. The first specific imagery that is to be utilized is end-result imagery.
3. Only if the above fail to produce significant results or if the condition to be achieved relates to a life-and-death situation should specific process images be instituted.

It is important to have trust in oneself. Most of the changes that take place initially are very subtle and will not be appreciated by the individual until that individual achieves the subtlety necessary to appreciate the changes. Dramatic experiences are not necessary and, in fact, may be detrimental to the development of important change. Therefore, one should practice these methods without judgment or criticism and as far as can be achieved without expectation. It is with this type of dispassionate practice that dramatic results may be attained.

Another important factor is the individual's commitment. One or two sessions a week with the therapist provides minimal chance for change when compared to the daily use of these procedures at home. We must learn to trust our own subconscious. It is this part of our mind that directs our bodily functioning anyway, without conscious interference on our part. As Maltz pointed out, all that is necessary is for us to provide the subconscious with a target and the subconscious will then direct all of our behavior toward achievement of the goal.[35] The goal will then be achieved usually with minimal, or no, conscious effort.

When experiencing a spontaneous image, it is important to trust the first image that appears. We find that it is common among our patients not to consciously feel that the first image that appears is suitable for their purposes, so they search for other images. This search is usually a conscious effort and a waste of time. It is important to stay with the original image. In this regard it seems to make little difference whether the original experience was fact, dream, or fancy.[9]

Remember that it is more important to be able to control the image rather than for the image to be lifelike and that the image should be experienced in all five senses for maximum effectiveness. If a person wishes to have the image be more powerful as well as more vivid, then the most important method is through repeated, dispassionate practice. As Samuels and Samuels state, it is most important to accept what appears without criticism and without preconceived notions as to what one should see. One should just believe that what is received is appropriate. They give a sequence of experiments to train one's visualizing ability, but it has been our experience that training in visualization techniques is very rarely essential before going on to specific therapeutic visualization. However, for those interested, their sequence is as follows:[30]

1. With the eyes open, visualize a two-dimensional object such as a triangle. Then close the eyes and attempt to visualize it.
2. Repeat exercise Number 1 for a three-dimensional object such as an apple.
3. Visualize one's childhood room.
4. Image large objects such as a house and move all around and through it.
5. Image a more complicated three-dimensional object from many angles, such as a teakettle or other object with multiple curves.
6. Go back to exercise Number 3, the childhood room, and do such things as picking up objects, turning off light switches, and even floating out the window.
7. Image a person.
8. Image yourself as if looking at a mirror.

Ahsen also agrees that an image can be strengthened by visualizing it repeatedly[47] or by utilizing a homopolar mechanism; that is, an image with underlying physiological or affective mechanisms that are similar to the desired physiology or affect.[48] Remember that when the image is repeated over and over again, the details become greater in number and clearer, particularly for an eidetic image.[9]

Lang has developed a hypothesis that he calls the bioinformational theory of emotional imagery, in which the image is conceived in the brain to be a "conceptual network, controlling specific somotovisceral patterns, in constituting a prototype for overt behavioral expression."[19] He devised response training, which enables average subjects to respond to imagery instructions in a way similar to those who have tested as good imagers. The response training essentially consists of adding to the usual verbalizations, which contain only stimulus propositions and response propositions. Therefore, a statement such as, "The wooden walls of the small room surround you, closing you in . . . " would be changed to "You tense all the muscles of your forehead, squinting . . . your eyes . . . dart left and right to glimpse the exit."[55] These principles can be utilized later in your practice by including expected motor activity in addition to merely suggesting only a sensory image.

Remember that a reported inability to image by the patient/client need not be accepted by you as an inability to create an adequate therapeutic milieu for effective response. By utilizing the above principles, even a so-called poor imager can benefit from these methods. And, as Sheikh and associates point out, "Even those individuals who do not have vivid imagery, with some encouragement and concentration, can visualize developmentally determined images from significant life situations in the past. These images . . . tend to open up the general imagination and fantasy process."[1]

If you are working with someone else, the differences in imaging ability and mode of imaging between the operator and patient become important. Lay[49] notes the difficulty that Socrates and Protagoras had in understanding one another. Protagoras had verbal-kinesthetic imagery, and Socrates, who "heard his daemon," was auditory. As Lay points out, "If one is auditory-linguistic, you should never enter into an argument with a motor-linguistic person, as in all topics except the most concrete facts, either will inevitably fail completely to understand the other. Words and their meanings are created and validated in a social context, while images and their meanings are personal creations."[49] That is to say, it is important to remember that not all people think or image like you; therefore, you must become adept at utilizing all modalities so that you will be able to tie into the perceptual and imageric system of your client/patient. Ample research validates and documents the differences among people with different modes of primary imagery.[50]

Introduction to specific uses of imagery _____

Section II will present the use of imagery in specific disciplines. This segment will serve primarily as an overview to demonstrate briefly the varied usefulness of these techniques.

Psychotherapy is a fertile field for the applications of imagery. Singer points out the central role imagery plays in psychotherapy by noting that "the ongoing nature of the private symbolic processes, when allowed freedom of development under controlled therapeutic conditions, are inherently curative."[6] In fact, imagery has been represented as an analog of free association and has been noted to be effective as an uncovering agent for suppressed events.[51] Reyher feels that the utilization of free imagery is much more effective than the verbal free associations popularized by Freud, in that images are more likely to circumvent the usual resistances and defenses.[52] He calls this method emergent uncovering therapy. We feel that even when using verbal free association, the verbal methods merely describe internal images. We agree with Sheikh that images are less likely to be filtered through the conscious critical apparatus.[1]

In light of the above, it is not surprising that a multitude of imagery therapies have been devised. In the following list we note many of these, with the name of the discoverer or popularizer of the therapy in parentheses. The methods are delineated more fully in the publications by Barber and Wilson[43] and by Bresler and associates.[53]

1. Systematic desensitization (Wolpe).
2. Covert conditioning (Cautela).
3. Basic ID technique (Lazarus).
4. Eidetic psychotherapy (Ahsen).
5. Guided affective imagery (Leuner).
6. Emotive-Reconstructive psychotherapy (Morrison and Cometa).
7. Primal therapy (Janov).
8. Guided daydream (Desoille).
9. Psycho-Imagination (Shorr).
10. Creative imagery (Levner).
11. Focusing (Gendlin).
12. Symbolic visualization (Gerard).
13. Psychosynthesis (Assagioli).

The vast quantity of various imagery therapies available attests to the usefulness of imagery in psychotherapy. In Chapters 9 and 10, our use of imagery in psychotherapy will be outlined, borrowing heavily from these therapies.

As Jung states, "When you concentrate on a mental picture, it begins to stir, the image becomes enriched by details. It moves and develops . . . and so when we concentrate on an inner picture and when we are careful not to interrupt the natural flow of events, our unconscious will produce a series of images which makes a complete story."[54]

As mentioned in previous chapters, imagery is an integral part of other types of therapies, such as *autogenic training* in its practice of autogenic meditation.[55] There is also a close relationship between hypnosis and imagery.[1] Hypnotic suggestions usually evoke imagery, and hypnotic responsiveness seems to be related to the ability of the individual to utilize fantasy and imagination.[56,57] Also, hypnosis appears to itensify the imagination process.[58] Sheikh and associates state that it is "safe to hypothesize that a wide variety of physiological effects of hypnosis are primarily due to the imagery involved."[1] The use of hypnosis and its association with imagery are pointed out even in behavioral methods such as systematic desensitization, in which hypnosis increases the ability of the individual to visualize the hierarchy.[59,60] Most studies seem to find that hypnosis enhances the ability of the individual to utilize imagery.[39,61,62] Imagery has proved to be of critical importance in such new fields as biofeedback, where it has been noted by the Greens that the movement of the machine itself is not important in producing the desired effect, but rather the imagining and visualization of what the movement signifies.[63]

The remainder of the specific uses of imagery all relate to the ability of imagery to change physiological phenomena. In earlier chapters, we presented the evidence that the body, in fact, will respond to these thought processes, and we agree with the Greens that imagery provides the quickest and surest way of programming the body, since it involves a global instruction rather than a neurological instruction.[64] The body then converts this into whatever nerve impulses are required for performance of the task. Therefore these methods can be used for any aspect of one's life or professional activity. They can be used to assist in the healing of a disease or disorder as well as in preventing the manifestations of disorders. They can be used from birth until death and probably even before birth. They can be used for success, creativity, and actualization, as well as for increasing ability and performance in such things as sports. All of these processes will be delineated in greater detail in Section II.

References

1. A. A. Sheikh, A. P. Richardson, and L. M. Moleski, "Psychosomatics and Mental Imagery: A Brief Review," in *The Potential of Fantasy and Imagination,* ed. A. A. Sheikh and J. T. Shaffer (New York: Brandon House, 1979), pp. 106–18.

2. M. B. Sterman, ed., "Neurophysiological and Clinical Studies of Sensorimotor EEG Biofeedback Training: Some Effects on Epilepsy," *Semin Psychiatry* 5 (1973), pp. 507–25.

3. M. Samuels and N. Samuels, *Seeing with the Mind's Eye* (New York: Random House Bookworks, 1975), p. *xi.*

4. M. J. Horowitz, "Image Formation: Clinical Observations of a Cognitive Model," in *The Nature and Function of Imagery,* ed. P. W. Sheehan (New York: Academic Press, 1972), pp. 281–309.

5. M. J. Horowitz, "Visual Imagery and Cognitive Organization," *Am J Psychiatry* 123 (1967), pp. 938–46.

6. J. L. Singer, "Imagery and Affect in Psychotherapy: Elaborating Private Scripts and Generating Contexts," in *The Potential of Fantasy and Imagination,* ed. A. A. Sheikh and J. T. Shaffer (New York: Brandon House, 1979), pp. 105–18.

7. C. M. Muses, "The Exploration of Consciousness," in *Consciousness and Reality,* ed. C. M. Muses and A. M. Young (New York: Avon Books, 1974), pp. 102–31.

8. I. Begg, D. Upfold, and T. D. Wilson, "Imagery in Verbal Communication," *J Ment Imagery* 2 (1978), pp. 165–86.

9. A. T. Dolan and A. A. Sheikh, "Eidetics: A Visual Approach to Psychotherapy," *Psychologia* 19 (1976), pp. 200–209.

10. E. Fromm, "An Ego-Psychological Theory of Altered States of Consciousness," *Int J Clin Exp Hypn* 25 (1977), pp. 372–87.

11. B. R. Bugelski, "Words and Things and Images," *Am Psychol* 25 (1970), pp. 1002–12.

12. W. S. Kroger and W. D. Fezler, *Hypnosis and Behavior Modification: Imagery Conditioning* (Philadelphia: J. B. Lippincott, 1976).

13. R. Gordon, "A Very Private World," in *The Nature and Function of Imagery*, ed. P. W. Sheehan (New York: Academic Press, 1972), pp. 63–80.

14. C. W. Perky, "An Experimental Study of Imagination," *Am J Psychol* 21 (1910), pp. 422–52.

15. P. R. Holt, "On the Nature of Generality of Mental Imagery," in *The Nature and Function of Imagery* (New York: Academic Press, 1972), pp. 6–33.

16. R. N. Shepard, "Form, Formation and Transformation of Internal Representations," in *Information Processing: The Loyola Symposium,* ed. R. L. Solso (Hillsdale, N.J.: Erlbaum, 1975).

17. S. M. Kosslyn and J. R. Pomerantz, "Imagery, Propositions and the Form of Internal Representations," *Cognitive Psychol* (1977), pp. 52–76.

18. Z. W. Pylyshyn, "What the Mind's Eye Tells the Mind's Brain: A Critique of Mental Imagery," *Psychol Bull* 80 (1973), pp. 1–24.

19. P. J. Lang, "A Bio-Informational Theory of Emotional Imagery," *Psychophysiology* 16 (1979), pp. 495–512.

20. T. R. Sarbin, "Imagining as Muted Role-Taking: An Historical-Linguistic Analysis," in *The Nature and Function of Imagery,* ed. P. W. Sheehan (New York: Academic Press, 1972), pp. 333–64.

21. U. Neisser, *Cognition and Reality* (San Francisco: Freeman, 1976).

22. P. J. Hampson and P. E. Morris, "Clinical Processing: Framework for Imagery Research," *J Ment Imagery* 3 (1979), pp. 11–12.

23. P. W. Sheehan, *The Nature and Function of Imagery* (New York: Academic Press, 1972).

24. A. Richardson, *Mental Imagery* (New York: Springer, 1969).

25. A. Ahsen, Eidetics: An Overview, *J Ment Imagery* 1 (1977), pp. 5–38.

26. D. P. Brown, "A Model for the Levels of Concentrative Meditation," *Int J Clin Exp Hypn* 25 (1977), pp. 236–73.

27. M. Panagiotou and A. A. Sheikh, "Eidetic Psychotherapy: Introduction and Evaluation," *Int J Soc Psychiatry* 20 (1974), pp. 231–41.

28. L. W. Doob, "The Ubiquitous Appearance of Images," in *The Nature and Function of Imagery,* ed. P. W. Sheehan (New York: Academic Press, 1972), pp. 311–33.

29. Samuels, *Seeing with the Mind's Eye,* pp. 21–37.

30. N. Lande, *Mind Styles, Life Styles* (Los Angeles: Price, Stern, Sloan, 1976).

31. W. LaBarre, "Anthropological Perspectives on Hallucinations and Halluci-nogens," in *Hallucination and Hallucinogens: Behavior, Experience and Theory,* ed. R. K. Seigel and L. J. West (New York: John Wiley & Sons, 1975), pp. 9–52.

32. M. J. Horowitz, "Modes of Representation of Thought," *J Am Psychoanal Asso* 20 (1972), pp. 793–819.

33. D. F. Marks, "Individual Differences in the Vividness of Visual Imagery and Their Effect on Function," in *The Nature and Function of Imagery,* ed. P. W. Sheehan (New York: Academic Press, 1972), pp. 83–108.

34. W. S. Kroger and W. D. Fezler, *Hypnosis and Behavior Modification: Imagery Conditioning* (Philadelphia: J. B. Lippincott, 1976).

35. M. Maltz, *Psycho-Cybernetics* (New York: Pocket Books, 1966).

36. M. Von Senden, *Space and Sight: The Perception of Space and Shape in the Congenitally Blind Before and After Operation* (London: Methuen, 1960).

37. R. A. Johnson, "Creative Imagery in Blind and Sighted Adolescents," *J Ment Imagery* 3 (1979), pp. 23–30.

38. R. G. Ley, Cerebral Asymetries, Emotional Experience, and Imagery: Im-plications for Psychotherapy," in *The Potential of Fantasy and Imagination,* ed. A. A. Sheikh and J. T. Shaffer (New York: Brandon House, 1979), pp. 41–65.

39. R. C. Gur and J. Reyher, "Enhancement of Creativity via Free-Imagery and Hypnosis," *Am J Clin Hypn* 18 (1976), pp. 237–49.

40. B. L. Forisha, "Mental Imagery and Creativity: Review and Speculations," *J Ment Imagery* 2 (1978), pp. 209–38.

41. Lande, *Mind Styles, Life Styles,* p. 63.

42. A. Richardson, *Mental Imagery* (New York: Springer, 1969), p. 116.

43. T. X. Barber and S. C. Wilson, "Guided Imagining and Hypnosis: Theoreti-cal and Empirical Overlap and Convergency in a New Creative Imagination Scale," in *The Potential of Fantasy and Imagination,* ed. A. A. Sheikh and J. T. Shaffer (New York: Brandon House, 1979), pp. 67–80.

44. D. Goleman, "Holographic Memory: Interview with Karl Pribram," *Psy-chology Today,* February 1979, pp. 71–84.

45. M. Ferguson, "Karl Pribram's Changing Reality," *Re-Vision* 1 (1978), pp. 8–13.

46. K. H. Pribram, "What the Fuss Is All About," *Re-Vision* 1 (1978), pp. 14–18.

47. A. Ahsen, "Endopolar Invigorative Image Response," *J Ment Imagery* 3 (1979), p. 130.

48. A. Ahsen, "Homopolar Image Confirmation," *J Ment Imagery* 3 (1979), p. 134.

49. W. Lay, "Mental Imagery," *Psychol Rev Monogr Suppl* 92 (1897), pp. 1–59.

50. A. Richardson, "The Place of Subjective Experience in Comtemporary Psychology," *Br J Psychol* 56 (1965), pp. 223–32.

51. J. Reyher, "Free Imagery, an Uncovering Procedure," *J Clin Psychol* 19 (1963), pp. 454–59.

52. J. Reyher, "Emergent Uncovering Therapy," in *The Power of Human Imag-ination,* ed. J. L. Singer and K. S. Pope (New York: Plenum, 1978).

53. D. E. Bresler, B. G. Pearse, and C. Wilson, eds., *Therapeutic Guided Imagery* (Pacific Palisades, Calif.: Center for Integral Medicine, 1979).

54. C. G. Jung, *The Symbolic Life*. Collected works, vol. 18, translated by R. F. C. Hull (Princeton, N.J.: Princeton University Press, 1976).

55. W. Luthe and S. R. Blumberger, "Autogenic Training," in *The Psychosomatic Approach in Medical Practice*, ed. E. D. Wilkower and H. Warnes (New York: Harper & Row, 1977), pp. 146-63.

56. T. X. Barber and L. B. Glass, "Significant Factors in Hypnotic Behavior," *J Abnorm Soc Psychol* 64 (1962), pp. 222-28.

57. P. W. Sheehan, "Hypnosis and the Manifestations of Imagination," in *Hypnosis: Research Developments and Perspectives*, ed. E. Fromm and R. E. Shor (Chicago: Aldine-Atherton, 1972).

58. M. B. Arnold, "On the Mechanism of Suggestion and Hypnosis," *J Abnorm Soc Psychol* 41 (1946), pp. 107-28.

59. J. Wolpe, *The Practice of Behavior Therapy* Elmsford, N.Y.: Pergamon, 1969).

60. E. Dengrove, "The Use of Hypnosis in Behavior Therapy," *Int J Clin Exp Hypn* 21 (1973), pp. 13-17.

61. V. L. Raikov, "The Possibility of Creativity in the Active Stage of Hypnosis," *Int J Clin Exp Hypn* 24 (1976), pp. 258-68.

62. S. Sanders, "Mutual Group Hypnosis As a Catalyst in Fostering Creative Problem Solving," *Amer J Clin Hypn* 19 (1976), pp. 62-66.

63. E. Green and A. Green, "General and Specific Applications of Thermal Feedback," in *Biofeedback: Principles and Practices for Clinicians*, ed. J. V. Basmajian (Baltimore: Williams and Wilkins, 1979), pp. 163-69.

64. E. Green and A. Green, *Beyond Biofeedback* (New York: Delacorte Press, 1977).

Chapter 5

Techniques: Introduction, general principles, and methods

This chapter presents some guidelines for incorporating the use of altered states of consciousness and imagery into specific medical and therapeutic clinical practice. The foundations have been laid to provide substantial bases from which the clinician can work within the realm of his or her expertise. A number of points will be considered in this chapter:

1. The physical and mental condition for optimizing ASC and imagery.
2. Safeguards and precautions.
3. Techniques for altered state induction, deepening, ego strengthening, general imagery, and awakening.
4. Questions often asked by clients.

We believe that personal experience with ASC and imagery is a major contributor to comfort and ease of use with clients.

General principles

When the therapist or clinician makes the decision to apply ASC and imagery within the therapy setting, the first thoughts usually pertain to technique, including altered state induction and deinduction. Inherent in the decision to use the techniques is the bias or expectation that some change will result from applying the techniques. It is important that the clinician examine carefully as many of those biases and expectations as possible that make up the particular belief system in question because the therapy and the outcome will be affected by them. In addition, the client brings into the therapy session many beliefs and expectations which affect the outcome. It is for this reason that the selection of clients who are ready for this type of work is of utmost importance. These techniques require a significant degree of motivation and self-responsibility. In describing the planned therapy to the client, the clinician will want to use language with which the client is comfortable and matching communication styles and linguistic preferences.

An important first step that will facilitate success in using the technique is to determine the client's major mode for experiencing the word; i.e., whether he is primarily visual, auditory, or kinesthetic. From Bandler and Grinder's work[1] we can cite the following examples of primary processing modes for perception:

1. Visual eidetic imagery (remembered images): "What is the color of your living room carpet?"
2. Visual constructed imagery: "How would I look with a mustache?"
3. Auditory eidetic imagery: "What are the words to your favorite song?"
4. Auditory constructed imagery: "What would you sound like if you sang?"
5. Kinesthetic imagery: "How do you feel when you wake up from a nap?" 'What does velvet feel like?"

By asking the client questions similar to these and judging the relative power of each type of imagery for the client, communication and linguistic preferences can be matched. From that point, communication will be clearer, and the imagery will be closely tied to the client's experiences with spontaneous imagery in the past.

The emphasis which we place on the state of the internal environment of each participant—clinician and client—is specific in light of the material presented in the previous chapters. The attitude of the clinician is a powerful influence acting upon the strength of the placebo response, i.e., comfort produces comfort and positivity facilitates positivity. One main goal of any therapeutic session is the maximization of the placebo effect. (Refer to Chapter 2.)

In setting up the external environment for relaxation and imagery sessions, it is important to remove as many distractions as possible, such as traffic, noise, and telephones, so that the client has the optimal opportunity to focus inward. Later, as the techniques become more incorporated into the patient's lifestyle, the distractions play a minimal role. The client could use a comfortable chair or chaise to rest upon, so that the body and head are comfortably supported. In the sitting position, the client should have both feet placed flat on the floor, the arms resting along the sides of the body with the hands in the lap. This position allows free movement of nerve impulses and blood circulation. The head should be supported by a small cervical pillow and slightly flexed forward. If the client chooses to recline, the position of choice is one in which the feet lie approximately 8 to 10 inches apart, tending to fall away from one another, with the arms resting comfortably.

It seems important in any clinical situation to establish a permissive attitude within which the client can function freely and explore personal spaces. The permissive attitude excludes commands, and includes the setting up of possibilities of alternatives, allowing the client to develop sensations and images independently. The freedom inherent in this attitude necessitates clinician expertise both in the realm of clinical practice and in personal experiences with ASC and imagery. With a background of personal experience with ASC, the clinician can refer to that experience when guiding the client.

Techniques

It is difficult to determine just when induction into ASC occurs for the client. We often feel that the mere presence of the clinician is enough to alter a client's state of awareness. Add an office setting, a client's nagging symptom, and the expectations and anticipations of the therapy, and the client is very likely in an altered state before any words are spoken. Depending upon the setting of the therapeutic encounter, induction may be as simple as asking a client to "close your eyes, if you will, and experience, for just a moment, what you are feeling"; or as simple as a classic hypnotic induction technique.

That range of possibilities must be researched and selected by the clinician. Of importance is the situation of the hospitalized patient, whose familiar lifestyle is markedly altered with little semblance of normalcy. From our experience within the hospital setting, we find that time spent in altered state induction can be minimized due to the change in the psychophysiology of the hospitalized person. For the hospitalized person, the normal sensations of everyday life have been altered (the sensation of regular clothing, the daily routine of activities, the usual sounds of traffic and home life). The patient may experience a reduction of overall stimulation, which produces mild sensory deprivation, or a change in the quality of sensory stimulation, which produces sensory overload. Refer to Chapter 3 for more details.

The clinician would be wise to prepare for induction processes by doing a bit of self-monitoring with regard to positivity and to vocal tone or quality. Nonverbal transmission of uncertainty is much more apparent to the hyperaware person who is experiencing ASC than to the clinician who is thinking of what the therapy session will contain. Being firmly positive and using a steady, calm, and reassuring vocal tone will do more to enhance session effectiveness than any specific verbalization. When proposing suggestions to the client, the clinician will find that indirect suggestions for changes will be more quickly and completely accepted by the client.

As noted by Erickson et al.,[2] both indirect and direct suggestions may affect the desired results but, due to the different methods of processing the input, the effects upon consciousness and volition are different. Direct suggestions propose a stimulus that identifies the responses desired. Thus we feel that there is little room for internal learning on the part of the client. On the other hand, with indirect suggestion the client is allowed more than just compliance. The client then uses less conscious ways of processing, relying on deeper centers of nervous system integration. For example: "You may find yourself breathing more deeply," which is an indirect suggestion, as opposed to "Breathe more deeply," which is a direct suggestion.

The choice to breathe more deeply is then that of the client, and any competition between client and clinician is minimized. This permissive and indirect approach is particularly effective with a person who becomes ambivalent or resistant at some subconscious level. It may be necessary at some point of ambivalence or resistance to set the client up for a therapeutic bind, which defines the possibilities of beneficial behavior. Again, using the works of Erickson et al.,[3] we can look to the concept of binds: "Forms of suggestion that offer patients the possibility of structuring their behavior in a therapeutic direction. A bind offers a free choice of two or more comparable alternatives in that whichever choice is made leads behavior in a desired direction." For example: "If you really wish to feel increased relaxation, you might find yourself breathing more deeply," or, "When you notice that you are breathing more deeply. . . ." Once again, the responsibility for change is placed with the client.

There are a number of cues which the client may demonstrate that will indicate to the clinician that relaxation is taking place. We generally include the following:

1. Decreased skeletal muscle tone, which may be dramatic or subtle.

2. Fewer, deeper respirations, which taper to fairly shallow respirations as relaxation continues.
3. Change in the color of face or lips.
4. Eyelid flickering.

At any point, the clinician may initiate appropriate imagery to continue to enhance the state of relaxation or to effect the therapeutic changes agreed upon by the client and clinician. Often it is desirable to have the client respond verbally to answer questions or to describe the image, and that can be accomplished by simply asking the patient, "Would it be all right for you to remain as relaxed as you appear to be, and talk with me?" Remember that the client is actually hyperalert due to the focusing of his or her attention and will hear and respond appropriately.

Whatever imagery is employed, we have found it helpful to use as many descriptive terms and words as possible relating to all five senses to achieve as much of a total body response as desired. If the client is a person who easily develops kinesthetic images and then can relate to finger movements, the fingers can be used for communication. This use of finger signal communication is a well-known hypnotic technique.[4] Idiomotor signaling is the response of a finger that is voluntarily made to indicate yes, no, or I don't know, in answer to questions posed by the clinician.

We believe that the most powerful imagery is *end-result imagery;* that is, developing as clear a picture as is possible of the goal or desired outcome. The clinician may suggest that the end-result image be experienced directly, "At this point you may experience what it is like to become relaxed in that stressful situation, by seeing with relaxed eyes, by standing with relaxed muscles," or experienced indirectly by viewing the end-result image on a television or movie screen. The end-result image is then worked with every day to reinforce its strength and to realize the unconscious fulfillment of that image by setting into daily practice all the individual steps that comprise the entire desired behavior or feeling state.

When the client has been guided through the desired imagery, session closure is initiated by suggestion. The types of suggestions which are offered to the client include (1) ego strengthening, (2) remaining in a relaxed state yet able to complete all desired activities, (3) willingness to practice techniques independently, and (4) the ability to develop imagery.

Basically, the ego-strengthening suggestions are for reinforcement of change taking place in the desired direction, for improvement of self-concept by affirmation, and for defining personal desires and goals. The closing suggestions for remaining relaxed yet active and for practicing independently have to do with changing lifestyle with a minimum of upheaval, which may be an ongoing goal of all therapy. The client is encouraged that imagery will develop spontaneously with daily practice and patience, and with the guidance given by the clinician. We refer you to Samuels and Samuels[5] for specifics on development of imagery processes.

Questions often asked

Following are some questions that are often asked by clients before, during, and after sessions spent in ASC. They are included to ease the incorporation of these techniques into clinical practice.

Q: Is imagery safe?

A: Imagery is a natural, universal, and spontaneous phenomenon of mankind, and serves as a basis of perception. Any image that can be created can be eliminated, since images are the product of brain function. Therefore frightening images can be modified, and positive, self-affirming images can be enhanced.

Q: Are the images I see, feel, and hear normal?

A: Imagery is a universal phenomenon in process only; content is an individual manifestation, so good-bad, right-wrong judgments are not considered valid.

Q: What happens if I fall asleep while practicing imagery?

A: If you fall asleep during a session, it might mean that you needed the sleep and thus gained the benefits of sleep. In order to gain the full benefits of imagery, prevent falling asleep by changing body positions, practicing before meals, or changing the time of your practice.

Q: What are the strange sensations that I sometimes feel?

A: If the sensations are those of losing awareness of body parts or of time distortion (which is an exaggeration of a common waking phenomenon) such that an hour feels like 5 or 10 minutes, then it is apparent that deep relaxation is taking place and your attention has been focused elsewhere. Other sensations may be the emergence of images in a kinesthetic mode or mere distraction.

Q: What if I don't come out of the state of relaxation?

A: It is very unlikely that you will stay in the relaxed state, as defined in terms of the relaxation session; however, there may be times when you reorient to the waking state at a time later than you had planned. While you are in a relaxed state, your perception of emergencies is actually heightened and you will be able to respond quickly and efficiently.

Q: What can I do about my wandering thoughts?

A: At first it seems as though your mind is jumping around from one thought to another more than it does in the waking state. More likely, you are simply more aware of the number of times your mind is distracted while you are experiencing ASC. The important thing is to just simply bring your mind back to the image, without criticism, and continue.

Images

As an introduction to the images at the end of this chapter, we propose here a few more concepts about the use of imagery.

1. In visualization or imagery, trust your own creative mechanism and deemphasize the conscious, cognitive effort in producing images. It is not necessary that the image be as real as life but that the image be controllable. (Refer to Chapter 4.)
2. Realize the imagery that is used on a daily basis. Be reminded of daily imagery: the layout of a room, the process of walking, the remembering of a song, the taste of a lemon, the aroma of freshly baked bread.
3. Accept noncritically the images which appear spontaneously, for those images have great power. (Refer to Chapter 4.)

Kroger and Fezler[6] have standardized many images for the achievement of specific results. For relaxation, they suggest beach, mountain, or garden scenes. For the development of control of internal states, they suggest cliff or volcano scenes. For temperature control, the hayloft scene is recommended. Because the specific verbalizations produce mental pictures in the client, certain specific effects are produced and controlled. We suggest the following narratives as examples of general imagery.

Breathing image

To heighten your client's awareness of breathing patterns as a way of inducing ASC, it is important sometimes to begin with a description of the breathing process, emphasizing the normal and effortless functioning of breathing. We have included an entire description that we feel is an important portion of the induction, and you can incorporate this into your induction as you see fit.

As you begin to settle your body into a comfortable position . . . realize that we always breathe . . . , We always breathe, but most of us do not use full capacity to breathe . . . and most of us are not even aware of what areas of our chest we might be using for breathing. . . . With correct breathing, the lungs can efficiently exchange air to replace oxygen . . . nitrogen . . . hydrogen . . . carbon dioxide in the appropriate quantities to nourish and cleanse the body tissues. . . . To accomplish easy breathing . . . first check your posture. . . . Poor posture is usually shown by continuous slouching . . . limiting the area in which the lungs can expand . . . and allowing the efficient transport of gases to and from the body. . . . So now you can allow your chest to expand fully and completely . . . in beginning the first exercise in breathing correctly. . . . The first exercise will provide you with the most complete utilization of the breath. . . . Begin to breathe slowly and deeply with the belly relaxed. . . . As the belly relaxes and the air moves into the lungs . . . the belly will expand slightly, just until it is comfortably full . . . and you can feel a slight buildup of pressure in the area of your chest. . . . That becomes the time to relax and let the breath go by exhaling . . . and as you exhale, feel the release of pressure . . . feel the relaxation . . . feel the effortless exchange of air into and out of your lungs. . . . Let your body breathe all by itself . . . and then begin to take a few deep breaths . . . and feel that as you breathe deeply . . . and comfortably you might be surprised to experience relaxation in all parts of your body.

Progressive relaxation

Now allow your body to assume a very comfortable position . . . one that you may have found comfortable before . . . or one that I have suggested previously . . . and then make any final adjustments. . . . Now comes your first activity . . . and that is allowing the body to rest. . . . Really allow the body to rest. . . . Cease all fidgeting and fluctuation. . . . Close the eyes . . . and notice that when you close your eyes . . . things begin to change right away . . . muscles begin to let go . . . the breathing evens out and becomes more regular and really becomes effortless . . . and that's exactly what these states are characterized by . . . effortlessness . . . ease . . . comfort. . . . And as you allow these changes to take place . . . you may find your mind wandering . . . beginning to experience images of its own . . . and that's all right . . . but what you want to focus on now is the state of your own internal affairs. . . . Begin to remember now how unique and how special you really are . . . as you begin to send your body the messages for relaxation. . . . Begin to do so now if you will . . . by sending all of your attention . . . all of your awareness . . . down to your feet . . . feel that comfort, however your mind and your body perceive that word to be . . . comfort . . . relaxation . . . ease. . . . Everybody has their own unique sensations . . . so just become aware of yours now . . . and when you know what those sensations are . . . allow them to become somewhat stronger . . . so that you really understand them. . . . I don't know how quickly or how slowly they will spread . . . but you might be surprised to feel that they are spreading above the feet . . . into the ankles . . . into the lower legs . . . inch by inch . . . moving up the body at your own rate . . . as you allow these sensations to be present . . . to become stronger. . . . And with each part of the body that you relax . . . nearby areas begin to relax. . . . The flow of relaxation is strengthened . . . and goes through every part of the body . . . on up to the knees . . . above the knees . . . into the hips . . . into the trunk. . . . The sensations might change . . . and that's all right, too. . . . Just let them change. . . . Enjoy this time . . . as you reinforce this relaxation . . . on . . . and on . . . and on . . . and truly, as you relax all parts of the body . . . the areas that are already relaxed will feel even more comfort with every moment that passes . . . with every breath that you take . . . and let go. . . . The relaxation strengthens itself. . . . Each part of the body that you are relaxing is learning the process . . . over . . . and over again. . . . Relaxation moving on up into the shoulders . . . down the arms . . . all of the way to the fingertips . . . loosening tension . . . discomfort . . . stress and strain . . . all of those feelings just leaving the body . . . more . . . and more . . . and more. . . . And, as you will . . . send that wave of relaxation back up the arms . . . into the shoulders once again . . . to relax the area between the shoulders and the neck . . . with greater and greater comfort . . . moment by moment . . . and then begin to relax the neck . . . just loosening all the tension there now . . . more and more comfort. . . . And as you do . . . you can begin to relax the scalp . . . relaxing the entire head . . . the brow feeling comfortable . . . the eyes relaxing deeply within their sockets . . . the entire face relaxing . . . and finally, relax the jaw. . . . Just let the jaw drop . . . and you may feel that when you relax the jaw . . . you can experience a tremendous spread of relaxation throughout the head . . . neck . . . and shoulders. . . . Just enjoy that state now . . . that feeling . . . keeping your mind focused for a few moments on this relaxation. . . . If the mind should wander . . . very gently . . . carefully . . . bring it back to the relaxation. . . . (Therapeutic intervention might be indicated at this point, or simply continuation of the relaxation process.) And now . . . as you begin to end this session of relaxation . . . realize that you have accomplished a great deal. . . . In learning relaxation . . . in developing awareness . . . you can have full strength throughout your body and mind . . . without having any excess tension. . . . Strength and tension do not equal each other. . . . So begin now to bring back the strength to the arms and legs . . . trunk . . . neck . . . face . . . head, in fact, all body parts. Begin to take deeper breaths now, bringing in more oxygen to rejuvenate the mind and body, realizing the benefits of your rest and relaxation. And then, whenever you are ready, simply open your eyes, feeling wonderfully relaxed, fully confident, alert, and happy.

Safe place

The safe place image is used as a therapeutic intervention or process image for general comfort and relaxation. Suggest to the client that the safe place has all the potentials of self-actualization or self-realization. It is important to stress to the client that the safe place is that image which appears initially and spontaneously and to caution the client not to search around aimlessly for the most ideal place to experience. The process by which the person gets to the safe place can vary; on occasion, we have used the image of being carried away by a very cool white fleecy cloud or simply asking the client to recall and remember a very safe place, one that had the cue words of peace, comfort, safety and happiness.

Now at this time, with the relaxation going on . . . and if you will . . . if you really wish to become even more completely relaxed and comfortable . . . just allow yourself to be transported across time . . . and across space . . . to a place that to you means peace . . . comfort . . . safety . . . and happiness. . . . This is the first place that you have in your awareness that means those things to you. . . . Begin to experience . . . if you will . . . all the sensations of peace . . . comfort . . . safety . . . and happiness . . . as you begin to look at all the things there are to see . . . and listen to all the sounds there are to hear . . . and smell all of the aromas . . . and taste and touch whatever you wish to taste and touch . . . knowing that as you experience all parts of this place . . . the feelings of peace . . . comfort . . . safety and happiness . . . are being taken deep within you . . . being moved around to all parts of you . . . so that all parts of you know these feelings. . . . Each moment you spend experiencing this safe place . . . the feelings become stronger and more a part of you. . . . Your enjoyment of this place can be heightened every moment that you spend there. . . . So for a few moments . . . just enjoy . . . experience . . . and ultimately know . . . all parts of this place and how those feelings interact with you. . . . In this place you can feel safe to experience all emotions in their proper perspective . . . and then realize that you can carry through your normal waking state . . . the ability to feel emotions clearly . . . completely . . . and enjoy the benefits of that skill . . . for in this place all potentials exist.

The closure of this safe place image can be general or specific, depending upon the therapeutic benefit desired. It is important to bring the client back across time and across space, to lighten his or her state of awareness, reoriented to this time and this place, and with full strength and resiliency regained. All the ego-strengthening suggestions can be made at this point, to bring him or her back to the normal waking state with the maximum of benefit.

The protective shield

At times it is important for a client to feel that he or she has a personal space, that there is somewhere that is safe for him or her to be, to feel protected from outside influences. We have developed this image of the protective shield specifically for this purpose and have found it particularly helpful for the hospitalized patient.

Now, at this time, you can find that position of rest for your body . . . make any final adjustments . . . loosen any tight clothing . . . and then once you have achieved a comfortable state . . . just allow your body to rest. . . . Close your eyes and feel once again how when you close your eyes you close out distractions . . . and those influences that keep you from looking within. . . . And now you can more clearly look inside yourself . . . with the light of your own consciousness . . . focusing first on your breathing . . . noticing how as you relax the breathing becomes more regular . . . more effortless . . . with less and less energy used . . . increasing comfort moment by moment . . . breath by breath . . . more and more relaxed . . . more and more comfortable . . . . And then, if you will, begin once again the relaxation of the body . . . the process through which you are going to lessen tension . . . going to increase comfort . . . and let the body rest . . . very completely . . . all parts of the body relaxing . . . so that as you send the messages of relaxation down to the feet . . . you become aware of those sensations again . . . those sensations that to you mean comfort and relaxation . . . and then you allow them to spread as you have done before . . . spread above the feet and into the legs . . . up . . . and up . . . and up . . . inch by inch . . . up the legs. . . loosening all muscle tension, opening the blood vessels, increasing comfort . . . up and up the legs . . . into the hips and trunk . . . all the way up to the waist . . . moving above the waist into the lower chest . . . where you feel your breathing once again . . . remembering to relax the back . . . the area between the shoulder blades . . . and the upper chest and shoulders. . . . Just send the messages of relaxation . . . and then feel those sensations develop . . . and, as you can . . . send that wave of relaxation down the arms . . . all the way down the arms to the shoulders . . . the elbows . . . through the wrists . . . into the hands and fingertips . . . more and more relaxed . . . more and more comfortable. . . . And keeping those sensations of comfort in the arms . . . send that wave of relaxation back up . . . once again into the shoulders . . . to begin the relaxation of the neck and head . . . relaxing the area between the shoulders and the neck . . . loosening tension . . . feeling increasing comfort . . . over and over again . . . then relaxing the neck area . . . all parts of the neck . . . front . . . sides . . . and back . . . and then relaxing the scalp . . . all over the scalp . . . feeling comfortable . . . as you let that wave of relaxation pour down over the brow . . . loosening all the lines . . . allowing the eyes to relax deeply within their sockets . . . then relaxing the remainder of the face . . . the nose . . . cheeks . . . lips . . . and tongue . . . and then, finally . . . relaxing the jaw . . . letting tension leave the jaw . . . increasing comfort in that area. . . . And now, as you may have noticed, there are areas of the body that are more easy to relax than others. . . . And now, if you really wish to become more comfortable and more relaxed . . . allow your attention to go back to an area of your body that you find to be the most comfortable . . . the most relaxed. . . . Send your attention there now . . . and find out just exactly what it is about that area that makes it most comfortable and most relaxed . . . and when you have identified those sensations of this most relaxed and comfortable area . . . allow them to spread . . . allow them to become stronger and begin to go out beyond that area . . . affecting all parts of the body. . . . Now the spread of this comfort may go as the rays of the sun would emanate . . . or as the rings of water spread out from where a pebble was dropped into a still pond. . . . However it does go, let it go to every cell of your body . . . let every cell feel this wonderful sensation . . . and with every moment that passes . . . the sensations become stronger in every cell. . . . Every cell knows these sensations . . . and once the entire body has felt this comfortable feeling . . . you can allow that sensation . . . that wonderful feeling . . . to go beyond the physical confines of your body . . . spreading out through the pores of your skin . . . out beyond your skin . . . to form a protective shield around you. . . . And you can let this feeling spread far . . . far beyond your own physical body . . . or keep it very close . . . as a second skin. . . . Since this protective bubble, or shield, is your own creation . . . you can do with it what you wish. . . . The uses of this shield are limitless. . . . It can act as a filter, to filter out those feelings . . . things that go on around you . . . situations that are uncomfortable . . . and allow you to let in those that you wish to experience. . . . It can act as an amplifier to help you understand people . . . and people to understand you. . . . It can be invisible . . . or invisible to a few people . . . or as many people as you wish. . . . However you wish to use this you may . . . because it is your creation. . . . You only need to practice developing the comfort in the body . . . allowing it to spread . . . and then allowing it to go beyond the confines of the physical body. . . . You can experiment with it . . . making it as large as you like . . . using it as a transport to other places . . . other times. . . . The more you use it, the stronger it becomes . . . the more diverse it becomes. . . . And now . . . placing it at whatever size or position you wish . . . realizing the full potential of what you can do here . . . increased stabilities and increased confidence . . . begin to lighten your state of awareness now . . . coming back to this time and this place . . . fully alert and responsive . . . as you know how to do . . . using your own speed to come back, bringing strength back into the body, alertness to the mind, responsiveness, full comfort remaining, without tension, and then whenever you are ready, simply open your eyes, feeling wonderfully relaxed and comfortable and happy.

Anxiety or pain as an object

One of the most important process images that we employ is one for symptom reduction, in a manner of objectifying the symptom, be it anxiety, stress, strain, or pain, and then reducing its size and therefore reducing its power or strength. As we will note later in the section on pain, there are a number of things to be taken into consideration before removing pain or reducing its intensity because pain and anxiety do serve as warning signals and must be recognized, not just blithely done away with without thought to the repercussions. The narrative of this image will be picked up in the process after relaxation has been induced in the client.

Now, many of us experience sensations that we would regard as unpleasant . . . pain . . . discomfort . . . tension . . . stress . . . strain. . . . We have already learned one method of dealing with these . . . and that is just breathing deeply and removing all parts of stress and strain. . . . Let us now use another image that can be utilized to deal with these symptoms. . . . These symptoms are all very subjective phenomena. . . . We feel them . . . but as we only know too well . . . it is very difficult to consciously modify feelings. . . . It is much easier to modify objects. . . . So what we will do here is change our unpleasant sensation into an object. . . . If you now have a pain or discomfort- . . . or if you feel somewhat tense or anxious . . . just take that pain- . . . tension . . . stress or strain . . . and give it a shape. . . . Imagine or visualize the shape. . . . It can be an abstract shape or a concrete shape . . . it could be an object or a geometric design . . it can be amorphous. . . . Whatever shape first came into your mind . . . that is the one that is appropriate. . . . Anything else is a conscious, judgmental effort. . . . Now, give that shape a color . . . and now give it a size. . . . You can give it a size just by knowing its size or by just picturing it next to some object of known size. . . . Now realize that this is a symbol of your tension or stress or strain . . . anxiety or discomfort- . . . and that it's obvious that the larger it is . . . the more severe the discomfort is . . . and conversely, the smaller and less vividly colored it is . . . the less severe and significant it is. . . . So practice by changing the size of the object. . . . First make it a little bigger . . . and then make it smaller. . . . If you have any difficulty making it smaller just by wanting it to be . . . then use a few tricks. . . . If it is a balloon you can put a needle into it . . . or kick it away . . . throw it away . . . put it on a boat or a truck or tie it to the tail of an airplane or bird and let it fly away with it. . . . And realize that as this symbol becomes smaller. . . the feelings associated with it become less intense. . . . And you can make it as small as it is comfortable for you to make it. . . . And practice making it larger and smaller . . . because remember, these are all skills, and as with any skill . . . the more you practice, the more proficient you become and the more practice, the more powerful the skill becomes.

The guide

The use of guides in any process of change has been a universal phenomenon for the human race. There are guides listed in every culture and expression of intellect, some of which have been written in fable form, others which have been passed down from generation to generation by word of mouth. It is important that the clinician realize that the guide can be used to give advice to the client, realizing that the advice is really coming from the unconscious of the client himself. The guide also provides support and protection, and provides some messages that will solve the problems that the client is having in a somewhat indirect manner. The guide also has the power to provide the patient with total symptom removal for brief periods of time, so that the client understands the power that the guide possesses. Use of the guide image usually begins with a safe place, one in which the client feels that he or she is comfortable and is able to experience all his or her potentials. This image fosters a process of centering, increasing the client's ability to observe his or her own intuitive aspects. We will take up the image of the guide after the safe place has been established.

As you begin to experience your safe place in greater and greater depth . . . feeling more and more comfortable with each moment in time that passes . . . more relaxed . . . more safe . . . more secure . . . allow yourself to become aware that you are not alone. . . . With you in this safe place is a living being that is very much concerned with your welfare . . . with your well-being. . . . If at first you don't know exactly where this living creature is . . . look around very carefully for any movement . . . listen for any sounds . . . and pay particular attention to any living being or creature that is paying particular attention to you. . . . The attention that you might see has the qualities of caring and concern . . . of intuitive and intellectual wisdom. . . . As you look around and as you experience your safe place . . . you can see and be aware of this living being . . . and if you look around and listen very carefully . . . and are not aware of one . . . it is even all right to pretend that there is a living being there with you that is very much concerned and wishes to help. . . . When you become aware and notice this guide . . . establish contact . . . by first perhaps finding out its name and what its purpose is . . . and this you can do by actually talking with the creature . . . or being . . . whether it be a person or an animal . . . and then telling the animal or person just exactly what you wish to get out of this encounter. . . . More than likely, the guide already knows and is there to serve as a facilitator or helper for you to understand those problems to which you are seeking answers. . . . You may ask one or two questions so that the guide can answer easily . . . and readily. . . . You may also ask the guide to demonstrate its power by taking away either partially or completely a symptom that you might be having . . . whether it be pain . . . discomfort . . . anxiety . . . or stress . . . thereby letting you know that it means to help you in the ways in which you feel you need help. . . . And you can stay with your guide as long as you wish . . . and when you are ready to part . . . make sure that you have definite plans to meet in your safe place . . . so that you two can continue working on increasing your awareness . . . and your ability . . . to control symptoms and changes in your own life.

References

1. R. Bandler, J. Grinder, and J. O. Stevens, eds., *Frogs into Princes: Neuro-Linguistic Programming* (Moab, Utah: Real People Press, 1979).

2. M. H. Erickson, E. L. Rossi, and S. I. Rossi, *Hypnotic Realities: The Induction of Clinical Hypnosis and Forms of Indirect Suggestion* (New York: Irvington, 1976).

3. Ibid., p. 62.

4. W. S. Kroger, *Clinical and Experimental Hypnosis in Medicine, Dentistry, and Psychology,* 2d ed. (Philadelphia: J. B. Lippincott, 1977).

5. M. Samuels and N. Samuels, *Seeing with the Mind's Eye* (New York: Random House Bookworks, 1975).

6. W. S. Kroger and W. D. Fezler, *Hypnosis and Behavior Modification: Imagery Conditioning* (Philadelphia: J. B. Lippincott, 1976).

Section II

Specific applications

Chapter 6

Application of imagery
to nursing practice

If one views healing and healers historically, it is possible to understand the power that can be wielded by a nurse in nearly any given situation. Samuels and Samuels relate such healing practices to visualization and mental imagery. They cite, as examples, the Hermetic tradition of visualization of perfect health as a means to cure disease and the shaman who reunifies the sick person with his or her soul by visualizing a journey in search of the soul.[1] The tradition is continued in the Christian Science Church with the belief that disease is a product of the human mind and therefore can be altered by the human mind.[2] Such important traditions must be acknowledged by nurses who wish to maximize their healing influence in such diverse situations as surgery, critical care, psychiatry, rehabilitation, emergency medicine, office practice, obstetrics, and laboratory work.

In the scope of the practice of nursing, communication through direct and indirect patient care services can be enhanced when the nurse is aware of—and practices—methods of altering states of consciousness and imagery. By utilizing specific techniques, the nurse can maximize the placebo response, which, according to Jerome Frank, triggers within the patient a healing visualization by persuasion.[3] As the nurse listens to and assesses the patient's linguistic and perceptual preferences, communication will naturally improve, and the patient's needs will be more effectively and efficiently met. Rather than obtaining partial information, or misinformation which can cause delays, the nurse can obtain quickly the necessary data which will facilitate the nursing care plan.

Nursing practice

Surgery

Preoperative management of any surgical patient can include suggestions of confidence in the medical and surgical care being rendered, as well as expectations that the surgery will progress without complications, that the postoperative problems of nausea, urinary retention, and pain will be diminished, and that the process of healing will be speedy and complete. Postoperatively, the patient can be guided into comfortable sitting, standing, and ambulation, with increased appetite. Crasilneck reported a decrease in the dumping syndrome postgastrectomy.[4] (Refer to Chapter 13 for more details of surgical applications.)

Intensive and critical care

Although many diagnoses are treated in intensive and critical care units, by far the most demanding for the nurse and potentially debilitating for the patient is the cardiovascular disorder. Beginning with the need for rest for the cardiac patient, the nurse can maximize the patient's rest by teaching progressive relaxation and images for calmness. The nurse can also begin the process of behavior modification that follows the myocardial infarction by having the patient rehearse the healthy response. Bernard Engel reported a number of studies in which patients have shown skills in controlling supraventricular arrhythmias, paroxysmal tachycardia, intermittent Wolfe-Parkinson-White syndrome, and ventricular ectopic beats.[5] Through imagery, we believe that medications can be potentiated in a shorter period of time. (Refer to Chapter 12 for more practical applications.)

Rehabilitation

The nurse who works in a rehabilitation unit has the unique opportunity to spend an extended period of time with one patient, from several weeks to several months. During that time the nurse teaches the patient preventative and restorative skills, including bed mobility, simple range-of-motion exercises, skin care, and personal care activities of daily living, all of which are maximized in the relaxed, comfortable patient who has a positive self-image and attitude toward the rehabilitation process. (Specific images for physical medicine and rehabilitation will be detailed later in Chapter 8.) We suggest using the slower evening hours for relaxation training, perhaps the time just before the evening meal. During the relaxation training, the nurse can reinforce the work done in the various therapies during the day; i.e., the nurse can ask the patient to remember what it felt like to walk before the onset of paralysis or amputation, therefore supplying positive input to the rehabilitation process. Similar ways of reinforcing occupational therapy, speech therapy, and other activities can be utilized. In some cases, say where the patient must learn bowel and bladder control, the control may occur more quickly and completely if the nurse guides the patient through relaxation and suggests the appropriate imagery; that is, the patient, having once learned such control, will now remember that learning, aided by end-result imagery.

Psychiatry

Often the use of imagery techniques has been dismissed as a part of the treatment of mentally disturbed persons, the rationale being that the addition of extraneous thought processes would disturb the psychotherapeutic rapport. In many situations now, where the patients are agitated or depressed, it is standard practice to use at least the relaxation imagery: "Remember how you felt, what you looked like, how you moved when you were very happy and your life was going well and you felt relaxed and comfortable." Further specifics on counseling will be detailed in Chapter 9.

Office practice

In the daily routine of a medical office, the nurse has frequent opportunities to utilize rapid relaxation and imagery techniques to facilitate positive results from the patients. By encouraging and teaching the patients the techniques of relaxation and imagery, the nurse can help the patient to see the importance of his or her favorable response to treatment and to daily life situations, of continuing self-reinforcement, and of a change of attitudes and values reflecting healthy emotional states.[6] When the teaching is provided within a permissive attitude, the patient can readily become motivated, confident, and trustful. Such opportunities arise each time an injection is given, a scope procedure done, a medication administered, and blood pressure taken. When a patient is anxious and begins to breathe in a shallow rapid manner, leading to hyperventilation, the nurse can guide the patient into a more normal breathing pattern. Specific techniques include:

Injection. By beginning the process through alternative language, the nurse can decrease anxiety and still be truthful to the patient, so that words like "This won't hurt" are replaced with "You might feel a pressure or a stick." By such substitution, the nurse has shifted the pattern of responses and opened up a new range of possible sensations. If the patient is one who has frequent injections, the response can be conditioned. The immediate area of the injection can be made temporarily numb by the technique of transfer of anesthesia as described in the chapter on pain (Chapter 7).

Endoscopic procedures. When a patient must have a sigmoidoscopy done, the nurse can readily prepare the patient by relaxation and assist during the scope by reinforcing muscle relaxation, easy and comfortable breathing, and by perhaps guiding the patient to dissociate to a pleasant mental space.

Medication. Whether medications are given by mouth, by injection into the muscle or viscera, or by intravenous transfusion, the effects can be enhanced by appropriate waking suggestion. One possible way to enhance the effect is to simply say that the medicine has been prescribed by the physician because of its many beneficial effects in many people. When medications must be given through intravenous transfusion and there is a problem with venous patency, suggestions can be given to enhance the health and strength of the venous walls. This skill is one that is especially facile in the conditioned patient.

Blood pressure. The use of altered states of consciousness and imagery in hypertension is well known (and detailed in Chapter 12), and the immediate use of these techniques in the monitoring of blood pressure is seen as a way to decrease the so-called white coat hypertension which results from the immediate anxiety of being in the physician's office. Care must be taken to avoid such effects that would give a false positive reading and mask potential problems. Following the monitoring of blood pressure, the nurse can then give training in relaxation in an attempt to decrease overall blood pressure status.

In the treatment of dermatological conditions, there is much that an office nurse can provide as assistant to the patient and physician. In case of neurodermatitis, glove anesthesia can be used to control itching. In the treatment of psoriasis, imagery that duplicates the sun and heat and facilitates the healing process can produce altered states within the skin.[7]
In the treatment of asthma and related chronic lung disease, simple

chest muscle relaxation can reverse the decompensating spiral of tension-muscle spasm. By far the most direct method of relaxation for lung disease patients is diaphragmatic breathing to a specific cadence.

It is anticipated that one of the most consistent and difficult problems that any nurse encounters is the efficient and thorough treatment of pain. There are easily adaptable images for pain control, detailed at the end of this chapter. (See also the methods of assessment and imagery on pain in Chapter 7.)

Emergency room

The majority of patients present in any emergency room are already in altered states of consciousness through shock and denial; therefore, imagery techniques can be readily applied with both the patient and the family. Utilization of whatever signs the patient is presenting is most important; i.e., if the patient is obviously hyperventilating, the nurse may pace her talking and breathing to a more normal rhythm, may ask the patient to remember a relaxed and comfortable time. By having the patient remember a more pleasant time, a dissociation takes place, and diagnostic procedures can more readily be accomplished, insertions of needles and catheters can proceed more easily, and a more clear history can be obtained in between suggestions of remembrances. By having the patient focus on a selected, nonthreatening spot on the wall or ceiling, or on a similarly noncharged piece of furniture or equipment, an altered state leading to increased relaxation can rapidly be achieved.

Images to be used in nursing practice

With nearly every hospitalized patient or patient undergoing procedures on an outpatient basis, the nurse has the opportunity to provide a special place, a place of refuge, or a personal space by using the images presented in Chapter 5—the safe place and the shield. With the intrusiveness of any hospital procedure, and the removal of normal privacy norms, it becomes very important for the nurse to provide some kind of feeling of privacy and safety for the patient in order to realize the maximization of all treatment care plans.

When a nurse is faced with starting and maintaining an intravenous infusion, it is important that he or she remember that the walls of veins and arteries have a certain tensile strength, which can be accentuated by use of imagery. The use of imagery is most effective in this way in a conditioned patient. Initially, the nurse can use the process of relaxation and imagery by approaching the patient with the positive attitude that there will be no difficulty in inserting the needle and maintaining a patent pathway into the vein or artery, and that it can be a very comfortable procedure. The overall effect of a relaxed nurse starting an intravenous transfusion is that the patient will soon pick up the nurse's confidence and respond favorably to the nurse and to the needle being inserted.

The use of appropriate relaxation and imagery techniques in nursing practice is felt to be an adjunct to the regular scope of nursing, and each nurse must decide how this series of new techniques will fit in best with his or her particular practice. It is anticipated that the nurse will use these techniques within the realm of his or her expertise.

Reference

1. M. Samuels and N. Samuels, *Seeing with the Mind's Eye* (New York: Random House Bookworks, 1975), p. 30.

2. Ibid., p. 33.

3. Ibid., p. 219.

4. H. B. Crasilneck and J. A. Hall, *Clinical Hypnosis: Principles and Applications* (New York: Grune and Stratton, 1975), p. 92.

5. J. V. Basmajian, *Biofeedback: Principles and Practice for Clinicians* (Baltimore: Williams and Wilkins, 1979), pp. 175–76.

6. W. S. Kroger and W. D. Fezler, *Hypnosis and Behavior Modification: Imagery Conditioning* (Philadelphia: J. B. Lippincott, 1976), p. 396.

7. Ibid., p. 342.

Chapter 7

Pain

Our experience in working with hundreds of people, on an inpatient as well as an outpatient basis has been that a holistic methodology that includes training in deep relaxation and imagery is the most effective and the most client-centered mode of treatment for chronic pain. Pain is a

> multi-dimensional experience which involves not only the discriminative capacity to identify the onset, duration, location, intensity, and physical characteristics of the stimulus, but also includes the motivational, affective, and cognitive functions leading to adversive behavior, with private experience of unpleasantness and the interpretation of the stimulus in terms of present and past experience.[1]

The problem of chronic pain as a major disabling condition of our times has reached staggering proportions in terms of money spent on treatment, days lost from work and meaningful avocation, and an unaccountable degree of suffering. The popular literature is filled with articles on disability from pain, and the chronic diseases and the newer methods of amelioration. Our methods are not new; their roots can be traced into history for thousands of years into many diversified cultures, which have made use of innate mechanisms for the voluntary control of pain in all its forms. In this chapter we delineate the forms of pains.

History of pain

Until 1965, there were two main theories of pain, which appeared to be in opposition to one another. The specificity theory and the pattern theory were derived from research begun in the 17th century by Decartes and in the 19th century by Von Frey and Goldscheider.[2] In the specificity theory, it was proposed that pain was a specific modality, like the other senses, with its own central and peripheral apparatus. Impulses were projected to a pain center in the brain by way of alpha-delta and C-fibers through free nerve endings. In the pattern theory, pain was described as being produced by intense stimulation of nonspecific receptors. In 1965, Melzak and Wall, after discussing the physiological basis for agreement and disagreement with the specificity and pattern theories, proposed a new theory, called the *gate control* theory. This theory encompasses the total interaction of the nervous system activity within a human being, and has been under scrutiny since publication. It continues to be a serious contender for the most accurate description of psychophysiological function.[2]

In the gate control theory of pain, there are two major components to be considered—the sensory-discriminative and the motivational-affective system.[3] According to Hilgard, in the sensory-discriminative system, there is carried the information concerning location and intensity of stimulation, with little attention given to quality of pain or stimulation. In the motivational-affective system, there is considerable attention given to the quality of pain, for structures close to the limbic system of the brain are responsible for mediation of the affective nature of pain. From the interrelation of these two systems, we have the result of pain modulation, so that impulses rising to the higher brain centers may be facilitated or inhibited according to the needs and motivations of the person experiencing the pain. Some central nervous system structures, namely the substantia gelatinosa, the dorsal columns, and the T-cells, activate and open or close the gates, while others are selective, but the presence or absence of pain is characteristically determined by the balance between the sensory and central inputs to the gate control system.

Some eight years after Melzak and Wall published their theory, three separate laboratories identified specific opiate agonists and antagonists binding to brain tissue, and two endogenous opioid peptides which were called enkephalins. It has been known for some 20 years that opiates derived from plant origins worked by attaching to sculpted tissue receptor sites, so that the proper three-dimensional configuration could produce analgesia and euphoria.

Acute versus chronic pain

Pain as a subjective response can be defined in terms of being acute or chronic, along a continuum from immediate acute, acute, subacute, moving into the chronic states. There is no rule which applies to the movement along the continuum, from acute to chronic or chronic with acute exacerbations. In any individual, acute pain resulting from an injury can be alleviated completely, or move inexorably toward chronicity, in as short a span of time as 24 hours. When pain is due to underlying pathology, appropriate diagnostic and therapeutic management has a potential for reducing pain and rectifying the abnormal condition. That appropriate care is given does not guarantee that the pain which accompanies the pathology will be relieved. The complexity of the pain experience belies predictability regarding whether the pain will be only acute or become chronic. In any individual the pain is a result of present and past experiences and perceptions, many of which remain within the unconscious mind.

Acute pain is characterized by

1. The presence of a definable disease or disorder.
2. The expectation of its being temporary and self-limited.
3. The state of being constantly informed about something which is wrong.
4. Sudden onset.

Chronic pain is characterized by the following:

1. The requirement of a period of time to develop.
2. A condition which precipitated the pain, which may or may not be clinically evident.
3. The expectation of continuation into states of suffering, a state of existence.
4. Constant or intermittent occurrence.

The management of acute pain can be relatively expeditious in minimizing the possibility of chronicity. If the learning component of pain can be avoided by treating the sensations adequately (with therapeutic doses of analgesics, education of the patient regarding the condition bringing pain, and rapid treatment of the condition), then many of the sequelae, such as persistent pain, fear, ignorance, and physical limitations and deformities can be eliminated.

An example of this point is as follows: A person is involved in a low-speed traffic accident and sustains a whiplash injury to the cervical spine. This person is taken to the emergency room of the local hospital. X-rays are negative for fractures. The person is given a soft cervical collar and a mild analgesic medication to take as needed and sent home. In one or two more weeks the person returns to the doctor complaining of neck, shoulder, and back pain, plus headaches, and may then be referred to physical therapy and given stronger analgesic medications. Physical symptoms are prominent and are rapidly approaching permanency and degeneration. Ignorance and fear may stem from some unfinished business regarding whether adequate care was actually given immediately after the accident. In short, a whole series of complicating events has ensued from a single incident and may lead to the persistence of pain and disability.

Acute pain needs to be managed thoroughly through evaluation and specificity of treatment. In a thorough evaluation, the characteristics of pain, the pain responses, the pain communication, the coping techniques, and the factors influencing the pain all must be considered.[4] Considerable time will be spent later in this chapter concerning the evaluation and treatment of chronic pain.

Management of specific pain conditions

Although the overall management of chronic pain is consistent, some different characteristics present themselves with specific pain conditions.

Headache

Each year, volumes are written by renowned medical specialists on the management of headache, both from a diagnostic and a therapeutic predominantly chemical) standpoint. In a recent issue of the *New England Journal of Medicine,* Caviness and O'Brian[5] presented the following statistics:

1. Approximately 80 percent of the population of the United States will experience headaches in a given year.
2. Approximately 50 percent of the 80 percent will have severe and disabling headaches.
3. Approximately 10 to 20 percent of the 80 percent will seek medical attention with headache as the primary complaint.
4. Three times as many women complain of headache as do men.
5. There is a familial incidence in 20 to 50 percent.

In this review article the headache syndromes are differentiated, the pathophysiology is discussed, and treatments are outlined. They indicate that education, supportive counseling, and reassurance can be adjuncts to the pharmacologic means of treatment. There is mention of biofeedback training and supervised exercise as nonpharmacological means of relief, and of psychotherapy in conjunction with pharmacologic agents. As in most other journal articles and books on the subject, the balance of the review concerns itself with chemical treatments. There is no mention made of hypnosis, relaxation, or imagery as primary or alternative methods of management.

As in all pain conditions, it is important in the management of headache that all possible diagnostic work be completed to the satisfaction of both physician and client. The therapist employing the techniques of relaxation and imagery must remember that the client's welfare is primary, and that guiding a person toward the reduction or removal of necessary pain is assuming responsibility beyond the scope of his or her expertise.

Once an appropriate candidate has been selected, the evaluation process begins. Since most clients who have headaches have had them for a substantially long period of time, it is important to follow some outline for the evaluation to establish clear communication.

History
1. The date and cause of the onset of headache.
2. The mode and intensity of the onset of headache.
3. Significant life experiences at the time of the onset.

Course
1. The frequency of headache, paying close attention to cyclic patterns.
2. Factors influencing the onset and/or relief of headache, mentioning activities, food, and feelings.

Previous Treatment
1. Include both self- and other-administered treatment.
2. Successes and/or failures.
3. Explorations of patients' concerns and fears.

Finally, some questions need to be asked to delineate how the client experiences the headache; i.e., what "pictures" there are for the client in as many sensory modes as is possible for the client to express; namely, visual, auditory, kinesthetic, gustatory, and olfactory.

From that point, treatment strategies can be selected which will maximize the client's self-responsibility, abilities for change, and control over somatic responses. Drawing upon the intensive research of Elmer and Alyce Green,[6] we have statistical evidence that thermal biofeedback can lead to decreased migraine response, with retention of skills for control over a five-year period of time. Budzynski[7] reported a study using electromyographic feedback in which headache activity was decreased and maintained five to seven months poststudy. Biofeedback is certainly one important tool in the management of headache. However, the biofeedback strategies are geared for muscle relaxation and handwarming, the latter for decreased overall sympathetic overflow in the autonomic nervous system, both of which can be done without the tool through use of progressive relaxation and appropriate therapeutic imagery.

One interesting introduction to the use of imagery in management of headaches was presented by Adam Smith in his book, *Powers of Mind*. The Great Central Philippine Headache Cure[8] was his term for the headache-curing practices of shamans in the central Philippines. In this process, the patient looks at the headache, decides upon the color, location, size, and movement, and if it were liquid, whether it would fit into a specific sized container. The patient is then told to pour the headache into the container. The process is repeated until the headache is gone.

Visualization of head pain is an important part of imagery, but for full expression, other senses can be included, especially sound and kinesthesia. Images for control of head pain will be discussed at the end of this chapter, but general guidelines that are useful include

1. Beginning the relaxation process at the feet so as to place distance between the site of pain and the first areas to be relaxed.
2. Utilizing specific breathing suggestions to enhance oxygen availability.
3. Approaching the relaxation of shoulder and neck areas slowly and repetitiously to allow sufficient time for "letting go," and avoiding suggestions that all of the relaxation must be done at once; i.e., accepting for yourself and the client what is actually done.
4. Initiating the experience in the supine position, with the head and neck comfortably supported by a small, soft cervical pillow.

Low back pain

The billions of dollars which are spent each year in the treatment of low back pain conditions indicate that the effectiveness of any preventive or curative measures today remains unquestionably poor. Low back pain is perhaps the most common, yet complex orthopedic problem faced today.

As outlined in the treatment of headache, evaluation of low back pain must be detailed and complete so as to provide for a well-rounded picture of the pain images. The location, movement, and size of the pain must be determined as the client experiences these parameters. It may take much questioning and reiteration in order to step by the client's reporting of what the doctors or therapists have told him or her about the condition. What matters is what pictures of the condition reside within the client's mind.

In the evaluative interview, the circumstances surrounding the initiation of the back pain must be delineated, whether through injury, illness, or disease. When injury is the precipitating mechanism, frequently the person will complain bitterly about seemingly poor emergency medical care and will continue to have "unfinished business"; both of these issues must eventually be confronted. If the injury was one resulting from repeated trauma, the issue of personal responsibility becomes part of the treatment focus.

Further into the evaluation, activities which aggravate and alleviate the back pain need to be detailed. These activities will become part of the imagery. A person whose back pain is alleviated by soaking in a hot tub will be trained to imagine those feelings of warm water to achieve relief.

Any other factors associated with the onset, perpetuation, and relief of the low back pain may be discovered in the diagnostic interview, or may arise from conversation about past therapeutic treatment or family discord, all of which can contribute to, or detract from, the effectiveness of the imagery.

Chest pain

Recently, it has become apparent that anginal pain has the potential, in selected cases, to be responsive to nonchemical, vasodilatative methods.[9] The use of handwarming images, monitored by temperature biofeedback, can be of additional therapeutic benefit to those patients who can accept the possibility of self-reliance and responsibility. Just as in the use of imagery for diminishing headache, the mechanism of control of blood vessel caliber from hand or fingertips to coronary arteries is not understood. It is wise, however, to recall from the previous chapters that sympathetic overactivity can be modulated by the use of relaxation and imagery processes, and that chest pain is frequently associated with myocardial ischemia, which is a direct reflection of sympathetic overactivity. As heart rate and blood pressures are decreased, the chance of reversal of myocardial ischemia is enhanced.

Behavior modification techniques

In the treatment of chronic pain, some considerable time and energy must be devoted to understanding the behavior patterns demonstrated by those with chronic pain. The behavior patterns which lead to dependence and disability are the manifestations of faulty coping mechanisms and of ways of controlling the environment, which includes not only families but friends, strangers, and the entire health care delivery system. Chronic pain occurs partially because of environmental consequences that reinforce the pain pattern; the pain therefore becomes contingent upon the results.

As an example of the learning pattern of pain, consider the reaction of one who observes a person with chronic pain. How does someone know that another person is in pain? Pain is known simply by the behavior pattern shown by the person with chronic pain. If a person of importance responds to pain behavior with concerns and extra time and favors, some elements of that response are contingent upon seeing pain behavior. If repeated often enough, soon the response of concern and attention is all that is needed to set into motion the pain pattern, regardless of whether the original pathology exists or not. At some time, all attention paid to the person with chronic pain has a potential for perpetuating pain behavior. In addition, certain circumstances or consequences may not occur when the person with chronic pain engages in pain behavior, and that avoidance then also reinforces the existence of pain. It is in the realm of behavior modification, therefore, that one must look for tools used to manage the manipulative behavior of the person with intractable chronic pain and in whom all previous approaches or treatment have failed.

We learn from behavior modification that to reward a behavior leads to reinforcement of that and similar behaviors. Conversely, to punish or ignore behavior is to encourage discontinuance of that or similar behaviors. In the treatment of chronic pain, the objectives are

1. Reduction of pain behavior by withdrawing positive reinforcement from such behavior.
2. An increase in activity or well behavior by programming positive reinforcement contingent upon increasing activity and exercise.[10]

The actual means of implementing this philosophy are less important than is maintaining a consistent treatment attitude. For success, the attitude must be present from all professionals working with the client and from significant others in the life of the client.

Our concept of a pain rehabilitation unit

Our concept of a multidisciplinary approach to the rehabilitation process is manifested in most specialized rehabilitation centers across the nation. We feel that chronic pain is a disease entity which must be included in the rehabilitation process so as to maximize the response by, and the process of change for, the person with chronic pain. The coordinated and integrated team effort of highly trained professionals representing medicine, rehabilitation nursing, physical and occupational therapy, recreation therapy, pharmacy, nutritional services, and psychiatry provides for an intensive education program for relearning living skills.

The Pain Rehabilitation Unit at Bay General Community Hospital is a specialized part of Bay Rehabilitation Center. The unit provides an inpatient medical treatment environment for evaluation and education of people who suffer chronic, disabling pain. The educational program focuses on providing chronic pain alternatives to pain behavior, including changing belief systems about illness and wellness and using the present health care system properly. In this inpatient setting, the person with chronic pain is provided with support and guidance from professionals who care and have enthusiasm for the treatment philosophy. The people who have had any contact with the pain rehabilitation team have remarked that they feel a certain cohesion and firm trust and communication among the team members. This feeling, combined with the presence of other patients with chronic pain, the relatively long hospital stay, and the intensive therapy, provides the greatest opportunity for the optimal outcome.

Each professional who works in the program does a thorough evaluation, which is written in the chart and reported at a case conference. After the evaluation has been completed, the professional plans a specific treatment program and a set of goals which are consistent with the desires and needs of the person participating in the program.

The protocol for our inpatient pain rehabilitation unit is described in the work of Wilbert Fordyce and his colleagues at the University of Washington Medical School, where they treated chronic pain by behavioral management. We refer the reader to Fordyce's papers for the specifics of management. The general principles include medication management, exercise and activity quotas, and family education.

Medication management

As an alternative to the use of multiple drug combinations, we provide, in a liquid medium, doses of methadone that approximate the patient's mixed medication pattern. This is a typical pattern for our clients. By using methadone in a liquid vehicle, we avoid withdrawal, the potentiation of mixed drugs, the euphoria usually associated with addictive narcotics, and the reward of having many pills or injections. The client is withdrawn from medication by approximately 20 to 30 percent a week, so that at discharge, most clients will be withdrawn from all pain medication. Other medications are the responsibility of the client. The habit of taking liquid is continued for at least one week after all medications have been withdrawn to insure reinforcement of nonpill, noninjection behavior. For those readers concerned about habit substitution and the development of a pattern of drinking addictive substances, it is felt that by the time of discharge, the client will have developed enough resources that the likelihood of that change is negligible. In addition, the client will be seen for long-term outpatient follow-up.

Exercise and activity quotas

Both physical and occupational therapy utilize the quota system for conditioning exercise, activity, and up-time (the time the patient is out of bed). Graphic progress charts are used to reinforce the increased activity levels.

Family education

Although each team member meets with the significant others of the client, it is of primary importance that the psychologist, the family counselor, and the leisure counselor meet regularly with and guide the family and significant others. The process of change affects all the participants.

Images for pain control

Following the evaluation of the person with chronic pain, it is important that the therapist select the appropriate images to be used during the sessions for maximum therapeutic benefit. The therapist must keep in mind that the patient has certain linguistic preferences and predominant modes of perception, and fit the images accordingly so that the patient can get the best result and be able to use them independently. Images for pain control are specific; the use of general pain control images for generalized pain is not recommended. Since pain is a specific phenomenon, which also is a warning signal, the therapist needs to be advised that the indiscriminate removal of pain can result in undiagnosed problems which can accentuate disability and lead not only to complications, but also to a disruption of the rapport with the patient because pain that is undiagnosed and indiscriminately removed will return at some point in time, perhaps rendering the patient unwilling or unaccepting of further treatment using imagery. Standard hypnotic induction and standard hypnotic suggestions are a part of the utilization of images for pain control. In the next few paragraphs we will be detailing the use of glove anesthesia or analgesia and a light switch image, both of which have been markedly successful in their amelioration of pain. (Chapter 12 refers to the use of the image of pain as an object.)

Glove anesthesia

Following the appropriate relaxation or induction techniques, the patient is instructed to use any one of several different methods for inducing apparent anesthesia and/or analgesia in one or both hands. The anesthesia or analgesia is then transferred to the body part that is painful. The method of inducing anesthesia or analgesia in any extremity, most significantly the hand, can be accomplished by a number of different methods; David Bresler has used in his work at the UCLA Pain Control Center and in his book *Free Yourself from Pain* the image of a person placing his or her hand into a bucket containing a very potent anesthetic solution. Additional ways of inducing a state of glove anesthesia or analgesia can include having the person imagine that his or her hand is encased in a very thick glove. The detail of the glove is important, and the more it is described as being thick, strong, and impenetrable, the more effective the result will be. The image of placing the hand in a snowdrift with the tingling sensation finally becoming numb is also very potent for producing a state of anesthesia or analgesia. Having the client remember what it feels like to have the dentist inject novocaine into the gum during dental procedures can be duplicated in the hand as the therapist touches the back of the person's hand lightly, indicating that with each touch the hand is becoming more numb and insensitive to pain. At the end of the use of any of these images for inducing glove anesthesia or analgesia, it is important that the client be instructed in restoring normal sensation in the part of the body to which the anesthesia or analgesia was transferred. The restoration of normal sensation to the hand can be accomplished very easily by having the client shake the hand briskly.

Light switch image

The use of the light switch image can be accomplished in a number of different ways, depending upon the level of sophistication of the client and according to the complexity of the pain problem. Many patients will do quite well if an image of a single rheostat-controlled light switch is suggested, such that there are wires leading into the bottom of the switch from the painful area, and one wire leading from the top of the painful area to the brain. When pain is felt the wires are glowing and obviously vibrating, alive with impulses, and the person can begin to turn the rheostat down. The dimmer switch is turned down and down until it reaches a certain point. The patient must determine what that point is. If it is possible, the patient may decide to turn the rheostat all of the way off and hear the click at the end so that the pain is completely gone. An extension of this image involves the use of an entire panel of switches, perhaps the toggle switch kind that would flip off a number of circuits. This image also includes wires leading from the painful body areas into each switch and allows the patient to have as many switches as he or she needs so that the awareness of pain from the body parts to the brain is cut off. In using both of these images, it is very important to remember that the client is going to work at his or her own speed, turning down the rheostat or flipping the switches at his or her own rate. The rheostat is important in that the person who is somewhat reluctant to give up the pain completely can have the control to dial as much pain away as he or she wishes to eliminate. Adaptations to each of these images can be made according to the individual responses of the client, and according to the preferences of the therapist.

References

1. K. L. Casey, "Pain: A Current View of Neuro-Mechanisms," *Am Sci* 61 (1973), pp. 194–200.

2. R. Melzak and P. D. Wall, "Pain Mechanisms: A New Theory," *Science* 150 (3699) (1965), pp. 971–79.

3. E. R. Hilgard and J. R. Hilgard, *Hypnosis and the Relief of Pain* (Los Altos, Calif.: William Kaufmann, 1975).

4. M. Johnson, "Assessment of clinical pain," in *A Source of Book for Nurses and Other Health Professionals,* ed. A. K. Jacox (Boston, Mass.: Little, Brown, 1977).

5. V. S. Caviness Jr,, and P. O'Brian, "Headache," *N Eng J of Med* 302, no. 8 (1980), pp. 446–49.

6. E. Green and A. Green, "General and Specific Applications of Thermal Feedback," in *Biofeedback: Principles and Practices for Clinicians,* ed. J. V. Basmajian (Baltimore: Williams and Wilkins, 1979), pp. 153–69.

7. T. H. Budzynski, "Biofeedback Strategies in Headache Treatment," *Biofeedback: Principles and Practices for Clinicians,* ed. J. V. Basmajian (Baltimore: Williams and Wilkins, 1979), pp. 134–45.

8. A. Smith, *Powers of Mind* (New York: Ballantine Books, 1975).

9. C. H. Hartman, "Responses of Angina Pain to Handwarming," in *Biofeedback and Self-Regulation* 4, no. 4 (1979), pp. 355–57.

10. W. E. Fordyce, "Operant Conditioning: Approach to Chronic Pain" in *A Source Book for Nurses and Other Health Professionals,* ed. A. K. Jacox (Boston: Little, Brown, 1977).

Chapter 8

Use of imagery in physical medicine and rehabilitation and in sports performance

The application of imagery and altered states of consciousness for the enhancement of physical performance has been increasing throughout the world. The rationale for augmenting physical performance with mental techniques arises from the studies of electrophysiology which indicate that the muscles have detectable amounts of electrical activity when one imagines a specific motor activity.[1] Later research has indicated that actual neural growth occurs and is related to experiential events involving imagery.[2] Such information lends support to the clinical training of physical performance using mental devices or practice. This type of training can be done in any organized clinical setting under the auspices of qualified personnel. Since the general goal of physical medicine and rehabilitation is the maximization of function, it is important for therapist and client alike to be clear about the means of achieving that goal. Many times function can be enhanced by simple relaxation alone, as Crasilneck states that anxiety about the physical state of being can be relieved by hypnosis.[3] He goes on to list other conditions that respond to hypnosis:

1. Patients who demonstrate poor motivation, anxiety, negativism, depression, death instinct, poor communication skills.
2. Phantom limb.
3. Headache.
4. Torticollis.
5. Blepharospasm.
6. Whiplash.
7. Low back pain and arthritis.
8. Tinnitus.

In his detailing of the applications of hypnosis to neuromuscular rehabilitation, Kroger referred to the Sister Kenny method of ideosensory conditioning for revitalization of paralyzed muscles. He indicated that when psychological suggestion reinforces a physiologic suggestion, there results a supramaximal motor response.[4] Thus, in working with a patient with a cerebral vascular accident, age regression can reestablish mental images of performance at a particular age.[5]

It has been documented in clinical practice that nearly all neuromuscular conditions can respond to the application of ASC and imagery using biofeedback monitoring. Clients with poorly controlled seizure activity showed a significant decrease in seizure activity after electroencephalographic biofeedback training.[6] As of 1972, there were more than 25 studies which reported the effectiveness of imagery in facilitation of perceptual motor skills.[7] In a study of seven patients with chronic fecal incontinence secondary to myelomeningocele, laminectomy, and diabetic neuropathy, all learned to control sphincteric responses.[8] In the treatment of stuttering, the hypno-behavioral model decreases the anxiety that contributes to the breakdown of feedback control systems for speech, thereby decreasing the stuttering.[9] Other neuromuscular conditions which appear to be amenable to mental practice include myositis ossificans, joint repair, frozen shoulder and tendon transfers,[10] facial nerve grafts, and masseter muscle grafts.[11]

In our own experience in the process of rehabilitation of a 16-year-old female who sustained closed head injury,[12] we have reported the treatment using hypnotic techniques and imagery in combination with the traditional physical rehabilitation by a multidisciplinary team. In this particular case, treatment was initiated within one week following injury and was consistently applied throughout the patient's inpatient stay, in the rehabilitation center, with follow-up on an outpatient basis. At the time of discharge, the patient had achieved age-appropriate levels of independence for verbal communication and personal care activities of daily living, as well as independence in gross motor skills, including ambulation without assistive devices. It was our belief that the patient was discharged from the hospital with significantly fewer residuals of her original neurologic impairment than is usually seen in most cases of such severe central nervous system damage.

In preparing to work with a client in rehabilitation, the therapist can use relaxation as a precursor to any treatment, to facilitate communication and to allow the patient to be more receptive to suggestions. By teaching relaxation first, the therapist is encouraging the patient to rely on internal cues and to become independently functional once again. As an example, consider the stuttering patient whose symptom is aggravated in difficult situations; that person can learn to reduce and release the tension in the oral-pharyngeal musculature that occurs in the prespeech anticipatory block, by repeated practice in nonthreatening imagery rehearsals in ASC. The concept in a programmed relaxation response is the revivification of comfortable feelings. Specific imagery for performance of physical motor skills begins with general stereotyped images that incorporate as many senses as possible (sight, hearing, feeling, olfaction, and taste), as well as memory. Images then become more specific and personal as the client becomes more adept at mental practice.

General images for rehabilitation can include

1. Relaxation
   a. Floating on a cloud, comfortably supported.
   b. Floating on water, gently flowing.
   c. Being like a rag doll, releasing, and becoming floppy.
2. Motor skill
   a. Deglutitive function: The patient is asked to remember in imagery all senses of ingestion of a favorite food or beverage, with additional suggestions to realize the full benefits of the nutrition contained in the food.
   b. Upper extremity activity: The patient imagines or remembers reaching for something, with the involved upper extremity, or combing the hair or brushing the teeth.
   c. Lower extremity activity: The patient is asked to remember kicking a ball, stepping up on a step or stair.
   d. Balance: The patient is asked to remember building a block tower, with each block being placed one on top of the other, and this can be imagined to be within the patient's body.
   e. Walking: The patient can be asked to remember what a puppet or marionette looks like as it walks along with strings assisting arms and legs in appropriate movements.
   f. Remembering a favorite activity such as walking in the park, playing golf, or swimming, to bring in more complex motor patterns of large and small muscles.

3. Cognition
   a. For speech and language, remembering the sounds and sights of reading a newspaper or book, or talking on the telephone.
   b. Remembering a time as a child learning numbers, perhaps standing at a chalkboard doing addition or subtraction.
4. Depression and anxiety
   The patient is given a safe place image to use so that he or she feels there is a personal space to retreat to.
5. Activities of daily living
   Imagery is employed to decrease the residuals of apraxia by imagining dressing a life-sized doll.

The therapist guides the patient into relaxed states and then describes the memory of the experience that will facilitate the desired motor pattern and responses. The description can begin as follows:

Now that you have become as relaxed as you can be at this point in time, I'm going to ask that you begin to remember a very simple activity that you might have done as a child, or perhaps an activity that you watched another child complete . . . and that is making a tower of building blocks. . . . The building blocks are small . . . maybe one-inch square . . . made of wood . . . very smooth . . . and as you begin to build the block tower . . . or watch a child build the block tower . . . you know that you must stack each one on top of the other . . . and that way provide a very strong and balanced tower. . . . Now you begin with one block . . . and move to the other . . . and the next . . . and each one in turn . . . and when the block tower is completely built . . . using all the blocks you have . . . I want you to imagine . . . imagine that the block tower is inside of you . . . along your spine . . . and it's going to help you balance your body . . . when you sit . . . and when you stand. . . ."

We believe that any patient can benefit from the mental practice of physical activity, even the receptively aphasic patient. The key in working with a patient who is receptively aphasic is repetition over a more prolonged period of time, with more frequent and shorter treatment periods.

Sports performance

The use of ASC and imagery for physical performance has been a recent addition to sports training regimens. The Russians and Germans have been using mental training techniques for their world class athletes for several decades, with amazing results. However, it is only recently that such methods have been put into practice in Western programs. Psychotherapists at the Advanced Mental Training Institute in the Soviet Union feel that the ordinary athlete realizes less than half of his or her potential unless the powers of the mind are utilized.[13] The importance of the mind in martial arts has been recognized for centuries.

Anecdotal and scientific evidence

For the true scientist, anecdotal evidence seems to hold little credibility; but when these reports reach staggering numbers, some credence must be given to them.

Jack Nicklaus estimates that the mental image is 50 percent of his golf game. He images the ball where he wants it to finish (end-result imagery), then he uses the process image of the path, trajectory, and shape of the ball during the shot.[14]

John Brodie, former quarterback of the San Francisco 49ers, has described situations that unmistakably involve ASC, such as dramatic improvement in perception and coordination and an uncanny type of clarity. In addition, there is the experience of time distortion, leading to the perception of the entire game unfolding as though in slow motion.[15]

The British golfer Tony Jacklin enters an ASC that he calls a "cocoon of concentration." In this cocoon he achieves a zen-like state in which he is "living fully in the present, not moving out of it . . . involved in what I'm doing at that particular moment."[16]

Former national women's skydiving champion, Susan Clements, describes her dives and maneuvers as the result of mental processes alone.[17]

Imagery was a significant part of the training of the foremost body builder of our time, Arnold Schwarzenegger. Recognizing the value of mental control over matter, he used end-result imagery, envisioning the actual physical maneuvers as a follow-through mechanism to remind himself of the image already in mind.[18]

The Swiss began using these methods in coaching their Olympic skiing squad in 1968. This change in training led the Swiss to win three medals in the 1968 Olympics and additional medals at the 1972 Winter Olympics.[19] They performed a study of the physiologic changes in skiers practicing imagery. They tested the physiology of skiers actually performing the giant slalom against those that only imaged this performance and found no significant differences.[20] The winner of three Olympic skiing gold medals, Jean Claude Killy, utilized imagery.[21]

Several years ago, the East German shotputter, Udo Beyer, had a personal record of 68 feet. By doing kinesthetic studies of Beyer, the East Germans were able to calculate that he could potentially perform a 72-foot shotput. They then created a video image of the form that he would need to put the shot 72 feet. In ASC he watched this image, and 18 months later, he was putting 72 feet. This increase of four feet in 1½ years was virtually unheard of at this level of world class competition.[22]

In addition to these well-known and well-quoted personal vignettes, numerous, less widely publicized stories have been told to us in the time that we've been teaching courses on imagery. Although much of the evidence has been accumulated on performers in individual events or on individual performers in team events, these methods are by no means limited to such participants. A high school football coach in our local area used the methods of end-result imagery (having the entire team walking on the school campus with their championship jackets) and process images (becoming familiar with a large stadium with a large crowd) en route to winning the city high school football championship with a team that most people regarded as too small and too slow. Several publications are now available outlining the use of many of these principles in specific sports, and we refer the interested reader to those publications.[21,23,24,25]

Many years before Richardson noted that improved performance resulted from mental practice,[26] Jacobson demonstrated a definite relationship of imagery ot the production of muscle action currents.[27] Cratty, who has noted the relationship of mental practice to motor learning, believes that "more complex skills, particularly those involving some kind of . . . hand-eye coordination, are most improved through mental practice."[28]

Those few controlled studies that have been performed have tended to validate the anecdotal evidence mentioned above. Garfield cites a Soviet Union study, as yet unpublished in English, which demonstrated that weight lifters could increase the size of their biceps muscle by imaging biceps curls as well as they could by actually practicing biceps curls.[20]

A representative study was performed on high school basketball players. One group was instructed to practice free throws daily for 20 days. The second group, serving as a control, would shoot free throws on days 1 and 20 and in between would do nothing. Group three would shoot free throws on days 1 and 20 and in between would image free throws for 20 minutes, a similar time to group one's practice of free throws. On day 20, group two showed no change in free throw accuracy; between groups one and three, however, there was no significant difference—group one improving 24 percent and group three improving 23 percent.[29] This demonstrated that mental practice of free throw shooting was as effective as the actual practicing of free throws.

Richardson reviewed studies as of 1972, in which more than 25 demonstrated the effectiveness of imagery in facilitating perceptual motor skills.[30] He also performed a study on athletes practicing a single-leg-up start on an Olympic highbar. His subjects were 31 men without previous experience on the highbar. They were rated in their performance by judges, the intercorrelations proving valid. These men learned this technique beautifully by the practice of mental imagery.[31]

Achievement of peak physical performance

Garfield, in studies of peak performers, not only in sports but also in other walks of life, has synthesized those qualities that are characteristic.[20] A major characteristic of these performers is their ability to be both relaxed and productive simultaneously; that is, the ability to perform with both passion and emotion while in a relaxed state. These are also characteristics of ASC.

Garfield also believes that performance on this level is inhibited by distress. As mentioned in earlier chapters, the achievement of ASC is a method of preventing the accumulation of harmful amounts of stress, thereby reducing the tendency to become distressed.

Most interesting, however, is what Garfield calls the special talents of peak performers. One of the talents is "relaxation and reflection." This is akin to what we have called ASC. Additionally, Garfield's studies of peak performers demonstrate that their supreme talent—and the most important element in the Soviet system of training—is "imagery and mental rehearsal."

As we have demonstrated in previous chapters, these abilities are well within the realm of all of us. In fact, Garfield states that nearly everyone has these qualities, not just those who are highly successful. The ways to achieve these levels of achievement are to remove the blocks that inhibit this performance, primarily by removing the chronic low-level distress and by engaging in such practices as relaxation and imagery.

Methods

If you were to learn new physical tasks the way you learned as children, books of this sort would be unnecessary. Imagine that you had just come to earth from another planet. You are the same age as you are now, with all of your abilities and knowledge, except that on the planet you previously inhabited, people crawled rather than walked. When arriving on this planet you noticed people, exactly like yourself, functioning as bipeds rather than quadrupeds. Because you noticed this, you desired to be like them. How would you go about doing this? If you were like most adults, you might first attempt to go to a bookstore and purchase a book on how to walk in five easy lessons, or you might enroll in a university extension course or evening school class in walking. Then you would begin your instruction, and during your first attempt at walking, you would fall. At this point, the critical and judgmental part of your personality, what Gallwey calls self 1,[32] would come into play. You would begin to tell yourself that you were clumsy and inept and therefore would be unable to walk. You would believe this and would then confine yourself to crawling for the rest of your existence on this planet. Children, however, would learn in a different manner. They would first observe the activity and would subsequently form a mental image. They would then begin to perform the task based on the entire mental image rather than attempting to break it down into smaller steps. The child also would fall but, instead of criticizing and judging, the child would begin to make very subtle changes. After a while, enough subtle changes would be made so that the child would become successful and thereby learn the new skill. And, as Gallwey states, "This process doesn't have to be learned; we already know it. All that is needed is to unlearn the habits and concepts which interfere with our natural learning ability, and to trust the innate intelligence of our bodies."[33]

These methods involve the utilization of the unconscious, the way we were meant to learn new skills. They involve experience rather than concepts. Gallwey and Kriegel note that this type of learning is by doing rather than thinking and by letting experience guide us.[34]

According to Gallwey and Kriegel, "the key to natural learning is to quiet the mind so that awareness is increased."[34] Add to this the statement of Garfield (see the previous section) that peak performance necessitates the use of antistress measures and the necessity of being relaxed while highly productive. This is all in keeping with our contention that it is important to establish a regular daily practice of elicitation of ASC. By doing this, one eliminates the low-level distress that interferes with performance. The importance of eliciting ASC in physical performance training has been accentuated by the Soviet coaches. They feel that one cannot bypass relaxation, and in fact, they utilize strict training in autogenics before ever beginning the use of imagery. Frequently, this involves 30- to 90-minute sessions of strict autogenic training. They note, however, that with practice, degrees of relaxation can be achieved in a few minutes that initially took much longer.

When utilizing imagery for physical performance, it is important at some point to bring in kinesthetic imagery. Jacobson noted that instructions in visual imagery would cause an increase in eye movement, whereas instruction in kinesthetic imagery would increase muscle motion.[27] To reiterate, we advise the use of imagery in all senses since we all image differently. Even if our primary mode of imagery is not kinesthetic, by using our primary mode of imagery the kinesthetic can be utilized later. A few examples of end-result imagery would be imaging where we want our serve to land in the service court (tennis), the ball in the cup (golf), successful completion of the individual act (high jump, pole vault, discus, and so forth).

Process images are also very effective in performance. In fact, this is the area of endeavor where process images may be the most successful. If one wishes to learn how to ski, one merely needs to see a good skier and then imprint that image into the mind. With mental practice one can become that image in all sensory modalities. This type of imagery can be applied to all types of physical performance. The vividness of the image is important, but of even greater importance is the controllability of the image. Commitment and persistence are also necessary to achieve optimal results from the use of imaging methods; occasional use of imagery will have only limited success.

References

1. E. Jacobson, "Electrophysiology of Mental Activities," *Am J of Psychol* 44 (1932), pp. 677–94.

2. A. Ahsen, "Eidetics: Neural Experiential Growth Potentials for the Treatment of Accidental Traumas, Debilitating Stress Conditions, and Chronic Emotional Blocking," *J Ment Imagery* 2 (1976), pp. 1–22.

3. H. B. Crasilneck and J. A. Hall, *Clinical Hypnosis: Principles and Applications* (New York: Grune and Stratton, 1975), p. 207.

4. W. S. Kroger, *Clinical and Experimental Hypnosis in Medicine, Dentistry, and Psychology,* 2d ed. (Philadelphia: J. B. Lippincott, 1977), p. 260.

5. Ibid., p. 263.

6. M. B. Sterman and L. R. McDonald, "Effects of Central Cortical Electroencephalography Feedback Training on Instants of Poorly Controlled Seizures," *Epilepsia,* 19 (1978), pp. 207–22.

7. A. Richardson, Voluntary Control of the Memory Images, in *The Nature and Function of Imagery,* ed. P. W. Sheehan (New York: Academic Press, 1972), p. 109.

8. B. T. Engel, P. Nikoomanesch, and M. M. Schuster, "Operant Conditioning of Recto-Sphincteric Responses in the Treatment of Fecal Incontinence," *N Eng J of Med* 290, pp. 646–48.

9. W. S. Kroger and W. D. Fezler, *Hypnosis and Behavior Modification: Imagery Conditioning* (Philadelphia: J. B. Lippincott, 1976), p. 234.

10. M. P. Baker and S. Wolff, "Biofeedback Strategies in the Physical Therapy Clinic," in *Biofeedback: Principles and Practice for Clinicians,* ed. J. V. Basmajian (Baltimore: Williams and Wilkins, 1979), p. 32.

11. F. Nahai, and D. M. Brown, "Further Applications of Electromyography Muscle Re-Education," in *Biofeedback: Principles and Practice for Clinicians,* ed. J. V. Basmajian (Baltimore: Williams and Wilkins, 1979), pp. 57–58.

12. K. Johnson and E. Korn, "Hypnosis and Imagery in the Rehabilitation of a Brain-Damaged Patient," *J Ment Imagery* 4 (1980), pp. 35–39.

13. S. Ostrander and L. Schroeder, *Superlearning* (New York: Delta, 1979), p. 157.

14. G. Leonard, *The Ultimate Athlete* (New York: Avon Books, 1977), pp. 115–16.

15. Ibid., p. 40.

16. Ibid., pp. 47–48.

17. Ibid., p. 41.

18. S. Ostrander and L. Schroeder, *Superlearning* (New York: Delta, 1979), p. 159.

19. Ibid., p. 153.

20. C. A. Garfield, "How to Achieve Peak Performance," paper presented at a workshop, San Francisco, May 1981.

21. T. Gallwey and B. Kriegel, *Inner Skiing* (New York: Random House, 1977), p. 119.

22. Ibid.

23. M. Spino, *Beyond Jogging: The Inner Spaces of Running* (Millbrae, Calif.: Celestial Arts, 1976).

24. W. T. Gallwey, *The Inner Game of Tennis* (New York: Random House, 1974).

25. M. Murphy, *Golf in the Kingdom* (New York: Viking, 1972).

26. A. Richardson, *Mental Imagery* (New York: Springer, 1969).

27. E. Jacobson, "Electrical Measurements of Neuromuscular States during Mental Activities"; "(IV) Evidence of Contraction of Specific Muscles during Imagination"; "(V) Variation of Specific Muscles Contracting during Imagination," *Am J Physiol* 96 (1931), pp. 115–21.

28. B. J. Cratty, *Movement Behavior and Motor Learning,* 3d ed. (Philadelphia: Lea and Febiger, 1973), pp. 372–79.

29. M. Samuels and N. Samuels, *Seeing with the Mind's Eye* (New York: Random House Bookworks, 1975).

30. A. Richardson, "Voluntary Control of the Memory Image," in *The Nature and Function of Imagery,* ed. P. W. Sheehan (New York: Academic Press, 1972), p. 115.

31. Ibid., p. 116.

32. T. Gallwey and B. Kriegel, *Inner Skiing* (New York: Random House, 1977), pp. 25–29.

33. Ibid., p. 6.

34. Ibid., pp. 39–40.

Chapter 9

Wellness, actualization, learning, and creativity

In the other chapters of Section II we explored methods of using imagery for solving situations that are considered to be problems. This chapter explores the uses of imagery in situations that range beyond the afflictions of the body-mind-spirit complex. Here we will explore the uses of imagery in attaining goals that many of us believe are the province of just a few. The subject matter covered in this chapter, however, is open to the experience of each of us. Whereas many people who are most successful in accessing these abilities apparently have done so without any concerted effort, most of us have to relearn those skills once known in childhood. These skills are the abilities to utilize potentials for change that are reorganized outside the realm of ordinary day-to-day reality. It is in this process that lies the magical nature of the abilities to be discussed below.

Promoting wellness

In the introduction and in early chapters of Section I, we stressed the concept that health is more than merely the absence of demonstrable

127

disease. In most of us, true health, or wellness, comes not merely by chance but as a result of the way we construct our lifestyles. This section is not intended to be an exhaustive treatise on health; it is an outline of the basic principles of promoting health, employing imagery as the primary promoting factor.

Optional functioning of the entire individual

Wellness depends upon the optimal functioning of the entire individual; that is, body, mind, and spirit. People who concentrate on only one portion of this whole usually are unsuccessful in promoting wellness because they never generalize to other parts of the system. It is possible, however, to start with any part; if managed optimally, the path will lead the individual to development of the other parts of the system and thus to the realization of wellness. Which part the person wishes to start with in his or her path toward wellness is an individual matter, but we would recommend utilizing as many different avenues as possible. Since this book deals with the mind and we presented evidence earlier that the mind-brain is the apex of the mind-body system, we feel that the most powerful tool we have at our disposal is the mind, if utilized correctly. The vehicle for the mind and its means to sense and interact with the environment is the body, which must not be neglected. Neglect of the body could lessen the mind's efficacy in achieving wellness.

One should begin working with the body at the same time one begins learning to use full mind capacity. Programming health through mental processes will eventually lead to institution of the proper diet and exercise, but not nearly as quickly as would be the case if the diet and exercise regimen were adopted at a more conscious level earlier.

The principles of dieting for weight control are very similar to those of dieting for health, regardless of one's weight and size. (Our nutritional and dietary recommendations are given in Chapter 11.)

Avoidance of toxins

In addition to eating in a healthful fashion, it is important to avoid the toxins that we frequently consume. In our common environment, unfortunately, it is almost impossible to avoid them completely—in other words, such things as air pollutants and chemicals in foods. But most of the toxins that we consume are well within our ability to avoid, such as alcohol, tobacco, large quantities of refined sugar, caffeine, and most prescription and nonprescription drugs. We believe that an individual cannot be truly well if he or she consumes significant quantities of these products.

Factors in fatigue

The way we move our bodies is the other important physical factor in wellness. It seems as though we are the only animal that voluntarily chooses not to exercise. One of the major complaints we see among patients is fatigue. We have found that, in most cases, fatigue is not due to any specific disease process, but rather that it is primarily due to one or any combination of the following factors: significant excess fat (obesity), lack of exercise, and unhappiness (possibly even to the point of depression). Except for treatment of severe depression, no medicine exists to combat these factors and cause the individual to feel energetic. The placebo injection of vitamin B-12 may work for a while, but like all placebos, it loses effectiveness with time.

Regular exercise program

In order for an individual's musculoskeletal system to be well, regular exercise is needed. This should include some form of cardiopulmonary exercise such as jogging, rapid walking, swimming, bicycle riding, other aerobic exercises (e.g., aerobic dancing, jazzercise), or cross-country skiing. In addition, to prevent the stiffness and immobility that usually accompanies the aging process, all the joints should be put through a complete range of motion on a daily basis. This consists of movement and posture positions best exemplified by yoga. Other similar methods include Arica psychocalisthenics, various movement therapies, and T'ai Chi Chuan.

Utilization of the powers of the mind

In the discussions in Section I, we observed that the apex of the mind-brain-body hierarchy is the mind. It is for this reason that we feel the utilization of the powers of the mind are paramount to the development of wellness. In earlier chapters, we noted the effects of altered states of consciousness in ameliorating or preventing the harmful effects of stress response and in promoting wellness. We believe that wellness is best achieved by the simultaneous cultivation of the mind and the body. However, utilization of the mind alone to accomplish these goals has been well documented. Peters and associates have studied the relaxation response in an industrial situation[1] in which 126 subjects were divided into three groups: group one practicing the relaxation response for 15 minutes twice daily; group two sitting quietly for 15 minutes twice daily; and group three, given no instructions, serving as control. The study lasted 12 weeks, and measurements were made of symptoms, illnesses, performance (energy, concentration, ability to handle problems, efficiency), sociability, satisfaction, and happiness. The group practicing the relaxation response demonstrated the greatest improvement in all indices.

Actualization

Actualization is defined as the realization of one's full potential. We feel that this is a corollary of optimal wellness because to utilize one's full potential one must be in a state of wellness, and visa versa.

Personal Orientation Inventory (POI). In a study of transcendental meditation, Seeman and associates studied subjects by means of Shostrom's Personal Orientation Inventory (POI).[2] In 6 of the 12 variables on the POI, significant differences were noted between the subjects and the control in the direction of self-actualization.

Study with transcendental meditation and actualization. Another study used Bendig's Anxiety Scale and Rotter's Locus of Control Scale, in addition to the POI, in studying TM and actualization. The experienced meditators were found to be significantly less anxious, more internally controlled, and more self-actualized.[3] In addition, Fehr and associates noted significant personality changes in meditators when age and sex norms were considered.[4] The most significant findings were decreased nervousness, decreased depression, decreased irritability, decreased tendency to dominate others, less inhibition, decreased neuroticism, and increased self-reliance. We find these changes compatible with the goals of wellness and self-actualization.

Psychosynthesis. Psychosynthesis, a psychotherapy developed from the work of Roberto Assagioli, has been shown to lead toward wellness and self-actualization. Psychosynthesis is defined as "that form of synthesis which expresses the will of the Higher Self and is achieved through wisdom and love. . . ."[5] Some of the methods of psychosynthesis include meditation and imagery.

Regular utilization of ASC. We believe that the use of altered states of consciousness alone on a regular basis, as mentioned in Chapter 5, is sufficient to lead to wellness and actualization. As we mentioned in the earlier chapters, it is not necessary to follow strictly the methods we outline. Any other methods, such as relaxation response, transcendental meditation, and progressive relaxation, can be used, as well as any of the general images mentioned in Chapter 5, particularly the safe place image. The important point is commitment and regularity of practice, with the idea that these methods will be practiced for the rest of one's life. For these goals to be achieved, it is more important to develop a few images and practice them consistently rather than have a wealth of images that are used haphazardly.

Utilization of end-result imagery.   If specific images are required—for wellness attainment and actualization, they rarely are—the next step would be the utilization of end-result imagery. This involves experiencing oneself as being well and having realized one's full potential. The experience, as mentioned previously, should be in all five senses and can be imagined in any of several ways, such as imaging oneself on a television or movie screen or in a picture gallery (Chapter 11). We do not recommend the use of specific process images for the goals of wellness and actualization because they would detract from the necessary time spent in the repetitive elicitation of altered states of consciousness and the use of general imagery, with or without specific end-result imagery.

Creativity

The methods of ASC and imagery have significant correlation with the creative process. Since great moments of creativity seem to be associated with these methods on a spontaneous basis, people can train themselves to be more receptive to the creative milieu by the practice of these techniques. Images, according to Gordon, are "the raw material of imagination."[6]

Examples of scientific discoveries through ASC

Noting that "altered states of consciousness have been responsible for all great successful scientific discoveries"[7] Muses cites as examples Nikola Tesla's discovery of the induction motor by means of a spontaneous vision; the physicist Max Born's discovery, in flashes, of significant quantum formulas and the relationships between wave mechanics and probabilities; the birth of the laser from a visionary experience occurring in a park; and the development of specific mathematic methods by Henri Poincare. The discovery of the benzene ring by Kekulé in the 1800s led to the birth of organic chemistry, for prior to that time no one had been able to delineate organic structures which required the concept of a ring rather than a chained compound. Kekulé's discovery came in the form of a dream, which, as in many cases, was somewhat abstract, that of a snake eating its tail. The application of this image to the specific chemistry problem in question was due to the ability of Kekulé to apply this dream in his own particular field of expertise.

Creativity by means of imagery

Creative images may appear in any of the perceptive modalities mentioned in earlier chapters. The philosopher Singer and the poet Lowell received such images primarily in the auditory mode; Nietsche was both auditory and visual; Einstein was visual and kinesthetic.[8] Samuels and Samuels point to the specific conditions which are most often cited by creative people: riding in a vehicle, walking, listening to music, dreaming, meditating, bathing or showering, reading, watching television, the hypnagogic state, states induced by drugs, and concentration on an object.[9] Most, if not all, of these conditions lead to ASC and are conducive to the experiencing of spontaneous imagery. Other conditions which we feel inspire the reception of creativity include certain types of physical exercise (jogging), odors, changes in temperature and climatic conditions, sensual or kinesthetic sensations (touch, massage); specific foods; a specific time of day or night. For stories of individuals describing their creative experiences we refer the reader to Samuels and Samuels' text.[9]

Stages of the creative process

The creative process has been divided into specific stages, though the stages may not be sequential (left-hemispheric analogy) but may occur more or less simultaneously (holistic, right-hemispheric analogy). These stages are

1. *Preparation.*   Collection of data, filing of images.
2. *Incubation.*   Releasing of the conscious hold on the problem.
3. *Illumination.*   Spontaneous occurrence of a solution.
4. *Verification.*   Working out of specific details so that the ideas are manifested in workable form.[10]

Stages 1 and 4 are both conscious processes, but stages 2 and particularly 3 are unconscious processes. The incubation stage can be aided by ASC and imagery. The illumination stage usually develops in ASC with the experience of spontaneous imagery.

Studies of ASC and imagery in the creative process

Studies demonstrate the effectiveness of ASC and imagery in the creative process. Gur and Reyher, for example, found that free imagery and hypnosis enhanced creativity, enabling the hypnosis group to outscore the control in overall creativity and figural creativity.[11] MacCallum administered the Torrance Test of Creativity to control subjects and practitioners of transcendental meditation. The creativity of long-term practitioners of TM was significantly better.[12]

Principles of using ASC and imagery for creativity

Using ASC and imagery for creativity is similar to using these methods for any goal. (See Chapters 4 and 5.) As Maltz recommended in *Psychocybernetics,* one should trust one's creative mechanism and not jam it by being too concerned or anxious or force it by too much conscious effort. In essence, just let it happen.[13]

Samuels and Samuels list four recommendations for enhancing one's receptivity to creative ideas:[14]

1. Learn the conditions in which you are most likely to have creative images, and then utilize these conditions frequently.
2. Learn to enhance your imagery.
3. After formulating the problem, allow the solution to just happen; that is, allow the incubation and illumination phases to take place, suspend judgment, and let go of ingrained thoughts and ideas.
4. Believe that the answer will come, and accept the idea, no matter what it is, including symbols and abstract ideas.

Recommendations for the use of ASC and imagery in creativity

The techniques for enhancing creativity through ASC and imagery are similar to the techniques of these methods for any other goal. First, it is most important to establish a regular daily practice of eliciting ASC. As has been shown by studies of transcendental meditation, the daily use of these techniques alone can enhance creativity. To this can be added the general images discussed in Chapter 5. End-result images may be used if specific creative goals are sought; e.g., imaging a piece of artwork, a musical composition, or a unique solution to a specific problem as already have been accomplished.

In their book, *Mind Games,* Masters and Houston list several images that can be utilized to further the creative process.[15] Generally, their images involve first induction and experiencing ASC, and then the enactment of the specific imagery.

Visionary Anthropology. Their mind game entitled "Visionary Anthropology" is applicable to this process.[15] Here the subject (or oneself, if practicing alone) is suggested to experience a rounding of the body until he or she is in the form of a sphere. The sphere begins to move rapidly across vast amounts of space, then slows down, and subsequently comes to a stop. The subject resumes normal shape and feeling but is located in a strange new world. One is asked to investigate this world and all of its animate and inanimate forms and to communicate with any types of intelligent creatures. The subject is asked to experience their music, art forms, laws, customs, philosophies and religions, and to take any direction at any time that appears to be promising. The individual could return again and again to these areas. As the sophisticated observer can see, this is merely a method to allow one to suspend judgment and open oneself to the creative processes that are within all of us but are usually camouflaged by the many barriers that we place in the way of these processes.

Image of communication with other imaginal life forms.   Another aid to creativity is Masters and Houston's image of communication with imaginal other intelligent life forms.[15] In this image they state that it is reasonable to suspect intelligent life exists elsewhere in space or in dimensions that overlap our own space-time frame. It is also possible that they can communicate with us by means of imagery. It is suggested that you then open yourself to the reception of communication with an intelligence other than human by becoming very relaxed and passive and drawing on these feelings and images.

The smashing of enslaving idols.   We feel that another of Masters and Houston's images, "The Smashing of Enslaving Idols," is helpful in the creative process by decreasing, if not eliminating, many of the barriers which have blunted our ability to experience things fully.[15] In this image you are asked to experience the world as if there were a sheet of glass between you and the world. Then, on the other side of the glass, you visualize a complete scene, but the glassy substance separating you from the scene blurs and somewhat distorts your complete sensing of the scene. You are then asked to smash the glass with a type of sledgehammer which is in essence "effectively smashing at the same time through habits and conceptualizations that have impoverished your sensory world, and whatever other elements are included in that glassy substance."[15] It is then suggested that you relax more deeply and go through a dark tunnel until you find some unwanted symbols and idols which "express certain values and attitudes and ways of feeling and thinking that were imposed on us in the past by someone else, or developed as products of our own error."[15] These idols may be fears, authority figures, or situations. As you smash the idols when you hit the glass, much of their power becomes destroyed.

Remember, images such as these are simply ways of getting past the barriers which we set up and which hinder our ability to be fully receptive to the creative processes that we all have within us. By using these methods on a regular basis, we systematically weaken and destroy the barriers, thus allowing ourselves to experience fully the range of creative processes that we all possess.

Learning

At its basic level, all of the contents of this book pertain to learning. In this section, we focus on those processes and phenomena that we usually associate with learning. Learning, in its basic sense, however, also involves mental processes, ASC, and imagery. Remember that these processes are all brain functions, and according to Frostig and Maslow, "the brain is the organ of learning. . . ."[16] The learning of motor processes has already been covered in Chapter 8.

Learning and twilight states of consciousness

Several studies have demonstrated the effectiveness of ASC in enhancing the learning process. Budzynski refers to the learning benefits of the twilight states of consciousness—hypnagogic, reverie, and transliminal states, or example.[17] He views these states of consciousness as useful because learning appears to be a holistic or intuitive phenomenon, the twilight states are relaxed rather than competitive states, they aid in absorption of formerly blocked material, and they assist in retrieval of information from less conscious mental processes.

Learning and hypnosis

Porter reviews numerous studies showing the benefit of hypnosis in recalling information, concentration, motivation, and enhancement of performance.[18] She then goes on to develop a method of success imagery and study problems utilizing contingency management, success imagery (similar to what we have called end-result imagery), specific study suggestions, and specific posthypnotic suggestions. For those who are interested in more detail, see Porter's article referenced above.

Learning and transcendental meditation

Transcendental meditation has been shown to facilitate the acquisition of information and to enhance recall.[19] It also has resulted in a significant increase in grade point averages in a study performed on undergraduate students.[20] In another study involving high school students, the practice of TM resulted in increased scores on various tests, including those on intellectual performance, and was associated with a decrease in anxiety.[21]

Learning and visual imagery

Persons possessing vivid visual imagery have been shown to have more accurate recall of visual material, and it has been stated that "visual imagery is the effective mediator of . . . improved recall."[22] Speidel and Pickens review studies relating the value of imagery in learning.[23] Additionally, it has been shown that visual imagery serves a function in the recall of material learned incidentally, i.e., unexpected recall.[24]

Learning methods utilizing both hemispheres

Lozanov pioneered a method of learning involving ASC with a focus on music.[17] In his method, the subject is presented with music, which is synchronized to volume and tempo changes, and suggestions are given synchronized with these changes. We feel that this is merely a variation of distractive or confusion forms of hypnosis pioneered by Milton Erickson. Erickson used metaphors, innuendos, and changes in voice tempo and inflection to carry two meanings, one to the conscious mind and one to the unconscious mind. Researchers in the linguistics field, such as Bandler and Grinder, have employed two people to do the work Erickson accomplished by himself, one person speaking concretely to the left hemisphere and the other speaking in metaphor to the right hemisphere and subconscious processes.[25,26,27,28] We feel that the same principle is at work in Lozanov's technique: The music is a distraction, so that the person cannot totally concentrate with his or her left hemisphere on the suggestions being given; thereby some of this material escapes the critical screening-out process of the left hemisphere and goes directly to the subconscious areas.

One can use the techniques of misdirection in teaching. Many forms of classical music can provide background for the suggestion material, as one's voice keeps cadence with the rhythm and volume of the music. Many of the traditional pieces of classical music can be used for this purpose. In addition, book and record stores carry various selections of music that are directed toward stimulation of meditative processes.

Most of the work associating imagery and learning, like most of the work involving imagery in general, has been with visual imagery. Lindauer points out that, in addition to the visual, the other most commonly studied mode of sensation—auditory—was found to be neither the highest in imagery nor the best in recall when compared to such things as taste, touch, and smell. [29] This is why, in order to access those modes most effective in any one individual, it is important to use all five models of sensation in imagery processes.

Learning and relaxation

In general, relaxation alone, due to its integrative functions on the central nervous system and thereby on learning processes, and by its effectiveness in allaying anxiety, will enhance learning. The daily practice of relaxation will allow the learning process to proceed and develop in a highly integrative fashion. In addition, the practice of specific relaxation prior to learning situations (reading, class attendance, and examination taking) will lead to enhanced performance in these activities.

Learning and end-result imagery

End-result imagery will enhance learning and especially performance. For example, to enhance performance in an examination, one should image the end-result of that examination, such as a diploma or the score on the test paper. For a license or state board examination, for example, particularly if the grades are received in the mail, one can image the receipt of the letter in the mailbox, the opening of the letter, and the reading of the material with the desired result. It is not very difficult to perceive this with all five senses.

Visual imagery paradigm (VIP)

Reid has developed a technique called VIP learning.[30] VIP, or visual imagery paradigm, is based on the idea that most learning relies on visual imagery. This technique has been used primarily for students with chronic poor attendance, but it can be adapted to any learning situation.

A hierarchy of positive imagery is constructed: simple tasks first; then more difficult procedures, leading to accomplishment of goals. Finally, this success is transferred from a classroom setting to all life processes. The method places emphasis on the use of metaphor; the role of symbolism in vocabulary and grammar; the role of school in transmitting values; the role of humor, myths, cliches, and poetry in communicating feelings; and the role of adjectives in allegory.

The method uses a combination of several existing psychotherapeutic frameworks: behavioral concepts to change maladaptive behavior to more effective responses and to improve faulty learning patterns; humanistic concepts to enhance the belief that all individuals have a positive, growth-oriented, and love-based innerself; existential concepts to lead to the finding of individual meanings in life; and interpersonal concepts.

The following monologue is used with permission of the author and can be utilized to music in the Lozanov-type method.

In order to listen more effectively to someone, the listener must learn selective attention to the speaker's words with selective inattention to both distracting outer noises and to distracting inner thoughts and emotions. Now, if you wish to relax you can use your imagination and feel all of my suggestions. Take it easy, just relax. As you relax, begin to really concentrate; just relax your whole body and as you relax, remember that if you do this, the better you will be able to hear what I am saying. The better you relax all over, the better you will be able to listen and respond to those suggestions which will be for your benefit in communicating with others. Each one is an individual personality and will be treated with both dignity and loving respect. Each one of you is a Very Important Person. Some of you might find it easier to relax and concentrate and listen if you close your eyes.

I cannot make you close your eyes unless you really wish to do so. I cannot make you listen and relax your whole body and concentrate unless you wish to do so. I cannot tell whether or not you are relaxing all over and concentrating more. Our relationship is based upon mutual respect and love. Our relationship is based upon mutual trust . . . a relationship that is a cooperation between equals. I am no better and no worse than you are. I am different from you and you are different from me, each person is unique—one of a kind— and we are all equal in our relationships.

Now, to improve your skills in communicating, you must first learn to follow very simple suggestions. Then, as you relax and concentrate, you may be surprised to find yourself learning more complicated tasks. Remember when you were watching some movie and became so involved in the movie that you forgot who was sitting next to you? You may remember that your feelings became very real—you might have felt like crying, or might have felt like laughing. Because you identified with the picture on the screen, you may have forgotten what city you were in, what time it was—you may have forgotten how fast time went by—yet you did react to the movie and your body felt many emotions. Now, if you let your imagination grow and as you follow my suggestions, you might be surprised at how easy it is for you to relax your whole body even more. The ability to deeply relax is already present, within you. I am merely a guide, to help you learn how to help yourself to more effective in communicating with others.

You can bring your communication skills to the surface. And you may choose to remember to forget or you might choose to forget to remember that you have such tremendous skills already inside you. It is not important for you to remember everything I've said—for you have that knowledge within you and you can trust yourself that you'll be able to use that knowledge whenever you need to. To use that knowledge in developing a more fulfilling life, and to feel like a Very Important Person, and to see others as Very Important Persons. To feel more confident in . . . (mention some of the positive adjectives listed by the subject in previous questioning) to see how nice it feels to be different from all others while at the same time being equal to all others. How assuring it feels to see yourself as capable and confident in making decisions.

And as your confidence grows from deep within you, your ability to effectively communicate with others will also grow. As you imagine yourself learning to relax your whole body when listening to someone else, you may be amazed at how well you can really, really hear them. And the more you picture in your mind that you are hearing someone else, the better you will picture feeling good about yourself and about your ability to communicate. The moments you spend listening to someone else will enrich your life. Now, when you deeply relax in the future, you can imagine yourself becoming super-alert and you can imagine yourself more clearly hearing whomever is speaking to you. This state of hearing clearly can be easily reached by you each time you relax your whole body while listening to someone else.

And now I would like you to become more aware of someone in the room that you would like to talk to for a while. Don't force yourself into a conversation but take your time, and if you must walk to another area, that's OK. Remember, each one of you is a unique, special, Very Important Person who is capable of developing your communication skills. You may want to discuss what you have just experienced in listening to me as a starting point.

References

1. R. K. Peters, H. Benson, and D. Porter, "Daily Relaxation Response Breaks in a Working Population," *Am J Public Health* 67 (1977), pp. 946–53.

2. W. Seeman, S. Nidichs, and T. Banta, "Influence of Transcendental Meditation on a Measure of Self-Actualization," *J of Counsel Psychol* 19 (1972), pp. 184–87.

3. L. A. Hjelle, "Transcendental Meditation and Psychological Health," *Percept Mot Skills* 39 (1974), pp. 623–28.

4. T. Fehr, U. Nerstheimer, and S. Torber, "Study of Personality Changes Resulting from the Transcendental Meditation Program: Freiburger Personality Inventory," in *Scientific Research on the Transcendental Meditation Program,* collected papers, vol. 1, ed. D. Orme-Johnson and J. T. Farrow (Livingstone Manor, N.Y.: Maharishi European Research University Press, 1977).

5. K. R. Pelletier, *Mind as Healer, Mind as Slayer* (New York: Delta, 1977).

6. R. Gordon, "A very private world," in *The Nature and Function of Imagery,* ed. P. W. Sheehan (New York: Academic Press, 1972).

7. C. M. Muses, introduction to *Consciousness and Reality,* ed. C. M. Muses and A. M. Young (New York: Avon Books, 1974).

8. B. L. Forisha, "Mental Imagery and Creativity: Review and Speculations," *J Ment Imagery* 2 (1978), pp. 209–38.

9. M. Samuels and N. Samuels, *Seeing With the Mind's Eye* (New York: Random House Bookworks, 1975).

10. C. Patrick, *What is Creative Thinking?* (New York: Philosophical Library, 1955).

11. R. C. Gur and J. Reyher, "Enhancement of Creativity via Free-Imagery and Hypnosis," *Am J Clin Hypn* 18 (1976), pp. 237–49.

12. M. J. MacCallum, "The Transcendental Meditation Program and Creativity," in *Scientific Research on the Transcendental Meditation Program,* collected papers, vol. 1, ed. D. Orme-Johnson and J. T. Farrow (Livingstone Manor, N.Y.: Maharishi European Research University Press, 1977).

13. M. Maltz, *Psycho-cybernetics* (New York: Pocket Books, 1966).

14. M. Samuels and N. Samuels, *Seeing With the Mind's Eye* (New York: Random House Bookworks, 1975).

15. R. Masters and J. Houston, *Mind Games* (New York: Dell, 1972).

16. M. Frostig and P. Maslow, "Neuropsychological Contributions to Education," *J Learn Disabil* 12 (1979), pp. 40–54.

17. T. H. Budzynski, "Biofeedback and the Twilight States of Consciousness," in *Consciousness and Self-Regulation: Advances in Research,* vol. 1, ed. G. E. Schwartz and D. Shapiro (New York: Plenum Press, 1976).

18. J. Porter, "Suggestions and Success Imagery for Study Problems," *Int J Clin Exp Hypn* 26 (1978), pp. 63–75.

19. A. I. Abrams, "Paired Associate Learning and Recall: A Pilot Study of the Transcendental Meditation Program," in *Scientific Research on the Transcendental Meditation Program,* collected papers, vol. 1, ed. D. Orme-Johnson and J. T. Farrow (Livingstone Manor, N.Y.: Maharishi European Research University Press, 1977).

20. D. P. Heaton and D. W. Orme-Johnson, "The Transcendental Meditation Program: An Academic Achievement," in *Scientific Research on the Transcendental Meditation Program,* collected papers, vol. 1, ed. D. Orme-Johnson and J. T. Farrow (Livingstone Manor, N.Y.: Maharishi European Research University Press, 1977).

21. H. Shecter, "The Transcendental Meditation Program in the Classroom: A Psychological Evaluation," in *Scientific Research on the Transcendental Meditation Program,* collected papers, vol. 1, ed. D. Orme-Johnson and J. T. Farrow (Livingstone Manor, N.Y.: *Maharishi European Research University Press, 1977).*

22. D. F. Marks, "Individual Differences in the Vividness of Visual Imagery and Their Effect on Function," in *The Nature and Function of Imagery,* ed. P. W. Sheehan (New York: Academic Press, 1972).

23. G. E. Speidel and A. L. Pickens, "Art, Mental Imagery and Cognition," in *The Potential of Fantasy and Imagination,* ed A. A. Sheikh and J. T. Shaffer (New York: Brandon House, 1979).

24. P. W. Sheehan, "A Functional Analysis of the Role of Visual Imagery in Unexpected Recall," in *The Nature and Function of Imagery,* ed. P. W. Sheehan (New York: Academic Press, 1972).

25. R. Bandler and J. Grinder, *The Structure of Magic,* vol. 1 (Palo Alto, Calif.: Science and Behavior Books, 1976).

26. J. Grinder and R. Bandler, *The Structure of Magic,* vol. 2 (Palo Alto, Calif.: Science and Behavior Books, 1976).

27. R. Bandler and J. Grinder, *Patterns of the Hypnotic Techniques of Milton H. Erickson, M.D.,* vol. 1 (Cupertino, Calif.: Meta Publications, 1975).

28. J. Grinder, J. DeLozier and R. Bandler, *Patterns of the Hypnotic Techniques of Milton H. Erickson, M.D.,* vol. 2 (Cupertino, Calif.: Meta Publications, 1977).

29. M. S. Lindauer, "Imagery and Sensory Modality," *Percep Mot Skills* 29 (1969), pp. 203–15.

30. R. Reid, "VIP Learning," *Personal Communication* (1980).

Chapter 10

Imagery in psychotherapy and counseling

In therapeutic intervention, which includes psychotherapy and counseling, each individual encounter between therapist and client has the potential to create change. We recognize that the direction of change is dependent upon a multiplicity of variables, not the least of which is the nature of each participant's imagery, which serves to form and cloak experiences from the conscious and the unconscious selves. Whether the therapist admits it or not, he or she is utilizing his or her own experiences with imagery to comprehend the process that the client is utilizing. In the process of psychotherapy, there exists the potential "to develop, to animate, or to re-animate as wide a range of imaginal experience as is possible."[1] The therapist has the responsibility to listen to the metaphors of the client's experience and to the analogies, dreams, and waking fantasies employed, and then to assist the client to limit the impact of excessive intensity or to widen the spectrum of experience. Imagery can provide valuable information during all phases of the therapeutic relationship, during evaluation and treatment, and during closure. During the evaluation, the therapist can discern the modes of perception that the client uses, the inner strengths, the needs and habits, and the pathway of a self-defeating lifestyle. In treatment, the therapist can devise image exercises to help the client create and accept change. During closure the therapist can provide the client with a plan or home program of imagery to reinforce the changes already made and to yet be made. As we have discussed in previous chapters, the relationship of imagery to hypnosis and to meditation in close, and deserving of some specific co-relationships. As Hilgard reported, the teaching of self-hypnosis can enlarge the area of the client's self-control and may strengthen his or her resolve to change some behaviors in the direction desired.[2] Kroger and Fezler suggest that hypnosis and imagery used in therapy can eliminate anxiety that is produced by the varied specific or nonspecific stressors and produce strong emotions, thereby making the situational stressors cues for relaxation, not anxiety.[3] As Crasilneck observed, in the hypnotic modification of anxiety, and with ego strengths being the reverse of anxiety, the patient's ability to cope with the general demands of life is enhanced.[4]

The literature from scientific studies of transcendental meditation lends further support to the use of techniques of altered states of consciousness in the counseling or psychotherapeutic process. Results on the Personal Orientation and Inventory indicate states of greater inner directedness and of more consistent presence in the here-and-now, and significant differences between subjects and controls in the direction of self-actualization.[5,6] A one-year study of 14 high school students measured by a Dutch Figural Reasoning Test demonstrated decreased neuroticism and increased intelligence.[7]

General uses of imagery in psychiatry were outlined by the Adlers and included addiction (offer alternatives to addictive and anxiety-relieving substances), usual feelings of being powerless, providing alternative ways of producing internal calm, hyperventilation, bruxism, phobias, insomnia, cardiac neurosis, character disorders, organic brain syndrome, and epilepsy.[8] Further applications were outlined by Fair to include obsessive compulsive behaviors, sexual dysfunction, tension and migraine headache, asthma, hypertension, Raynaud's Disease, insomnia, and cardiac arrhythmias.[9]

The techniques of hypnosis, ASC, imagery, and visualization have been used by many psychotherapists since the time of Freud for many diverse reasons and conditions. From Samuels and Samuels we have the following examples of therapeutic interventions:[10]

A. Beck: Taught control of spontaneous visualization and forward time projection (which has been called end-result imagery in previous chapters), to enable the patient to see beyond the moment of anxiety to a time when the source of anxiety is past.

Wolfgang Kretschmer: Described meditative techniques that included general body relaxation and symbolic fantasies with colors and objects to attain symbolic representations of ideas.

Carl Happich: In the 1920s and 1930s, developed a theory of a level of consciousness called symbolic consciousness, which is between the conscious and unconscious and is where the collective unconscious expresses itself with symbols; he used a meadow meditation.

Hans Carl Leuner: Created guided affective imagery (which relaxation and visualization of a meadow), which was his first of 10 standardized imaginary situations.

Roberto Assagioli: Used symbolic visualization such that a man building a personality equals a man building a house; his main thrust was psychosynthesis.

R. Desoille: Directed daydreams, also called psychic wandering.

C. Jung: Called his form of visualization active imagination, in which the patient meditates, remaining free of goals or programs, inviting images to appear, and not interfering. The patient could interact by asking questions or talking with the images, and subsequently discussing these images with the therapist.

Joseph Wolpe: Developed systematic desensitization in which the patient uses relaxation and visualizes a series of situations related to a source of anxiety or places a phobia in a hierarchy, moving from the least frightening to the most frightening.

Another way of dealing with phobias through systematic desensitization was discussed by Kroger and Fezler. The method they used was successive approximations, which were outlined by B. F. Skinner, such that the patient can imagine being or doing whatever desired while remaining deeply relaxed.[11] At no time is the patient to experience anxiety. This makes it necessary for the therapist to construct as many subdivisions as needed for a smooth transition from step to step. The patient is then instructed to practice so many times each day for so many minutes, relaxing and imagining, and switching off the imagery at the first hint of anxiety to return to a relaxing one. It is known that practicing self-hypnosis increases a person's ability to visualize and to establish this hierarchy for systematic desensitization.

Preparation of the client for ASC and imagery can include analysis by the therapist of his or her own images in all of their extensive and differentiated forms. This will enable the client to realize how fluid image systems are and how change can result. In general, rigidity will be decreased and control of images increased as the initially impoverished image systems of the therapist and client are changed so that a sense of unique identity is developed for each person. The process is described as a time in which each person who images can clear the static that occurs with prolonged, unchanging listening to oneself, decrease negative images, and increase spontaneity and confidence. During a session of imagery, it is important that the therapist utilize whatever the patient presents for attitudes, thoughts, or feelings, that the patient be respected in the inevitable changing process. The therapist must keep in mind the linguistic preferences shown by the client.

Specifically for the counselor or psychotherapist, the imagery sessions can be used to help the client

1. Find his or her own inner strengths to live life and accept change.
2. Take an inventory of needs, wants, and habits.
3. Define the inner and outer noise that constitutes listening to oneself.
4. Exercise the new skills.
5. Change a self-defeating lifestyle.

The client can also learn to identify the origins of lifestyle images, those which are innate and those which are learned. The innate images appear to be related to intuition and feeling—much more primitive sources than the ego. The learned images relate to problem solving and are conditioned by the culture.

Basically, with ASC and imagery, the therapist helps the client identify what feelings are present, what hurts, what the wants are, and what can be done to achieve resolution. An example might be a rehearsal of a difficult situation in which the client images and decides what feelings are present in the situation, what is so difficult about the situation, what wants could be present, and what should be the method of resolution, all done within a realm of increased self-respect. The therapist then has the task of helping the patient evaluate the results. Ideally, the family would also be encouraged to learn relaxation and use it with the client.

Images

The images to be used in psychotherapy and counseling are as varied as the personal experience of each therapist and client. In general, however, there are several images that can be applied universally (with slight modifications for each individual situation): the shield, rehearsal of a difficult situation, and systematic desensitization.

Shield

As was discussed in the chapter on general techniques, the use of a protective bubble or shield can promote in a client a feeling of safety, of peacefulness, and of a personal space in which thoughts and decisions can be made with somewhat less of a risk of rejection or vulnerability. Realizing, of course, that the therapist use this protective bubble or shield in a selective and therapeutic manner, consistent with the process of change for the client, remembering that walling off or closure from the outside world is not advantageous, the therapist can devise a way of initially using this safe space and then allowing the client to experiment with thoughts and feelings and new decisions, and then working through in a more realistic life situation, without the shield. The shield can be developed through expansion of an internal state of calm, developed through progressive relaxation, or by having a source of beautiful white light coming from the universe and enveloping the person. The individual resources and abilities of each client are first assessed to decide whether he or she can best develop the shield from the inside or have it come from the outside.

Rehearsal of a difficult situation

In a relaxed state, in which a client may feel that he or she is in a very comfortable personal space, a rehearsal of participating in a very difficult situation can be made very comfortable, and the client can be prepared then to do the situation in real life with less anxiety. The rehearsal of this difficult situation can take place on a television screen, such that the client is observing the situation and is not that intimately involved in it; or if the client has some degree of greater confidence, he or she can actually participate in the situation, yet realize that this is rehearsal and that it is the practice of a new skill. Of course, the main emphasis here is on letting the client know that this is an entirely safe situation and that the reactions that he or she may experience in the difficult situation can be conditioned and modified to be less destructive to overall health.

Systematic desensitization

In a relaxed and comfortable state, the patient is asked to list in order of level of anxiety various steps that lead up to a conditioned fear response or a phobia. Each step along the way is then confronted while the person is in a relaxed and comfortable space, and the therapist tells the patient at each step, "Check your body for tension. Are you ready to go on to the next step? As long as you can remain relaxed, you can go on to each successive step." The therapist then has the responsibility to keep track of how far the patient is able to go and to help the person back to a safer level of comfort and relaxation if at any time some anxiety responses should occur.

References _____

1. P. W. Sheehan, ed., *The Function and Nature of Imagery* (New York: Academic Press, 1972), p. 74.

2. E. R. Hilgard and J. R. Hilgard, *Hypnosis in the Relief of Pain* (Los Altos, Calif.: William Kaufman, 1975), p. 253.

3. W. S. Kroger and W. D. Fezler, *Hypnosis and Behavior Modification: Imagery Conditioning* (Philadelphia: J. B. Lippincott, 1976), p. 88.

4. H. B. Crasilneck and J. A. Hall, *Clinical Hypnosis: Principles and Applications* (New York: Grune and Stratton, 1975), p. 225.

5. L. D. Dick and R. E. Ragland, "A Study of the Transcendental Meditation Program in the Service of Counseling," in *Scientific Research on the Transcendental Meditation Program*, collected papers, vol. 1, ed. D. Orme-Johnson and J. T. Farrow (Livingstone Manor, N.Y.: Maharishi European Research University Press, 1977), p. 603.

6. W. Seeman, S. Nicich, and T. Banta, "Influence of Transcendental Meditation on a Measure of Self-Actualization," *J Counsel Psychol* 19 (1972), pp. 187.

7. A. Toja, "Some Evidence that the Transcendental Meditation Program Increases Intelligence and Reduces Neuroticism As Measured by a Psychological Test," in *Scientific Research on the Transcendental Meditation Program*, collected papers, vol. 1, ed. D. Orme-Johnson and J. T. Farrow (Livingstone Manor, N.Y.: Maharishi European Research University Press, 1977), p. 365.

8. C. S. Adler and S. Morrissey-Adler, "Strategies in General Psychiatry," in *Biofeedback: Principles and Practice for Clinicians*, ed. J. V. Basmajian (Baltimore: Williams and Wilkins, 1979), pp. 189–94.

9. P. L. Fair, "Biofeeback Strategies in Psychotherapy," in *Biofeedback: Principles and Practice for Clinicians*, ed. J. V. Basmajian (Baltimore: Williams and Wilkins, 1979), p. 112.

10. M. Samuels and N. Samuels, *Seeing with the Mind's Eye* (New York: Random House Bookworks, 1975).

11. W. S. Kroger and W. D. Fezler, *Hypnosis and Behavior Modification: Imagery Conditioning* (Philadelphia: J. B. Lippincott, 1976), p. 90.

Chapter 11

Habits and phobias

Anxiety

Anxiety is a normal human emotion and one of the most common, so the anxieties we all experience at some time in our lives is not necessarily indicative of emotional illness. Anxiety is, however, one of the most common concomitants of mental disorders such as neuroses. It is a manifestation of fear, and the fear itself is directed toward an internal object related to past experiences, memories, and/or fantasies. Present situations are then unconsciously associated with certain past situations, and anxiety is thereby produced.

Although psychotherapy can be helpful in modifying anxiety, particularly the type associated with phobias or severe neuroses, frequently, the methods of altered states of consciousness, with or without the application of appropriate imagery, are sufficient in allaying the harmful effects of anxiety. (See Chapter 2, Stress, and Chapter 9, Promoting Wellness, for further material associating ASC and imagery with modification of the harmful effects of the stress response.)

Considerable experimental evidence validates the use of these techniques as antianxiety measures. Hypnosis was found to be as effective as psychotherapy and more effective than drug therapy in the treatment of anxiety.[1] Some even feel that hypnosis may be the treatment of choice for this problem.[2] Physical relaxation may cause a decrease in the "anticipation of anxiety concerning a threatening image."[3] This physical relaxation is a concomitant of all of the methods of induction of ASC (see Chapter 3).

Transcendental meditation resulted in significant improvement on the State-Trait Anxiety Inventory, A-State Scale only six weeks after instituting the practice.[4] This practice also led to a significant decrease in anxiety, as measured by Bendig's Anxiety Scale.[5] With TM there is also a significant (P <.001) decrease in nervousness, as measured by the Freiburger Personality Inventory.[6] As yet another demonstration that there is marked interchangeability of all forms of inducing ASC, biofeedback of both the electroencephalographic and the electromyographic type has resulted in significant benefit in the therapy of anxiety states.[7]

In the therapy of anxiety states by the use of ASC and imagery, the single most important factor is the instruction in and daily practice of the elicitation of ASC alone. To this can be added the safe place image as described in Chapter 5. Since a common symptom of anxiety is rapid, shallow breathing, it would be beneficial for the subject to learn deep, relaxed, diaphragmatic breathing either as part of the induction of ASC or afterwards. This breathing can then be extrapolated into the waking state. In fact, Spiegel has noted that "any stimulus can induce relaxation by being paired with relaxation."[8] By linking such things as relaxed breathing and a safe-place image to the relaxation experienced while in ASC, the subsequent use of this relaxed breathing and/or the thought of the safe place while in the waking state can eventually result in the same feelings of relaxation experienced in ASC. Other stimuli that can be paired to relaxation and then recovered in the waking state may be the use of physical cues, such as touching the thumb and little finger of the nondominant hand together or verbal cues, simple words such as *relax, calm,* or *safe.* By the appropriate practice of these cues while in ASC, power and potency can be developed for their use in the waking state. These methods may be used for anxiety in general or for anxiety associated with other situations, such as neuroses, habits, tests in school, public speaking, and job interviews.

Phobias

Since phobias involve anxiety in a specific, rather than global mode, the anxiety in phobias is "bound more to a specific object or situation, which is often symbolic of some hidden, unconscious thought or buried memory."[9] In the past it was thought that insight and working through the original unconscious memories were necessary to achieve lasting resolution of a phobia without substitution of other problems. However, it now appears that phobias are primarily habits, and the long-buried psychodynamics are relatively empty. Kroger has stated that "hypnotherapy without insight is as effective in dealing with symptomatic behavior as those therapies which provide insight."[10] He furthermore goes on to state that most deep-seated conflicts are forgotten with the passing of time, and insight is never achieved.[10] In phobias, therefore, symptom removal is not only appropriate but usually long-lasting.

Many behavioral techniques have been developed to aid in symptomatic therapy of phobias. Such therapies as systematic desensitization[11,12] involve the use of imagery and are more highly effective when performed in ASC.

We would first suggest training of the individual in relaxation. As mentioned previously, this is frequently all that is necessary in allaying anxiety. Then, desensitization can be accomplished by having the individual go through, in step-by-step fashion, the situation to which anxiety is attached. For example, for specific fears, such as fear of flying, we would have the person proceed methodically from the time of purchasing an airline ticket to the time of arriving successfully at his or her destination. The number of steps are determined by the intensity of the fear and the difficulty of mentally experiencing earlier steps without anxiety. Each step is imaged while in ASC until the person can easily image that step without anxiety. If anxiety is experienced, even in a mild degree, the subject is asked to experience that scene from afar; that is, in a dissociated fashion. For example, instead of experiencing the scene directly, the subject would be asked to view the scene as though it were part of a movie or television show. As each step is experienced without anxiety, the person continues to the next step. When all the stages in the desensitization are experienced without anxiety, the subject is asked to experience them in reality, using the appropriate antianxiety mechanisms, such as cues, breathing, and safe place.

For more global phobias, such as acrophobia (fear of heights), the client would be asked to draw a hierarchy of several situations that would lead to the experience of the anxiety. Once again, the number of scenes in the hierarchy would be determined by the severeity of the symptom and the difficulty in calmly experiencing each step. The scenes would then be ranked by the subject according to the intensity of fear which they provoke. The therapist would then start with the scene of the least fear-producing intensity and desensitize them in the same manner as mentioned in the previous chapter. The more senses utilized in the imagery, the more effective and long-lasting the results.

In certain phobias, such as giving speeches, escalators, elevators, and so forth, end-result imagery alone has been extremely effective.

Insomnia _____

One of the most distressing of all human symptoms is the inability to sleep, a problem which seems to increase in intensity as people become older. As a person ages, he or she needs less sleep, but the long-ingrained thoughts of the necessity of a certain amount of sleep lead to a neurotic sleep preoccupation. The inability to sleep is associated with anxiety.

Normal sleep consists of four stages—1, 2, 3, and 4, with 4 being the deepest level. With age, there is a progressive decrease in stages 3 and 4. These stages are called non-REM, as contrasted to the REM (rapid eye movement) stage, which is associated with dreaming. REM occurs about four to six times per night and encompasses one fifth to one fourth of the total sleep time. Most medications used to induce sleep cause REM deprivation, and, when used on a long-term basis, seem to be ineffective in promoting a normal sleep pattern.[13]

Research has demonstrated that many methods of inducing ASC are helpful in the therapy of insomnia. These include progressive relaxation,[14,15] transcendental meditation,[16] and hypnosis.[17] In fact, it has been stated that "often a single session (of hypnosis) is effective in restoring the sleep cycle."[17] Also, the use of biofeedback has been demonstrated to decrease an individual's need for sleep.[7]

Method

We believe the client should be instructed in the use of ASC alone, by methods outlined in Chapter 5. Frequently, this is all that is necessary to remove the symptom of insomnia. In addition, some *behavior modification* may be in order. We agree with Kroger and Fezler that the person should use the bed for sleeping, and not for other activities such as watching television, eating, or reading. The bed should be behaviorally associated with sleep. We feel that the individual should avoid taking naps in the daytime, since sleep at some other part of the day will lead to greater difficulty in sleeping at night. We believe that any person with sleep disturbances should be on a regular exercise program. Exercise in general is important for good health, and physical fatigue will lead to more normal sleep patterns.

One of the most common symptoms of *depression* is sleep disturbance, which usually is manifested by early awakening within a few hours of going to sleep. The proper therapy of depression will lead to alleviation of this type of sleep-disturbance pattern.

If further image therapy is indicated beyond that of simple induction of ASC we believe *repetitive mental images* are the most helpful. The age-old adage of counting sheep is a very good example of a repetitive image.

If this is performed on a regular basis, normalization of sleep patterns should occur.

End-result imagery, such as dissociating and seeing oneself asleep and then seeing oneself awakening the next morning refreshed and alert, is also beneficial. Kroger suggests a law of reverse effect that utilizes suggestions and imagery "toward the need to keep awake!"[17] The more intensely a person *tries* to fall asleep, the less likely he or she is to fall asleep; therefore, reasons Kroger, if the person imagines that he or she must stay awake as long as possible it will become increasingly difficult to do so. He recommends the image of an airplane spotter who must actively assimilate all sounds which come into auditory range.[19]

Other images of an appropriate nature, as suggested in Kroger and Fezler's textbook,[20] include scenes of a garden, a mountain cabin, a farm, and a thundershower.

Tics

Tics are spasmodic movements that may involve any part of the somatic musculature. They are probably related to anxiety and may be triggered at their onset by some particularly distressing emotional trauma.

Behavior modification therapy in the form of massed practice (rapid repeating of the tic) and operant conditioning have been successful in ameliorating tic behaviors.[21] It appears that tics are less likely to occur when the general anxiety level is lowered, and therefore the induction of ASC alone, by its antianxiety effect, can help. Imagery may be used to transform symptoms; for example, a distressing symptom might be moved to an area that will be less disabling. Also, some images, such as the safe-place image (see Chapter 5), are helpful in giving one a sense of calm and comfort.

Drug abuse

Narcotics

Most of the studies on ASC in the therapy of drug abuse have been performed on practitioners of transcendental meditation. We feel that these studies can be directly extrapolated to other methods of inducing ASC, as described in Chapter 3.

Schilling demonstrated a significant decrease in marijuana and hashish use ($P = .043$) and in total drug use ($P = .077$).[22] In another study,

Winquist demonstrated that 83 percent of 525 subjects discontinued all drugs after instituting the regular practice of meditation.[23] Of the remainder, 15½ percent decreased their drug use by more than half, and only 1½ percent continued to use drugs regularly. Other studies have demonstrated a significant decrease in the use of hashish[24] and marijuana.[25] In a large-scale study of 1,862 respondents, Benson and Wallace demonstrated that decrease in drug use seemed to be related to the number of months meditation had been practiced.[26] This study included the use of marijuana, hashish, LSD, narcotics, amphetamines, and barbiturates.

Since drug abuse is a very complex and devastating condition, we feel that multiple methods of therapy should be used. Standard psychotherapeutic and behavioral techniques as well as counseling should be combined with the regular practice of ASC.

Some success in decreasing the need for drugs has been obtained by having the person recreate the beneficial feelings they get from the drugs without actually utilizing the drugs. Such images as the safe place and the shield (see Chapter 5) are extremely effective in problems of this type because of their ability to instill in the individual a sense of safety and protection.

Alcohol

Alcoholism is a psychodynamically complex disorder with a very low rate of successful therapy. Some of the problems that must be faced are dependency, regression, compulsivity, and slow suicide. Psychotherapeutic techniques and behavior modification methods have been somewhat successful in the therapy of alcoholism. One of the most successful forms of therapy is group therapy based on the methods of Alcoholics Anonymous. We believe that all of these methods can be combined with the use of ASC and imagery to increase their effectiveness. Several studies have demonstrated the ability of ASC induced by transcendental meditation to decrease the dependency upon alcohol.[22,26,27]

We feel the first step in the use of these methods in treating alcoholism is the instruction in the induction of ASC. We strongly believe that it would be helpful to utilize this in the context of group therapy and/or individual psychotherapy, and possibly even in an alcoholic rehabilitation unit.

Images that we have found particularly effective are the general images of a safe place and shield. In fact, in one case the use of the shield image alone, without any other therapy, was effective in leading to the cessation of a 20-year alcoholic habit, a cessation which has lasted now for five years. The individual modified the shield image that we suggested to him by allowing that shield to have pseudopods. These pseudopods would grab alcohol bottles and smash them. By repeatedly practicing this he was able to eliminate the need for alcohol use.

End-result imagery is also helpful therapy for this condition. This would involve the image of being a well-functioning, healthy person, accomplishing those things which the individual wishes to accomplish.

Kroger and Fezler suggest the positive imagery of having the subject image himself or herself in a situation in which alcohol is usually consumed. The subject is then instructed to imagine his or her favorite alcoholic beverage, then to smell it, resist it, and walk away. "The moment he sees himself resisting or avoiding liquor, he reinforces the avoidance response by immediately recalling one of the pleasant, relaxing images. Avoidance is reinforced with relaxation."[28] They also suggest emotional as well as sensory recall, and recommend that resisting liquor be accompanied by recalling feelings of elation. This merely involves the addition of a kinesthetic mode to the other modes already in use.

Use with prisoners

We feel that it is necessary to include this section since the use of ASC and imagery have been helpful in the rehabilitation of prisoners. It is included in this chapter because there are certain similarities between the manifestations and dynamics of some prisoners and the manifestations of anxiety.

Transcendental meditation has been shown to be helpful in rehabilitating prisoners by decreasing nervousness, decreasing irritability, increasing sociability, decreasing the tendency to dominate, decreasing neuroticism, and so forth.[6] Other studies on TM have shown a significant decrease in aggression.[22]

Four studies have been performed on the use of meditation with prisoners, all of which led to satisfying results. In Lompoc, California, meditation was shown to decrease anxiety and increase positive behavior in prisoners.[29] In New Mexico, increased physiologic stability and psychological adaptability were noted.[30] In Stillwater, Oklahoma, the results were decreased anxiety, decreased numbers of rules infractions, increased participation in educational and recreational activities, and decreased parole violations.[31] And a study on juvenile prisoners in Tennessee discovered decreased anxiety, increased self-regard, and improved behavior.[32]

Spear performed a study on 49 borderline recidivist prisoners. By the use of ASC and imagery, the recidivism rate was decreased significantly.[33]

It seems obvious that the instruction of prisoners in ASC and imagery, particularly such imagery as the shield and safe place techniques (see Chapter 5), would be extremely helpful in the rehabilitation of a group of people in whom rehabilitation has been something less than overwhelming in the past.

Smoking

Cigarette smoking is a major health problem in the world today. There is a cause-and-effect relation between smoking and lung cancer, heart disease, and chronic obstructive lung disease. It is also linked with diseases of the peripheral blood vessels and somewhat with cancer of the mouth, larynx, esophagus, pancreas, kidney, and bladder. Unfortunately, traditional approaches to curbing smoking, which may have an initial success rate of 40 to 89 percent, have a low long-term success (20 to 25 percent in one year).[34]

Many forms of behavior therapy have had some success in leading to cessation of the smoking habit. ASC techniques, such as meditation, have also been demonstrated to aid large numbers of people in reducing cigarette consumption.[26] Numerous publications have substantiated the effectiveness of hypnosis in the control of the smoking habit.[35]

We feel that it is important to internalize the commitment to health, since this will lead to a cessation of smoking. Smoking is one of the habits that can be eliminated by will power. However, the forceful, conscious cessation of the habit does nothing to change the internal milieu leading to the habit in the first place. Therefore, the strict use of will power to stop a habit such as smoking will frequently lead to other problems, such as weight gain or increased anxiety. When a commitment to health is internalized by ASC and imagery, the cessation of smoking will become a natural event rather than one viewed as an elimination of something pleasurable.

Stanton utilized imagery techniques in a one-session therapeutic milieu, which, in 75 clients, led to a significant number of them quitting their habit.[36] (45 stopped smoking, and 34 were still nonsmokers six months later).[36] His methods involved

1. Establishment of a favorable mental state.
2. Induction of ASC.
3. Ego strengthening.
4. Specific verbal suggestions against smoking.
5. Red balloon image—A red balloon is imaged as lifting away the container with cigarettes.
6. Success visualization—what we would call-end result imagery.

We would recommend a combination of behavioral methods with ASC and imagery. Some of the behavioral methods include inconvenience, such as holding the cigarette in the left hand and placing cigarette butts near the bed; and methods such as keeping a chart or book to increase the awareness of the number of cigarettes smoked and the conditions under which they are used. The daily practice of induction should decrease the overall anxiety level and lead to normal functioning, thereby resulting in a decrease and eventually cessation of cigarette intake. End-result imagery, including a commitment to health and life, are important. Imagery pairing relaxation with nonsmoking may be helpful, and cues could be used, such as touching one's little finger to the thumb of the nondominant hand, thereby recreating relaxation at a time when the individual feels an urge for a cigarette.

The end-result image of health and vitality can be imagined even in the individual's waking state as a method of reinforcement. This would be particularly effective when the individual feels the urge for a cigarette. We would not even recommend that the individual consciously or willfully fight the urge for a cigarette, but rather, before actually taking the cigarette, image the health that was visualized under ASC. We believe that repetitive use of this image will lead to internal changes that will subsequently lead to behavioral changes. Forced changes tend to be short-term, whereas natural changes tend to be true, lasting changes in one's personality.

Obesity

Obesity is one of the most serious and common problems affecting Western society. It has been determined by the United States Public Health Service that of Americans over the age of 30, 25 to 45 percent are more than 20 percent overweight.[37] Obesity is seven times more common in lower socioeconomic groups and is definitely associated with an increase in mortality and a decrease in life span.

Although metabolic changes such as hyperinsulinism, increased cortisol production, decreased somatotrophin production, and insulin antagonism have been described in obesity, these may be secondary rather than primary phenomena. We believe that obesity is primarily a behavioral problem, even though different people may metabolize at different rates. Overeating serves as a coping mechanism ingrained in many of us since early childhood. The repeated reinforcement that we get from eating leads to strengthening of this learned behavior over long periods of time. Food can be used as a mechanism for reducing tension, anxiety, and/or depression from any source. We have been rewarded with food both as children and at times of festivity, such as holidays and birthdays. Many of us use food as a substitute for love, and, in fact, we may have learned this at a very early age.

No matter what the psychodynamics of excessive food consumption are, in essence, when a person reaches adult years, most of the overeating tendencies persist merely as learned behavior. Behavioral mechanisms associated with the mental processes of ASC and imagery can lead to effective changing of maladaptive habit patterns into adaptive and functional ones.

Many studies have validated the effectiveness of ASC in the therapy of obesity. Hypnosis is an effective adjunct in the therapy of obesity.[38,39,40,41,42,43] Weldon and Ron demonstrated the effect of meditation on obesity in a group of 76 subjects.[44] The applicability of extrapolating data from one technique of inducing ASC to others, as noted in Chapter 3, was validated in a recent study by Wadden and Flaxman,[45] who found that three different methods of ASC induction all produced similar weight loss. First was hypnosis with direct suggestion, to which goal-directed imagery was added. This imagery included slow eating, increased enjoyment of food, imaging oneself as thin, and imaging the benefits of weight loss. The second method was the behavioral technique of covert modeling, which also included instruction in progressive relaxation and goal-directed imagining without hypnotic induction. The third method was relaxation-attention control, which simply consisted of progressive relaxation associated with imagery for relaxation only and not imagery related to weight reduction. We believe that this important study documents our contention that various methods of inducing ASC, as well as imagery techniques, are equally valuable and interchangeable.

Since beneficial weight reduction takes a considerable amount of time and hopefully will be integrated into a lifelong living pattern change, motivation has been a problem. Stanton has given us some direction in this regard in his study on hypnosis and weight control. He discovered that clients paying fees had a significantly greater weight loss than patients not paying them.[46]

In the subsequent sections of this chapter, we will present our comprehensive approach to weight control. Although this text is devoted to the use of ASC and imagery, because other forms of therapy are even more effective when combined with these methods, we feel all should be included in this section.

Diet

Most diets are doomed to failure because of the negative connotation of the word *diet*. The diet that will be most successful is the one requiring the least amount of restriction for the longest time, in fact, for the rest of one's life. In essence, we all are on diets, that is, what we eat is our diet. By permanently changing dietary habits and integrating the change into a lifelong pattern, diets cease to have a restrictive and negative connotation.

Expectations concerning diets are frequently unreasonable. It requires approximately 3,500 calories of energy expenditure to lose one pound of fat, and fat loss, rather than weight loss, is what we should be concerned about. The average, relative sedentary American uses about 1,500 to 2,000 calories per day. Even if an individual were to go on a total starvation diet, he or she would not lose more than one pound of fat every two days. Diets which lead to a weight loss in excess of this usually involve the loss of fluid, which tends to be a transient, unhealthy situation.

We feel that diets which eliminate certain types of foodstuffs such as carbohydrates are basically unhealthy. An evaluation of the average American diet shows that we eat slightly too much protein, significantly excessive fat, and less carbohydrate than is optimal. This is unfortunate, since fat contains nine calories per gram whereas carbohydrate and protein have four calories per gram; that is, fat, for an equivalent amount of food substance, has more than twice the caloric content of carbohydrate and protein. The average American consumes between 40 and 60 percent of all of his or her calories in the form of fat. We feel that the preferred diet should contain no more than 20 percent fat. By merely making these adjustments, a person can realize a significant decrease in caloric intake with no significant decrease in bulk and satiability.

We feel that individuals should become aware of all they eat, an awareness that can be adequately accomplished only by means of a diary. At the same time, they need to study composition of food tables to become aware of the exact content and composition of the food they consume. In this way people will begin to understand that a tablespoon and a half of butter contains as many calories as a rather large potato. Only with this kind of information imprinted in the consciousness can they begin to understand where the problem spots are.

Once again, no one can compare his or her food intake to that of anyone else. We are all individuals, and only when we stop the comparisons and start working on our own situations can permanent results be obtained. Because we tend to compare ourselves with those who have a lifestyle that seems more pleasing to us, we experience frustration, helplessness, and hopelessness and eventually cease all reasonable attempts to maintain proper eating habits and weight control.

It is also important to remember that although obesity constitutes a health risk, frequent significant weight changes pose an even greater risk to the individual. It is less healthy to continually gain and lose considerable weight than to maintain a baseline level of obesity.

Exercise

Since weight loss is a matter of tipping the weight equation (weight = caloric intake − caloric expenditure) in the direction of increased expenditure as well as decreased intake, it would seem reasonable that exercise would be conducive to weight loss. The problem with exercise is that we tend to understand it on a short-term rather than long-term basis. For example, one would have to jog approximately one mile in 10 minutes to burn off 100 calories. This may seem frustrating and insignificant, since a piece of pie has anywhere between 400 and 600 calories. Unfortunately, we believe this is a case of short-sightedness and a result of a pessimistic rather than an optimistic viewpoint. That is, it is a matter of seeing the glass half empty rather than half full, or noting the weather to be partly cloudy rather than mostly sunny.

When one looks at the long-term effects of exercise, merely walking everyday at a rather rapid pace for 30 minutes will lead to a 10-pound weight loss over the period of about a year, without any change in caloric intake. Accordingly, we advise our patients to undertake a program of regular physical activity (see Chapter 9). There are many opportunities for increased expenditure of energy in our daily lives. We advise people to walk the stairs both up and down rather than take elevators. Parking at the far end of a parking lot rather than directly in front of the store will increase energy expenditure. In fact, it may frequently be possible to walk to the store rather than take an automobile at all. If distances are too far for walking, one might consider using other modes of humanpower, such as a bicycle.

Behavior modification

The efficacy of behavior modification therapy for obesity is well documented.[47] In fact, many franchise weight control centers use behavior modification as the primary focus of their therapy. We believe that certain behavior modification techniques are essential in any program for weight control.

A major problem for many obese people is rapid food consumption. There is a difference between feeling full (stomach distension) and being satiated. Gastric fullness depends strictly on the quantity of food presented to the stomach. Satiety necessitates the food getting from the stomach and into the small intestine, being absorbed in the portal system, and eventually making its way to the satiety center of the brain. This process takes a significant amount of time, possibly as long as 15 minutes. Therefore, if a person eats rapidly, he or she will tend to eat a fullness rather than to satiety. By merely slowing the rate of food intake the individual can then train himself or herself to appreciate the subtle changes of satiety rather than the more gross discomfort of fullness. Some tricks to eating slowly include placing the fork or utensil back on the plate in between mouthfuls, making sure one mouthful is completely chewed before swallowing and taking another mouthful, and even timing each mouthful.

Food should be served in portions rather than family style. People eat more when second courses are available. In addition, it is important to learn not to finish everything on the plate. Many of us have been indoctrinated since childhood to leave an empty plate. For behavior modification therapy of obesity, it is important to leave a certain portion of all foodstuffs presented.

When eating, full attention should be devoted to the meal. When people read or watch television at mealtimes, the food intake seems to increase until the end of the chapter or program is reached.

As mentioned above, a food-intake diary will help a person to gain knowledge of the exact quantities of food and calories consumed, the times at which he or she is most likely to eat, and, if feelings are recorded, the exact feeling states that are particularly apt to lead to snack or binge eating.

A behavioral method designed to take advantage of the satiety factor is to eat a low-calorie snack such as vegetables about 15 to 30 minutes before sitting down for a meal. This will lead to stimulation of the satiety center prior to the meal and is likely to result in less intake.

The concept of reward is essential in any behavior modification therapy. Initially, the reward is for weight loss itself; but Stern and Hoch point out that diets tend to fail in maintaining the weight loss because, after the desired weight has been achieved, there are no more rewards. They state that "to lose weight successfully, you must reward yourself for the actions that caused you to lose weight, and not just for the weight loss itself. After a while these acts will be ingrained in your mind, become habits, and take over automatically."[48]

An important concept that needs to be internalized by those who overeat is that of enjoying food. The desire to overeat tends to be external in origin; that is, the eating seems to be stimulated by situational and emotional reasons. When the desire to eat is internal, it is stimulated by true physical hunger. Paradoxically, externals usually don't get as much pleasure from eating. This is because they tend to eat rapidly with much less mastication. When a person learns to eat more slowly and chew the food well, more enjoyment is derived from each bite, and the locus of eating seems to be changed from external to internal.

We also feel, contrary to many other programs, that repeated daily weighing is detrimental. First of all, most diets produce an initial rapid weight loss associated with salt and water loss, but later, when the weight loss becomes correlated primarily with fat loss, scales will not give the same degree of positive reinforcement. In fact, if some diets are overly restrictive to begin with, that great initial loss of salt and water may be reconstituted at a later date, resulting in weight gain, although the weight gain is not fat. If an individual reaches a plateau, and particularly if he or she begins to gain weight while on what they consider to be a restrictive diet, the tendency will be to discontinue the weight control program. Also, since weight control is a long-term process, day-by-day fluctuations are totally meaningless. Women can gain as much as five pounds premenstrually, all of which is related to fluid retention. We feel that scales should be utilized no more than once or twice a month or, at maximum, once a week. Without using scales, people can learn to develop their own internal locus of perception and will be able to feel when they are losing weight by their internal feelings as well as by changes in the fit of their clothes. People who are on a physical exercise program at the same time they are on caloric restriction may gain weight while losing inches because, on a volume basis, muscle weighs more than fat.

ASC and imagery

As mentioned in the first paragraphs of this section, the induction of ASC alone can lead to weight reduction in obese people. We feel this is because of the general anti-anxiety effects of these states of consciousness as well as a positive reorienting of the individual toward a state of greater health and harmony.

Then, by the use of imagery, the effects of ASC can be enhanced and intensified. Stern and Hoch relate that an extensive mind change is necessary to achieve permanent weight control. By the use of imagery, they report more than 70 percent of their clients lost significant amounts of weight and 75 percent of them had not regained the weight in a one-year followup.[49] They feel that the imagery "accelerate[s] mind change and . . . [is] incredibly efficient in instilling new eating patterns."[49] They relate that imagery can also "enable uncovering of deep-rooted psychological reasons for overeating, discover and eliminate obstacles, change detrimental eating habits, test new methods of eating, instill new coping behaviors to deal with previously difficult eating situations, act as internalized self-rewards, and lead to a sense of well-being."[50]

End-result imagery

We believe that the most important type of image used in weight control is end-result imagery. The following image (from *End Result Imagery* © 1980 by Errol R. Korn) is one we use for many purposes, but the last part of the image enables a person to develop the end-result image of being thin, which is much more powerful than merely thinking thin.

The early parts of the image allow a person to attain a true perspective of his or her self-perception. The image can be used in full, or any of its parts may be used separately for other specific purposes. Other methods for end-result imagery of this type would be the incorporation of an imaginary television set, movie screen, or mirror in which a person could view himself or herself.

Imagine now that you are in a very large, private . . . comfortable . . . room of an art gallery. . . . All of the walls are empty except for one . . . and on that wall there are three empty frames of identical size and structure . . . placed side . . . by side . . . by side . . . Approach the first frame . . . and as your attention focuses on that blank space . . . let there appear an image . . . an image of you . . . as you perceive yourself to be. . . . As you previously learned . . . let whatever image that appears spontaneously . . . be the one that you study. . . . And even if it is indistinct . . . just appreciate whatever of its essence that you are able to perceive. . . . And appreciate not only the visual image . . . but the feeling . . . that you get as you study it . . . and any other sensations that pervade your consciousness. . . . Study the image intensely and if you can, even . . . allow the image to move . . . so that you can see it from various sides so that you can . . . appreciate . . . not just the static qualities . . . but the movement qualities as well. . . . All of these will add to the sense . . . of what this image really conveys. . . . And spend a few moments studying the image . . . in all its fine detail. . . .
. . . Move your attention now to the second frame . . . and allow an image spontaneously to appear there . . . of you . . . as you really are. . . . Take a few moments now . . . to fully perceive . . . this image . . . in the manner that you perceived image number one. . . . And now compare . . . and contrast . . . images one and two. . . . or most people there are differences . . . and these differences . . . represent the fact that our own . . . perception of ourselves . . . is very rarely the same . . . as we really are. . . . From time to time . . . by going back to these two images . . . you may be able to judge . . . progress . . . in becoming more aware of yourself . . . as you really are. . . .
. . . Now become aware of the third frame . . . and allow spontaneously to appear there . . . an image of . . . how you wish yourself to be. . . . And as you previously have done with frames one and two . . .allow yourself to . . . fully study and appreciate . . . the image of how you . . . wish to be. . . . Then compare and contrast the second and third images . . . how you really are . . . with how you wish yourself to be . . . and become keenly aware of the . . . similarities. . . and . . . differences. . . . By periodically . . . reevaluating

. . .these images . . . you will be able to perceive . . . changes
. . . that you have made. . . . You will be able . . . to appreciate
. . . the progress. . . . The method of instituting these changes . . . is
by . . . identifying clearly . . . with the third image . . . not just by
looking at it . . . but by feeling it . . . merging with it . . . actually
feeling your consciousness . . . become that image. . . . Remember,
the language of the brain is pictures . . . and by using this particular
picture . . . the one in the third frame . . . you send the message to the
brain . . . of what you desire. . . . The brain controls . . . all bodily
functions . . . and has the ability to translate these desires . . . into
the changes in habits . . . lifestyle . . . activity . . . etc. that will
lead to the attainment of your goal.

Process images

Stern and Hoch's book, *Mind Trips to Help You Lose Weight,* presents
many process images that we have found extremely helpful in weight
control through both general purposes and for specific problems.[48] We
will outline a few of the most effective of these images.

Eating drama.[51]   This image consists of watching a TV or movie of
your eating processes and enables you to detect a general theme of your
eating, to look at your life in general, and possibly to discover insights.

Jungle doors.[52]   This image involves walking through a jungle and
finding a door, behind which is a stumbling block that acts as a barrier to
the achievement of your goal. By opening the door you are then able to
study what the block is and subsequently program success. This image
leads to the discovery of hidden psychological obstacles to losing weight.

Mountain climbing.[53]   In this image, the rocks and boulders in your
way as you climb the mountain are metaphors for obstacles to permanent
weight loss. Each one is either removed or bypassed until you reach the
top.

Emotional closet.[54]   This image involves a house in which a closet is
experienced that brings back a *déjà vu* sensation. This emotional closet
contains stored-up ideas and feelings about food and eating habits that are
reexperienced when you open the closet. This differs from jungle doors in
that it reveals concrete rather than metaphorical blocks to the realization
of your goal.

Chat with a famous person.[55]   In this image, you are at a meal when a
famous person sits at your table and you begin to talk with that person.
The purpose of this is to enable you to interrupt or stop the eating process

by becoming interested in something else. This allows you to eat more slowly and to decrease the inertial forces leading to overeating.

Slow motion.[56]   This image is designed to reverse some faulty eating habits in restaurants. It is an image of being in a restaurant, placing a reasonable order, engaging in conversation but utilizing methods of time distortion, that is, the impression that everything except the conversation is in slow motion and in a relaxed situation until the actual eating begins. At that point, everyone else seems to be eating in old-time movie rapid motion while you continue in a relaxed, calm situation.

Immersion.[57]   This image is designed for a specific trouble food. In a room you see your favorite food in large quantities, filling up the entire room. This is a negative image, involving your walking into it, crawling in and through the food, which subsequently flows all over your body. You grab large amounts into your mouth and it drips down your mouth. At this point, you mentally say, "Stop," and go to the safe-place image (Chapter 5). In the second part of the image, you go to a door behind which is a table piled high with a favorite food. You then begin to eat it compulsively, using your hands even though you are full. Your jaw begins to hurt, and your stomach stretches until your body begins touching the walls and ceiling and then bursts. At that point you mentally imagine pulling together and leave the room in a calm, controlled manner, and go to the safe place.

Metamorphosis.[58]   In this image, you become your obsession, that is, your trouble food. You notice your location and packaging and all other things in the environment. You fully experience how it feels to be that food. This may sound somewhat ridiculous, but at the level of primary processes, the level at which the unconscious works, this is a perfectly reasonable image that produces lasting effects.

These are just a sampling of the many images and patterns of the use of imagery for losing weight. Other sections of Stern and Hoch's book include images on finding solutions, developing a better body image, handling one's feelings, changing thought patterns, and feeling good about oneself. Essentially, anyone can construct process images geared to his or her own specific needs and preferences. The effectiveness of the imagery is limited only by one's own imagination.

References

1. A. C. Isham, "Hypno-Relaxation: Therapy for Tension State," *Am J Clin Hyp* 14 (1971), pp. 63–64.

2. M. L. Armstrong, "The Treatment of Anxiety States by Hypnotherapy," *Aust J Med Sophrology Hypnotherapy* 2 (1974), pp. 21–25.

3. A. Ahsen, "Relaxation and Image Anticipation," *J Ment Imagery* 3 (1979), p. 150.

4. S. Nidich, W. Seeman, and W. Seibert, "Influence of the Transcendental Meditation Program on State Anxiety," in *Scientific Research on the Transcendental Meditation Program,* collected papers, vol. 1, ed. D. Orme-Johnson and J. T. Farrow (Livingstone Manor, N.Y.: Maharishi European Research University Press, 1977), pp. 434–36.

5. L. A. Hjelle, "Transcendental Meditation and Psychological Health," *Perceptual and Motor Skills* 39 (1974), pp. 623–28.

6. T. Fehr, U. Nerstheimer, and S. Torber, "Study of Personality Changes Resulting from the Transcendental Meditation Program: Freiburger Personality Inventory," in *Scientific Research on the Transcendental Meditation Program,* collected papers, vol. 1, ed. D. Orme-Johnson and J. T. Farrow (Livingstone Manor, N.Y.: Maharishi European Research University Press, 1977), pp. 420–27.

7. L. G. Fahmi, EEG Biofeedback, Multichannel Synchrony Training and Attention," in *Expanding Dimensions of Consciousness,* ed. A. A. Sugarman and R. E. Tarter (New York: Springer, 1978), pp. 155–82.

8. H. Spiegel, "A Single Treatment Method to Stop Smoking Using Ancillary Self-Hypnosis," *Int J Clin Exp Hyp* 18 (1970), p. 235.

9. H. P. Crasilneck and J. A. Hall, *Clinical Hypnosis: Principles and Applications.* (New York: Grune and Stratton, 1975), p. 236.

10. W. S. Kroger, *Clinical and Experimental Hypnosis,* 2d ed. (Philadelphia: J. B. Lippincott, 1977), p. 381.

11. W. S. Kroger and W. D. Fezler, *Hypnosis and Behavior Modification: Imagery Conditioning* (Philadelphia: J. B. Lippincott, 1976), p. 251.

12. J. Wolpe, *Psychotherapy by Reciprocal Inhibition* (Stanford, Calif.: Stanford University Press, 1958).

13. A. Kales and J. D. Kales, "Sleep Disorders," *N Eng J Med* 290 (1974), pp. 487–99.

14. T. Borkovec and D. Fowles, "A Controlled Investigation of the Effects of Progressive and Hypnotic Relaxation on Insomnia," *J Abnorm Psychol* 82 (1973), pp. 153–58.

15. J. Geer and E. Katkin, "Treatment of Insomnia Using a Variant of Systematic Desensitization: A Case Report," *J Abnorm Psychol* 71 (1966), pp. 161–64.

16. D. E. Miskiman, "The Treatment of Insomnia by the Transcendental Meditation Program," in *Scientific Research on the Transcendental Meditation Program,* collected papers, vol. 1, ed. D. Orme-Johnson and J. T. Farrow (Livingstone Manor, N.Y.: Maharishi European Research University Press, 1977), pp. 296–98.

17. W. S. Kroger, *Clinical and Experimental Hypnosis,* 2d ed. (Philadelphia: J. B. Lippincott, 1977), p. 316.

18. W. S. Kroger and W. D. Fezler, *Hypnosis and Behavior Modification: Imagery Conditioning* (Philadelphia: J. B. Lippincott, 1976), p. 204.

19. Ibid., p. 317.

20. Ibid., p. 205.

21. Ibid., p. 245.

22. P. B. Schilling, "The Effect of the Regular Practice of the Transcendental Meditation Technique on Behavior and Personality," in *Scientific Research on the Transcendental Meditation Program,* collected papers, vol. 1, ed. D. Orme-Johnson and J. T. Farrow (Livingstone Manor, N.Y.: Maharishi European Research University Press, 1977), pp. 453–61.

23. W. T. Winquist, "The Transcendental Meditation Program in Drug Abuse: A Retrospect of Study," in *Scientific Research on the Transcendental Meditation Program,* collected papers, vol. 1, ed. D. Orme-Johnson and J. T. Farrow (Livingstone Manor, N.Y.: Maharishi European Research University Press, 1977), pp. 494–97.

24. E. Brautigaur, "Effects of the Transcendental Meditation Program on Drug Abuse: A Perspective Study," in *Scientific Research on the Transcendental Meditation Program,* collected papers, vol. 1, ed. D. Orme-Johnson and J. T. Farrow (Livingstone Manor, N.Y.: Maharishi European Research University Press, 1977), pp. 506–14.

25. M. Shafu, R. A. Lavely, and R. D. Jaffe, "Meditation and Marijuana," *Am J Psychiatry* 131 (1974), pp. 60–63.

26. H. Benson and R. K. Wallace, "Decreased Drug Abuse with Transcendental Meditation: A Study of 1,862 Subjects," in *Drug Abuse: Proceedings of the International Conference,* ed. Z. J. D. Zarafonetis (Philadelphia: Lee and Fediger, 1972), pp. 369–76.

27. M. Shafu, R. A. Lavely, and R. D. Jaffe, "Meditation and the Prevention of Alcohol Abuse," *Am J Psychiatry* 132 (1975), pp. 942–45.

28. W. S. Kroger and W. D. Fezler, *Hypnosis and Behavior Modification: Imagery Conditioning* (Philadelphia: J. B. Lippincott, 1976), p. 188.

29. M. Cunningham and W. Koch, "The Transcendental Meditation Program and Rehabilitation: A Pilot Project at the Federal Correctional Institution at Lompoc, California," in *Scientific Research on the Transcendental Meditation Program,* collected papers, vol. 1, ed. D. Orme-Johnson and J. T. Farrow (Livingstone Manor, N.Y.: Maharishi European Research University Press, 1977), pp. 562–68.

30. D. Orme-Johnson, J. Kiehlbauch, R. Moore et al., "Personality and Autonomic Changes in Prisoners Practicing the Transcendental Meditation Technique," in *Scientific Research on the Transcendental Meditation Program,* collected papers, vol. 1, ed. D. Orme-Johnson and J. T. Farrow (Livingstone Manor, N.Y.: Maharishi European Research University Press, 1977), pp. 555–61.

31. D. Ballou, "The Transcendental Meditation Program at Stillwater Prison," in *Scientific Research on the Transcendental Meditation Program,* collected papers, vol. 1, ed. D. Orme-Johnson and J. T. Farrow (Livingstone Manor, N.Y.: Maharishi European Research University Press, 1977), pp. 569–76.

32. J. P. Childs, "The use of the transcendental meditation program as a therapy for juvenile offenders," in *Scientific Research on the Transcendental Meditation Program,* collected papers, vol. 1, ed. D. Orme-Johnson and J. T. Farrow (Livingstone Manor, N.Y.: Maharishi European Research University Press, 1977), pp. 577–84.

33. J. E. Spear, "The Utilization of Non-Drug Induced Altered States of Consciousness in Borderline Recidivists," *Am J Clin Hyp* 18 (1975), pp. 111–26.

34. E. L. Wynder and D. Hoffman, "Tobacco and Health: A Societal Challenge," *New Eng J Med* 300 (1979), pp. 894–903.

35. H. P. Crasilneck and J. A. Hall, *Clinical Hypnosis: Principles and Applications* (New York: Grune and Stratton, 1975), pp. 167–68.

36. H. E. Stanton, "A One-Session Hypnotic Approach to Modifying Smoking Behavior. *Int J Clin Exp Hyp* 26 (1978), pp. 22–29.

37. G. A. Bray, M. B. Davidson, and E. J. Drenick, "Obesity: A Serious Symptom," *Ann Int Med* 77 (1972), pp. 797–805.

38. R. T. Oakley, "Hypnosis with a Positive Approach in the Management of Problem Obesity," *J Am Soc Psychosom Dent* 7 (1960), pp. 28–40.

39. H. Stanton, "Weight Loss through Hypnosis," *Am J Clin Hyp* 18 (1975), pp. 34–38.

40. F. S. Glover, "Use of Hypnosis for Weight Reduction in a Group of Nurses," *Am J Clin Hyp* 3 (1961), pp. 250–51.

41. H. Mann, "Group Hypnosis in the Treatment of Obesity," *Am J Clin Hyp* 1 (1953), pp. 113–16.

42. L. Wollman, "Hypnosis and Weight Control," *Am J Clin Hyp* 4 (1962), pp. 177–80.

43. F. W. Hanley, "Treatment of Obesity by Individual and Group Hypnosis," *Can Psychiatr Assoc J* 12 (1967), pp. 549–51.

44. J. T. Weldon and A. Ron, "The Transcendental Meditation Program and Normalization of Weight," in *Scientific Research on the Transcendental Meditation Program,* collected papers, vol. 1, ed. D. Orme-Johnson and J. T. Farrow (Livingstone Manor, N.Y.: Maharishi European Research University Press, 1977), pp. 301–6.

45. T. A. Wadden and J. Flaxman, "Hypnosis and Weight Loss: A Preliminary Study," *Int J Clin Exp Hyp* 29 (1981), pp. 162–73.

46. H. E. Stanton, "Fee-Paying in Weight Loss: Evidence for an Interesting Interaction," *Am J Clin Hyp* 19 (1976), pp. 47–49.

47. W. S. Kroger and W. D. Fezler, *Hypnosis and Behavior Modification: Imagery Conditioning* (Philadelphia: J. B. Lippincott, 1976), p. 213.

48. F. M. Stern and R. S. Hoch, *Mind Trips to Help You Lose Weight* (Chicago: Playboy Press, 1976), p. 63.

49. Ibid., p. 76.

50. Ibid., pp. 77–78.

51. Ibid., pp. 91–92.

52. Ibid., pp. 93–95.

53. Ibid., pp. 95–97.

54. Ibid., pp. 98–100.

55. Ibid., pp. 103–4.

56. Ibid., pp. 105–6.

57. Ibid., pp. 108–10.

58. Ibid., pp. 114–15.

Chapter 12

The uses of imagery in medicine, psychosomatics, and dermatology

Earlier in this book, we described how the health of an individual is affected by stress. We also noted the use of altered states of consciousness and imagery in directing and changing physiological patterns. In this chapter, we will discuss the applications of ASC and imagery in the treatment of medical and dermatological disorders. The prevention of these disorders is found in Chapter 9.

The role of the mind in disease processes

The influence of the mind over the body has been a subject of interest in psychosomatic medicine. A number of diseases have been delineated which are considered to be either psychosomatic in origin or have psychosomatic components. However, a list of this sort negates the role of psychic influences on the soma with respect to all other diseases and tends to propagate Cartesian dualism. This theory, as mentioned in early chapters, has fostered an artificial separation of the mind from the body and has led to models of disease and therapies which have been somewhat inadequate. Therapies involving the mind, such as ASC and imagery, can affect not only the emotional factors of an illness but the physical and biological factors as well.

Kaufman and Margolin note that emotional factors are of importance during every stage of every illness, varying only in their intensity and importance in each particular situation.[1] Linn states that there are three sources of symptoms from all illnesses: *biological, psychological,* and *social.*[2] The biological factors refer to the physical manifestations such as the inflammatory response, psychological factors are the attitudes and feelings not only of the patient but of the significant others, and the social factors are factors relating to the social environment such as school, work, community interactions.

Leigh and Reiser more recently have developed a nonlinear field systems model of disease which adds to the previous factors the individual's own constitutional and genetic factors.[3] The basic components in this model include constitution, genetic factors, sociocultural factors, interpersonal (psychological) factors, and physical environment.

In the modern practice of medicine we tend to pay excessive attention to the biological factors and significantly less attention to the psychological, and frequently we overlook the social factors entirely. Numerous studies have shown that psychosocial processes do influence even such things as susceptibility to infections and neoplasms, possibly by altering immune responses, both humoral and cell-mediated.[4,5]

Pelletier writes that stress is the common denominator in the development of these psychosomatic illnesses.[6] If stress becomes excessive, it will cause alterations in mind-body function. Then, if serious life-change events occur or if stress becomes extreme, a disease or disorder can be precipitated. At this point, the individual's personality will determine what type of disease is manifested. Pelletier notes that our basic instincts, (sex, hunger, sleep, fear) are diencephalic, whereas our emotions (pity, shame, hope, guilt) are cortical elaborations of these basic instincts.[6] Excessive stresses, writes Simeons, cause the usual diencephalic reaction; however, the symptoms produced are interpreted by the cortex as abnormal rather than as responses to stress. For example, fright (a diencephalic instinct) may cause an inability to sleep—a normal reaction. If the fright is unrecognized by the individual, he or she may interpret the inability to sleep as insomnia. A similar example would be the misinterpretation of fright-induced tachycardia as palpitations or heart disease. This can then develop into a feedback loop in which the symptom causes more of the basic instinct (fright), which causes increased symptoms, and on and on. Additional evidence for the role of the mind in the development of somatic illnesses, even those not usually classified as psychosomatic, can be found in the Holmes and Rahe Life Change Index (see Chapter 2) and Friedman and Rosenman's studies with the type A personality in the development of cardiac disease.[7]

Use of ASC and imagery with medical problems _____

Principles

A major use of these techniques is to alleviate the excessive elicitation of the stress response. This response leads eventually to psychosomatic illnesses and plays a significant role in other illnesses where the psychological factors are less clear. The effectiveness of these techniques in stress reduction is well documented in Chapter 2. The stress-reducing characteristics of these techniques are also important in the prophylaxis of disease as well as in decreasing the stress-related propogation of disease processes. We also feel that these methods can be utilized for earlier diagnoses, since the individual practicing these methods is more attuned to his or her own bodily processes. The techniques can also lead to an individual's understanding of the meaning of the disease processes[8] and the need for self-instituted lifestyle changes.

Alleviation of symptoms (including pain) is an important application of these methods (see Chapter 7). People with medical problems may need changes in their food intake; appetite may be stimulated by these means; obesity may be controlled (see Chapter 11). The methods can be used to treat associated sleep disturbances, anxiety, or depression.

Healing may be promoted by the utilization of ASC and imagery (see Chapter 13). In fact, according to Samuels and Samuels, imagery as a method of healing probably existed in ancient times.[9] In primitive civilizations, these methods are still the mainstay of healing.

Vascular instability, highlighted by overreactivity of the sympathetic division of the autonomic nervous system, is associated with many disorders. The condition can be stabilized by regular use of ASC and imagery. This aspect of the use of imagery has found clinical usefulness in the treatment of migraine headaches (see Chapter 7) and other vascular phenomena.

Methods and images

It would be superfluous to delineate specific images for every specific disorder. In fact, adherence to the techniques and therapeutic sequences outlined in Chapters 4 and 5, supplemented with liberal use of one's imagination, will yield imagery of therapeutic impact. (See Chapters 4 and 5 for the sequence and types of images that can be used for medical problems. For healing, we would also suggest an image based on the work of Jack Schwartz—see Chapter 13.)

Additional useful images may be found in Kroger and Fezler's text.[10] Image 15, the Mansion Scene (pp. 121–22), allows one to gain autonomic and somatic control. Control over the visceral and musculoskeletal systems is emphasized in Image 17, the Picnic Scene (pp. 123–24). The gastrointestinal and circulatory systems are represented by Images 18 and 19, the Shangri-La Scene (pp. 124–25) and the Chalk Cliff Scene (p. 125). The circulatory system is emphasized in Image 22, the Hayloft Scene (p. 129).

Masters and Houston utilized the healing effects of ancient healing rites to create an image which we think is therapeutically useful; that is, the image of an ancient healing temple.[11]

White Light Healing Image.   The following image (© 1980 by Errol R. Korn) allows one to consciously channel forces in the body toward health and healing. By translating our desires into images, we can direct those forces that have central nervous system direction but that usually have been beyond our conscious directional ability.

Allow yourself to concentrate . . . on an area in the midportion of your forehead . . . so that you may even begin to feel . . . a tingling sensation. . . . As you do so . . . you are bringing all your attention . . . all your consciousness . . . to this area. . . . By centering your consciousness . . . you can bring the . . . full power . . . of it to . . . enhance . . . the establishment of . . . wellness . . . in the body-mind axis. . . . Now allow the spot of attention . . . to become as small as you possibly can . . . so that all your consciousness is . . . concentrated . . . in a very small area. . . . Now project this point . . . to an area about a foot above your head . . . and let it expand . . . to the size of a baseball. . . . Let this sphere obtain the appearance of . . . a glowing sphere . . . of radiant . . . fiery . . . white . . . light. . . . Perceive the glowing and fiery nature . . . feel the warmth . . . and maybe even hear . . . the vibratory qualities of this object. . . . Now let it begin to slowly . . . expand . . . until it achieves the size of a moderately sized melon . . . still radiant . . . fiery . . . glowing . . . white. . . . Allow the bottom to open . . . as though the top were hinged . . . and as it does . . . begin to see the downpour of fiery . . . white . . . radiant . . . light energy. . . . Feel and see the energy entering the body through the top of the head . . . and flowing downward through the entire body . . . from the head . . . into the neck . . . down the arms to the hands . . . back up the arms . . . down the chest . . . both front and back . . . the remainder of the trunk . . . front and back . . . down into the legs . . . the feet . . . and out the feet . . . into the ground. . . . Permit yourself not only to see the energy pour through the body . . . but feel it . . . and also hear it. . . . True health and wellness will be exemplified by a . . . free flow . . . of this fiery . . . radiant . . . white . . . light . . . energy through the body. . . . If there are problems in the body such as diseases or discomforts . . . whether they be consciously realized or not . . . they can be manifested by some impotence . . . or even a complete blockage . . . of the flow of this fiery . . . radiant . . . white . . . light . . . energy . . . through that particular area or areas of the body. . . . When these areas are perceived . . . you may be able to feel and see these areas being fragmented . . . and consumed . . . by this fiery . . . radiant . . . white . . . light . . . energy. . . . It is as though the debris and garbage of the body . . . were being incinerated . . . by this . . . healing force. . . . When the discomfort . . . disorder . . . or diseases have been fragmented–and consumed . . . by this fiery . . . radiant . . . white . . . light . . . energy . . . the result will be . . . free flow . . . of energy . . . through this area. . . . Continue to feel . . . and perceive . . . through this downpour . . . coming from that sphere . . . above the head through the entire body . . . and out the feet . . . and into the floor . . . until the free flow . . . of this fiery . . . radiant . . . white . . . light . . . energy . . . has been established through the body . . . so when this free flow has been established . . . it will represent the elimination of all toxins . . . wastes . . . and debris . . . that interfere with the . . . maintenance of health. . . .

When this free flow has been established . . . allow the sphere to close . . . and the downpour to cease. . . . Then allow the sphere . . . to get larger . . . approximately three feet in diameter . . . and allow it to rotate . . . very slowly . . . around its vertical axis. . . . As it rotates . . . allow it to descend . . . very slowly . . . so that it descends . . . around the entire body . . . from head . . . to toes. . . . The function of the sphere at this time . . . is to absorb any accumulated debris . . . that has been left behind by the radiant . . . light . . . downpour. . . . When it reaches the feet . . . the entire body should be cleansed of all debris . . . detrimental to maintenance of physical . . . and emotional . . . wellness. . . .

Now let the sphere begin to . . . slowly . . . rotate . . . in the opposite direction . . . around its vertical axis . . . and let it slowly begin to ascend . . . the body. . . . The function . . . of the sphere . . . at this time is to . . . instill . . . new . . . and vitalizing . . . energy . . . into the body. . . . Not only is the energy being instilled into the body . . . but it is being instilled . . . into a body . . . which

has been completely freed . . . of all forces which would hinder the
. . . complete assimilation and utilization . . . of this energy. . . .
When the sphere reaches the top of the head . . . then ascends . . .
above the head . . . the entire . . . body-mind axis . . . can be free
. . . of all debris . . . and filled with a vitality . . . and energy
. . . heretofore rarely if ever experienced. . . .

   The sphere can now . . . stop rotating . . . and begin to . . .
shrink . . . in size and eventually . . . return to the body as a point
of . . . concentrated consciousness . . . in the forehead region.
. . . Then, with a few deep breaths . . . this consciousness can travel
throughout the body . . . and you can return slowly to the waking state
. . . as you have done . . . in previous exercises.

   Pain or Anxiety as Object. This image (© 1980 by Errol R. Korn) is
utilized to give abstract sensation such as pain, discomfort, anxiety, or
disease a more concrete image with which we can work to change the
subject's feelings as represented by the symbol.

   Most of us at one time or another . . . experience . . . sensations
. . . that we would regard as unpleasant . . . such as pain, discomfort,
tension, stress and strain. . . . Just by relaxing and concentrating on
the . . . exhalation phase . . . of respiration, we have already learned
one method . . . of alleviating . . . these uncomfortable sensations.
. . . These sensations are all subjective phenomena. . . . We feel them
. . . but as we know only too well . . . it is very difficult to . . . consciously . . . modify these . . . feelings. . . . We usually find it
easier to modify concrete objects . . . so the purpose of this image is
to . . . change our unpleasant sensation . . . into an object . . .
which is a . . . symbol . . . of the sensation. . . . If you now have a
pain . . . discomfort . . . tension . . . or disease . . . or even if you
don't . . . going through the procedure anyway at this time will enable
you to use it later . . . when these problems do develop. . . . Take the
pain . . . tension . . . stress . . . strain . . . anxiety . . . or   disease . . . and . . . give it a shape . . . by imagining or visualizing the
first shape . . . that comes to mind. . . . The shape may be . . . abstract . . . or concrete. . . . It can be an object . . . inanimate form
. . . a geometric design . . . or it can be amorphous. . . . The first
shape that comes to your mind is the . . . appropriate one . . . to work
with. . . . Anything else tends to be conscious . . . judgmental ef-
forts. . . . Next . . . give the shape a color. . . . Now . . . give it a
size. . . . You can establish a size just by knowing it . . . or by picturing next to it . . . an object of known size. . . . Realize that the shape
is a symbol . . . of your tension or discomfort . . . and the larger it
is . . . the more vibrantly and vividly colored it is . . . the more in-

tense the discomfort it represents will be . . . and conversely . . . the smaller . . . and less vividly colored it is . . . the less severe . . . and less significant . . . the discomfort will be. . . . So practice . . . by changing the size of the object. . . . Because we usually are able to increase the discomfort much more easily than decrease it . . . make the object larger. . . . Make it as large as you need to make it . . . to feel somewhat more uncomfortable . . . and when it is as large as it needs to be . . . make it . . . smaller. . . . If you have any difficulty in making it smaller by just wishing it . . . to be smaller . . . then . . . you can attempt to kick it away . . . or throw it away . . . place it on a boat . . . or on a truck . . . or tie it to an airplane . . . and let it fly away. . . . Or if it is a balloon . . . you can put a needle into it . . . and deflate it. . . . Realize that as the symbol becomes smaller . . . the feelings associated with it become . . . less intense. . . . You can make it as small as it is comfortable for you to do so. . . . Practice making it larger and smaller, because these are skills and, as with any skill . . . the more you practice . . . the more . . . powerful . . . the skill becomes.

Internal Progressive Relaxation. In Chapter 5, we outlined a somatic mental relaxation procedure. This tends to relax the skeletal musculature and may even stabilize the autonomic nervous system. It may also cause visceral relaxation by a direct route or by the autonomic stabilization. However, particularly in people with visceral disorders, a guided internal relaxation can be used. We would suggest this image (© 1980 by Errol R. Korn) be used as an addendum to the somatic relaxation discussed in Chapter 5.

Now . . . with the body and mind relaxed . . . we can begin to focus our attention inward . . . enabling the internal organs . . . to become as relaxed . . . as we feel externally. . . . You can allow the internal organs of the body to become more relaxed . . . by thinking of the organs . . . and by feeling . . . the relaxation . . . deepen . . . every time . . . you exhale. . . .

You can allow that glow . . . that wave . . . of comfort and relaxation . . . to travel down the food pipe . . . or esophagus . . . as though you had just swallowed a potent . . . magic . . . elixir . . . containing all the ingredients necessary . . . to alleviate all the distress . . . of any tissue . . . with which it comes into contact. . . . And as it travels . . . down . . . the food pipe . . . it can also lead to relaxation . . . and healing . . . of the adjacent organs . . . the trachea and bronchial tubes . . . the heart and major arteries . . . and the lungs . . . enabling all of them to function more leisurely . . . and more effectively. . . . It is not even necessary for you to know . . .

consciously . . . what these organs look like. . . . Deep in the mind
. . . you have a precise . . . unconscious . . . knowledge . . . of the
functioning and structure . . . of all the organs. . . .

And feel the relaxation . . . travel into the stomach . . . relaxing
it . . . and the nearby organs of the spleen . . . and the upper left of
the abdomen . . . the liver . . . and the upper right of the abdomen . . . and the pancreas . . . lying deep . . . in the upper abdomen. . . . And enable the relaxation wave . . . to travel through the
small intestine . . . all 24 feet of it . . . coiled up in the midportion of
the abdomen. . . . And it now . . . can travel through the large intestine . . . six feet of structure . . . in the right . . . upper . . . and
left portions of the abdomen. . . . Then the relaxation can ex-
tend . . . to the kidneys . . . the ureters . . . connecting the kidneys
to the bladder . . . the bladder . . . and the genital organs. . . . At
this point . . . the internal organs and structures of the body . . . can
be as relaxed . . . comfortable . . . and healthy . . . as the muscles . . . blood vessels . . . bones . . . and joints . . . already are.

Specific medical disorders   The techniques of ASC and imagery, we
feel, can be an adjunct to the therapy of *any* medical disorder, or problem.
The basic principles mentioned above and in earlier chapters apply to all
situations. In general, research in imagery has been directed toward
learning situations and psychotherapy. Satisfactory research in the uses
of imagery with respect to medical and surgical disorders is unfortunately
lacking. However we believe we can extrapolate some of the research in
other applications of ASC.

Cardiovascular disorders

The influence of the mind on the development of cardiovascular disorders, particularly, such a debilitating disorder as ischemic heart disease,
has been well documented by Friedman and Rosenman.[7] They describe
the type A individual as one who is competitive, time-urgent, impatient,
aggressive; who judges accomplishments in terms of numbers; who
strives for deadlines; and whose hostility, which may be well rationalized,
is easily aroused. This is in contrast to the type B individual, who lacks
time urgency, can relax without guilt, understands his or her own
strengths and weaknesses, works for personal satisfaction, is free of
hostility, and considers alternatives. The type A personality is a strong
factor in the development of coronary heart disease.

Sudden death, which may be caused by lethal cardiovascular events, is
probably psychological in origin.[12] In other words, there may be circumstances that are impossible to ignore, leading to an overwhelming re-

sponse of excitability or giving up. Situations causing sudden death may be the impact of the death of a close other, the mourning or anniversary thereof, loss of status or self-esteem, personal danger or threat, the period after a personal danger or threat has passed, or even reunion, triumph, or happy endings.

Using ASC and imagery can lead to a modification or decrease in type A characteristics, an increase in type B characteristics, and smoothing of the effects of overwhelming life stress events, thereby decreasing the propensity to develop cardiovascular disorders or limiting the seriousness of the problems once developed. Other risk factors such as obesity can also be managed with these techniques.

Although well-controlled studies on the effectiveness of these techniques in altering the pathophysiology of coronary artery disease are lacking, there is initial evidence that the imagery techniques of hand-warming (used to stabilize the autonomic nervous system) may be of value in the symptomatic therapy of angina pectoris.[13] In addition, biofeedback research has demonstrated that mental techniques can be used to decrease the heart rate in sinus tachycardia and to control the heart rate in patients with various arrhythmias (paroxysmal super-ventricular tachycardia, Wolff-Parkinson-White syndrome, atrial fibrillation, and premature ventricular contractions).[14]

Another serious cardiovascular problem is hypertension. The techniques of ASC and imagery can decrease the chronic ongoing stress which may be a causative factor in hypertension and can decrease the risk of hypertension by reducing obesity. The use of ASC in directly lowering blood pressure has been well summarized by Shapiro et al.[15] Such methods have been given the names of biofeedback, progressive relaxation, autogenic training, hypnosis, Zen meditation, hatha-yoga, transcendental meditation, relaxation response, and combinations thereof. Other studies have also documented the effectiveness of the practice of these methods in controlling hypertension.[16,17] Since many antihypertensive medications have detrimental side effects, any lowering of the medication requirement by mental techniques would certainly be an important addition to our therapeutic armamentarium.

Thermal biofeedback by means of handwarming has been utilized for the therapy of migraine headaches (see Chapter 7). Handwarming can be accomplished by imagery techniques without the use of a biofeedback device. In fact, in a well-controlled study, hypnosis with handwarming suggestions caused greater peripheral vasodilitation than did biofeedback.[18] Adler and Adler feel that hand temperature is a very good indicator of general sympathetic tone and that the results we get from this vascular control are not just from shifting of blood but from actual normalizing sympathetic homeostasis by means of the hypothalamus.[19]

These methods have been applied to vasospastic disease and have been used successfully for therapy of Raynaud's phenomena.[20,21] We have utilized these methods successfully in cases of Burger's disease and sympathetic reflex dystrophy. Other forms of ASC (hypnosis) have been utilized successfully for therapy of these vascular phenomena.[22,23]

Hemorrhage

The uses of ASC and imagery in controlling hemorrhage are outlined in Chapter 13. Because of the effects of these methods on the control of vascular tone, the vascular factors in hemorrhage can be modified. Studies with hemophiliac patients suggest the ability of these techniques to alter the interactions of the coagulation factors as well.[24]

Gastrointestinal disorders

The gastrointestinal system has long been associated with psychosomatic influences. Such disorders as peptic ulcer disease, inflammatory bowel disease, and irregularities of bowel function such as constipation and diarrhea long have been thought to have significant psychic influences. The effect of ASC in altering gastrointestinal function has been well documented with respect to the lower esophageal sphincter,[25] the anal sphincter competence,[26] vomiting states,[27,28] control of acid secretion,[29] and functional diarrhea.[30]

In our experience, these methods have been extremely useful for maintenance of a disease-free state after traditional forms of therapy have healed peptic ulcer disease. We have also had experience with patients with inflammatory bowel disease, refractory to standard methods of therapy, who have obtained complete symptomatic and endoscopic amelioration of the problem by means of imagery. We have had success with these methods in an overall program of management of patients with severe disabling postgastrectomy syndromes such as dumping, postvagotomy diarrhea, and persistent nausea and vomiting.

Rheumatic and autoimmune diseases

There is increasing evidence that emotional factors play a role in the onset or aggravation of rheumatic and autoimmune diseases.[31] Because of this association, we feel that the techniques of ASC and imagery can reduce psychosocial influences on the diseases and also effect tissue healing. In addition, the techniques are important in the management of pain. Objective studies of the techniques used with these diseases are still lacking, however.

Pulmonary disorders

Pelletier has noted that when an individual is under stress, his or her breathing becomes very shallow and irregular.[6] ASC such as meditation can be used to actually increase airway conductance, a measure of the ease of airflow.[32]

Asthma is considered to be a very important psychosomatic disorder of the respiratory factors, and evidence indicates that psychological factors can change pulmonary functions.[33] Numerous reports exist of the successful treatment of asthma by the use of ASC such as hypnosis,[34,35] progressive relaxation,[2,36,37,38] and meditation.[39,40]

An image that we have utilized with success in asthma is that of the bronchial tree as a faucet. Instead of water, this faucet would control the ingress and egress of air. When the faucet is closed down, it would be very difficult to move air through the pipe, whereas the converse is true with the value open. We would have the client practice by turning the value down and actually inducing feelings of respiratory difficulty that were completely under his or her control. By learning that one has the ability to control the disorder in one direction, one can learn one has the ability to control it in the other, preferred direction.

Neurological disorders

In this section we devote our attention primarily to epilepsy. A more complete discussion of neuromuscular uses of imagery appears in Chapter 8.) Since ASC have a stabilizing effect on the electroencephalogram, it would seem that these methods would be beneficial in the therapy of epileptic disorders.[41,42,43] In fact, hypnosis has been reported to decrease the frequency of psychomotor seizures.[44] Most reports of the use of hypnosis with epilepsy, however, are limited to case reports. Other forms of ASC have demonstrated significant ability in controlling epileptiform seizures such as control of the sensorimotor EEG rhythm by the use of electroencephalographic biofeedback.[45] We certainly feel that more research is needed in the potential of this important use of imagery.

Dermatology

The skin is strongly influenced by emotional effects, and ASC such as hypnosis and suggestions have led to the production of dermatological lesions.[46,47] Conversely, neutral hypnosis (analogous to ASC without direction) and hypnosis with suggestion can decrease harmful reactions in the skin.[48,49] There is a body of literature attesting to the effectiveness of hypnotherapy in dermatologic disorders.[50] However, other ASC such as dreams, direct suggestion, and waking suggestion were equally as successful as hypnosis in regressing condyloma acuminata.[51] This report plus our own experience lead us to believe it is the induced state of consciousness, associated with a particular imagery, that results in the alleviation of the dermatological problem. The well-known effectiveness of hypnosis in therapy of warts is accentuated by the vivid use of imagery.[52]

We also feel that these techniques are helpful in most other dermatologic disorders, particularly such disorders as psoriasis and herpes simplex. In alleviating the symptomology and physiological manifestations of oral herpes, we have used direct process images involving the immune system attacking the herpes virus (given a symbolic image by the patient). This is very similar to the imagery used by the Simontons in their cancer therapy. Images of heat and especially coolness are helpful in many dermatoses, particularly such things as photosensitivity dermatitis and other dermatitides where there exists a significant change in skin temperature.

Summary

The techniques of ASC and imagery serve as a valuable adjunct in the prevention and therapy of medical disorders. If the harmful effects of excessive stress response are alleviated, disease can be prevented or ameliorated. The direct physiological effects of imagery can lead to healing of disease processes in addition to amelioration of symptomology and enhancement of feelings of well-being. Since double-blind controlled studies are frequently lacking, we feel this is a fruitful area for research and hope that funding authorities will see fit to investigate this nonmutilating, nonpharmacological form of therapy.

References

1. M. R. Kaufman and S. G. Margolin, "What is Psychosomatic Medicine?" *Medical Clinics North America* (Philadelphia: W. B. Saunders, 1948), pp. 609–11.

2. L. Linn, "Basic Principles of Management in Psychosomatic Medicine," in *Psychosomatic Medicine: Its Clinical Applications,* ed. E. D. Wittkower and H. Warnes (Hagerstown, Md.: Harper & Row, 1977), pp. 2–14.

3. H. Leigh and M. F. Reiser, "Major Trends in Psychosomatic Medicine," *Ann Int Med* 87 (1977), pp. 233–39.

4. M. Stein, R. C. Schiavi, and M. Camerino, "Influence of Brain and Behavior on the Immune System," *Science* 191 (1976), pp. 435–40.

5. G. F. Soloman, "Emotions, Stress, the Central Nervous System and Immunity," *Ann N.Y. Acad Sci* 1611(2) (1969), pp. 335–43.

6. K. R. Pelletier, *Mind as Healer, Mind as Slayer* (New York: Delta, 1977).

7. M. Friedman and R. H. Rosenman, *Type A Behavior in Your Heart* (New York: Alfred A. Knopf, 1974).

8. W. S. Kroger, *Clinical and Experimental Hypnosis*, 2d ed. (Philadelphia: J. B. Lippincott, 1977), p. 191.

9. M. Samuels and N. Samuels, *Seeing With the Mind's Eye* (New York: Random House Bookworks, 1975).

10. W. S. Kroger and W. D. Fezler, *Hypnosis and Behavior Modification: Imagery and Conditioning* (Philadelphia: J. B. Lippincott, 1976).

11. R. Masters and J. Houston, *Mind Games* (New York: Dell Publishing, 1972), pp. 113–16.

12. G. L. Engel, "Sudden and Rapid Death during Psychological Stress," *An Int Med* 74 (1971), pp. 771–82.

13. C. H. Hartman, "Response of Anginal Pain to Handwarming," *Biofeed and Sel-Reg* 4 (1979), pp. 355–57.

14. B. T. Engel, "Behavioral Applications in the Treatment of Patients with Cardiovascular Disorders," in *Biofeedback: Principles and Practice for Clinicians*, ed. J. V. Basmajian (Baltimore: Williams and Wilkins, 1979), pp. 170–79.

15. A. P. Shapiro, G. E. Schwartz, D. C. E. Fergusen et al., "Behavioral Methods in the Treatment of Hypertension," *Ann Int Med* 86 (1977), pp. 626–36.

16. C. Patel, "Twelve-Month Follow-Up of Yoga and Biofeedback in the Management of Hypertension," *Lancet* 1 (1975), pp. 62–65.

17. C. Patel and W. North, "Randomized Controlled Trial of Yoga and Biofeedback in the Management of Hypertension," *Lancet* 2 (1973), pp. 93–95.

18. A. F. Barabasz and C. M. McGeorge, "Biofeedback, Meditated Biofeedback and Hypnosis in Peripheral Vasodilitation Training," *Am J Clin Hyp* 21 (1978), pp. 28–37.

19. C. S. Adler and S. M. Adler, "Biofeedback—Psychotherapy for the Treatment of Headaches: A Five-Year Follow-Up," *Headache* 16 (1976), pp. 189–91.

20. A. M. Jacobson, T. P. Hackett, O. S. Sherman et al., "Raynaud Phenomenon: Treatment with Hypnotic and Operant Technique," *JAMA* 225 (1973), pp. 739–40.

21. A. Norris and P. Huston, "Raynaud's Disease Studied by Hypnosis," *Dis Nerv Syst* 17 (1956), pp. 163–65.

22. D. Shapiro and R. S. Surwitt, "Learned Control of Physiological Function and Disease," in *Mind/Body Integration: Essential Readings in Biofeedback*, ed. E. Peper, S. Ancoli, and M. Quinn (New York: Plenum Press, 1979), pp. 7–46.

23. H. B. Crasilneck and J. A. Hall, *Clinical Hypnosis: Principles and Applications* (New York: Grune and Stratton, 1975), pp. 127–28.

24. W. L. LaBaw, "Autohypnosis in Haemophilia," *Haematologia* 9 (1975), pp. 103–10.

25. M. M. Schuster, "Operant Conditioning and Gastrointestinal Dysfunctions," *Hosp Prac*, September 1974, pp. 135–43.

26. B. T. Engel, P. Nikoomanesh, and M. M. Schuster, "Operant Conditioning of Rectosphincteric Responses in the Treatment of Fecal Incontinence," *New Eng J Med* 290 (1974), pp. 646–49.

27. J. D. White and D. Taylor, "Noxious Conditioning As a Treatment for Rumination," *Ment Retard* 5 (1967), pp. 30–33.

28. V. S. Lait, "A Case of Recurrent Compulsive Vomiting," *Am J Clin Hyp* 14 (1972), pp. 196–98.

29. R. Eichorn and J. Tractor, "The Effects of Hypnotically Induced Emotions upon Gastric Secretion, *Gastroent* 29 (1955), pp. 432–38.

30. S. Furman, "Intestinal Biofeedback and Functional Diarrhea: A Preliminary Report," *J Behav Ther and Exp Psychiatry* 4 (1973), pp. 317–21.

31. A. M. Freedman, H. I. Kaplan and B. J. Sadsock, "Rheumatoid Arthritis (Psychophysiological Musculoskeletal Disorder)," in *Modern Synopsis of Comprehensive Textbook of Psychiatry* (Baltimore: Williams and Wilkins, 1972), pp. 471–73.

32. P. W. Corey, "Airway Conductance and Oxygen Consumption Changes Associated with Practice of the Transcendental Meditation Technique," in *Scientific Research on the Transcendental Meditation Program*. Collected papers, vol. 1, ed. D. Orme-Johnson and J. T. Farrow (Livingstone Manor, N.Y.: Maharishi European Research University Press, 1977), pp. 94–107.

33. P. H. Knapp, "Psychotherapeutic Management of Bronchial Asthma," in *Psychosomatic Medicine: Its Clinical Applications,* ed. E. D. Wittkower and H. Warnes (Hagerstown, Md.: Harper & Row, 1977), pp. 210–19.

34. W. S. Kroger, *Clinical and Experimental Hypnosis,* 2d ed. (Philadelphia: J. B. Lippincott, 1977), p. 207.

35. H. B. Crasilneck and J. A. Hall, *Clinical Hypnosis: Principles and Applications* (New York: Grune and Stratton, 1975), p. 122.

36. A. B. Alexander, D. R. Micklich, and H. Hershkoff, "The Immediate Effects of Systematic Relaxation on Peak Expiratory Flow Rates in Children," *Psychosom Med* 34 (1972), pp. 388–94.

37. A. B. Alexander, "Systematic Relaxation and Flow Rates in Asthmatic Children: Relationship to Emotional Precipitance and Anxiety," *J Psychosom Res* 16 (1972), pp. 405–10.

38. A. D. Sirota and M. J. Mahoney, "Relaxing on Cue: The Self-Regulation of Asthma," *J Behav Therapy and Exper Psychiatry* 5 (1974), pp. 65–66.

39. J. W. Zamarra, I. Besseghini, and S. Wittenberg, "The Effects of the Transcendental Meditation Program on the Exercise Performance of Patients with Pectoris," in *Scientific Research on the Transcendental Meditation Program,* collected papers, vol. 1, ed. D. Orme-Johnson and J. T. Farrow (Livingstone Manor, N.Y.: Maharishi European Research University Press, 1977), pp. 270–78.

40. A. F. Wilson, R. Honsberger, J. T. Chin et al., "Transcendental Meditation and Asthma" *Respiration* 32 (1975), pp. 74–80.

41. J-P. Banquet, "Spectral Analysis of the EEG in Meditation," *Electroencephalography and Clinical Neurophysiology* 35 (1973), pp. 143–51.

42. J-P. Banquet and M. Sailhan, "EEG Analysis of Spontaneous and Induced States of Consciousness," in *Scientific Research on the Transcendental Meditation Program,* collected papers, vol. 1, ed. D. Orme-Johnson and J. T. Farrow (Livingstone Manor, N.Y.: Maharishi European Research University Press, 1977), pp. 165–72.

43. P. H. Levine, J. R. Hebert, C. T. Haynes et al., "EEG Coherence during the Transcendental Meditation Technique," in *Scientific Research on the Transcendental Meditation Program,* collected papers, vol. 1, ed., D. Orme-Johnson and J. T. Farrow (Livingstone Manor, N.Y.: Maharishi European Research University Press, 1977), pp. 187–207.

44. B. B. Raginsky, "Hypnosis in Internal Medicine and General Practice," in *Hypnosis in Modern Medicine,* 3d ed., ed. J. M. Schneck (Springfield, Ill.: Charles C. Thomas, 1963).

45. M. D. Sterman, "Neurophysiological and Clinical Effects of Sensorimotor EEG Biofeedback Training: Some Effects on Epilepsy," *Semin Psychiatry* 5 (1973), pp. 507–25.

46. L. F. Chapman, H. Goodell, and N. G. Wolff, "Changes in Tissue Vulnerability Induced during Hypnotic Suggestion," *J Psychosom Res* 4 (1959), pp. 99–105.

47. Y. Ikemi and S. A. Nakagowa, "Psychosomatic Study of Contagious Dermatitis," *J Med Sci* 13 (1962), pp. 335–50.

48. M. Dennis and M. J. Phillipus, "Hypnotic and Non-Hypnotic Suggestion and Skin Response in Atopic Patients," *Am J Clin Hyp* 7 (1965), pp. 342–45.

49. L. Fry, A. A. Mason, and R. S. B. Pearson, "Effects of Hypnosis on Allergic Skin Responses in Asthma and Hayfever," *Brit Med J* 1 (1964), pp. 1145–48.

50. H. B. Crasilneck and J. A. Hall, *Clinical Hypnosis: Principles and Applications* (New York: Grune and Stratton, 1975), p. 268.

51. D. M. Ewin, "Condyloma Acuminatum: Successful Treatment of Four Cases by Hypnosis," *Am J Clin Hyp* 17 (1974), pp. 73–78.

52. Ibid., pp. 268–71.

Chapter 13

The uses of imagery in surgery and with surgical patients

As we mentioned in Chapter 12, research in imagery and imagery processes has been applied in the fields of psychology and the development of enlightened consciousness, but there is a distinct lack of scientific investigation into the uses of imagery in medical practice. However, by extrapolating some of the medical research on hypnosis, which we know has a distinct relationship with imagery, and by drawing on general knowledge about imagery, we can reach certain conclusions as to the usefulness of these techniques in surgical situations.

We will not include many specific verbalizations of suggestions and images in this chapter. Expressions of that sort will be easily developed if the practitioner has a firm grounding in the principles and uses of imagery as mentioned in the earlier chapters.

Preparation of the patient

Most surgeons agree that emotional and psychological preparation of the surgical patient is important in determining the outcome of the procedure. Although no studies have compared the importance of psychological preparation to physiologic preparation of the patient, we need only look at the power of the placebo response to know the importance of properly preparing the patient. The patient who is confident of the necessity for the procedure and the expected outcome and who has confidence in the person or persons associated with the performance of the procedure is likely to have a more successful outcome. The explanation of the procedure and its inherent benefits and risks is a method of communication and as such depends upon the principles of suggestion and imagery, both the images of the person explaining (surgeon, anesthesiologist, and so forth) and the images developed in response by the patient. These images can lead to successful outcomes (placebo) or can hinder the success of the procedure (nocebo). The medical practitioner who is well versed in the principles discussed in Section 1 of this text will be in a better position to benefit his or her patient. Unfortunately, training in these principles is very rare in modern medical practice. In an esteemed textbook of surgery, less than one page is devoted to the psychological preparation of the patient, imagery is not even hinted at.[1]

Before an operation, there are subtle benefits which are produced by the positive placebo effect of the interaction between the professional and the patient and which can be enhanced by relaxation and imagery. The apprehension that is naturally associated with impending surgical procedures can be significantly alleviated by the practice of simple relaxation techniques with a therapist or a prerecorded tape or by the patient alone. Thus the influence of anxiety on the outcome of a procedure is minimized, and the relative ease with which the patient can experience the procedure may be enhanced.

Behavioral therapists have taught us the value of techniques such as rehearsal in alleviating the anxiety-producing effects of phobias. We believe rehearsal methods can be applied directly to situations that produce anxiety but would not necessarily fit the psychological classification of phobias. This application certainly has been demonstrated for such phenomena as enhancement of physical performance and creativity (see Chapter 8 and 9) and can be applied to the alleviation of anxiety and its detrimental sequelae with respect to surgery.

While in a relaxed state, the patient can be guided by the appropriate health professional (physician, anesthesiologist, or nurse) through a rehearsal of the procedure from the preoperative phase, through the operative phase, and into the recovery phase. The appropriate use of imagery in all five senses can be invoked and can be performed in sequence. The patient's reaction to each step can be assessed in the sequence by observing the patient for covert and overt signs of anxiety. The next step in the sequence should be accessed only when the previous step can be experienced without anxiety. If anxiety does develop, it can be minimized by having the person become an observer of the event rather than by experiencing it as a participant. The observation may be as remote as necessary. One-stage removal is watching the procedure being performed; two-stage removal is watching the procedure on television or on a movie screen.

The preparation should be carried to its conclusion; that is, not only through successful performance of the operation but also through healing and recovery. This is readily accomplished by end-result imagery of the individual doing whatever he or she reasonably could be expected to do. This may include the preoperative level of employment and physical activity, or, if appropriate, an even higher level of performance than was possible preoperatively. As is generally true when imagery is used, imagery in this manner is limited only by the imagination of the therapist.

Informed consent

Ethically and legally, the patient has a right to know the potential benefits and risks of any surgical procedure. However, what comprises reasonable information is quite variable. Recently, it seems that the trend is surgical specialties, somewhat promoted by larger awards in malpractice cases, has led to a disclosure of every possible risk and complication contained in the literature. We feel that the imagery evoked by such explanations will lead to a significant worsening of the outcome by means of the negative placebo effect. A patient certainly has the right to know, and this right can be protected by reasonable descriptions. A preoperative discussion of the risks of a procedure may also contain positive suggestions of the beneficial outcomes.

We have always hoped that a study would be performed which could scientifically demonstrate the effect of the reasonable, informed consent on placebo response. As far as we know, such a study has not been performed. This study would be relatively easy and would be designed, in a double-blind fashion, to compare the results of similar surgical procedures, the only major variable being the difference in obtaining informed consent. In one group, the consent would be obtained in the usual way, as stated above, and the other group would have largely positive suggestions implanted at the time of informed consent. The study could be designed so that both groups would receive information in keeping with the highest legal and ethical standards and still have distinct differences to yield valid conclusions. Until this happens, we believe that practitioners can be selective in their preoperative information sessions lest they be a tool in leading to a negative outcome.

Preparation of the surgeon

In the early chapters of this text we commented that the principles contained herein were not solely for use with others but were extremely important to the life and efficiency of performance of the individual practitioner. We believe that the use of altered states of consciousness and imagery can assist in the development of surgical skills. Many of the comments on creativity (Chapter 9) and musculoskeletal proficiency (Chapter 8) are directly applicable to the training of a surgeon. Certainly, the relaxation and positive mind-set can be important in the acquisition and performance of surgical skills. Additionally, the ability to image primarily visually and kinesthetically will aid in the learning of surgical procedures, just as these methods allow one to become more proficient in any motor skill. Many surgeons reading this may find themselves remembering times during their internship and residency training when at night they would just lie in a relaxed state and mentally image a new surgical procedure that they had learned or one that they were about to perform the following day. Many will realize the importance of this image rehearsal in the performance of the actual procedure.

Anesthesia

The use of ASC and imagery is not only a reliable method of analgesia for minor procedures, but is also of value for major procedures. The literature supporting this is largely limited to hypnosis, which is sufficiently analogous to be used in support of imagery.

James Esdaile, prior to 1850, performed hundreds of surgical procedures using only hypnoanesthesia. At that time, no chemical anesthesia was available, and the mortality rate of operations was about 40 percent, whereas Esdaile's mortality rate was less than 5 percent.[2] The literature is replete with the successful use of ASC such as hypnosis in surgical procedures, only a selected few of which are listed in the references.[3,4,5,6] Chemical anesthesia and analgesia are relatively safe and extremely effective. We are in no way advocating the use of ASC and imagery as a substitute for chemical anesthesia, since, for most purposes, ASC and imagery are more applicable in preoperative and postoperative care of the patient. However, for minor procedures, nonchemical analgesia of this type may be all that is necessary and, in certain selected cases, can be used for even major procedures. This techniques are by no means all-or-none phenomena, and they may be combined with chemical anesthesia in order to produce beneficial effects.

If the amount of chemical anesthetic and preoperative and postoperative medication are decreased, many surgical complications such as nausea and vomiting can be reduced. Additionally, breathing and coughing can be more readily regulated, thereby decreasing postoperative pulmonary complications. Communication can be more readily established with the patient during the procedure rather than with the impersonality of drug-induced anesthesia. Certainly, suggestions given during surgery may be of benefit even with patients under chemical anesthesia. Pearson demonstrated that patients receiving suggestions while "unconscious" had a hospitalization stay of 2.4 days less than the control group.[7] Indeed, this ability to perceive certain sensory phenomena while unconscious has been helpful in critical care situations (see Chapter 6). Other references testify to the fact that patients undergoing chemical anesthesia can remember the events of the surgery, events that can be used creatively as well as detrimentally.[8,9,10,11,12,13]

Unfortunately, in the chapter on anesthesia in a major surgical textbook, no mention is given to other than chemical anesthesia.[14] There are, however, certain anesthesiology training programs that are incorporating imagery techniques.[15]

Although most considerations for the anesthetic uses of ASC and imagery involve a therapist and a subject, this is by no means necessary. Of interest is a case report in the use of self-hypnosis by a dentist during a cholecystectomy. The dentist, was well trained in heterohypnosis.[16] It is interesting that, even with all of the rehearsal, the events at surgery were completely unexpected. Imagery of a rather spontaneous nature was utilized for the successful outcome. Said Rausch: "I can mentally direct the flowing sensation to any area and achieve complete control, and still be totally aware of every step of the operation. I would simply allow sensations caused by the surgery to rise to the surface and cancel them by mentally directing this apparent flowing force to the area in question. It was like establishing an equilibrium or balance in a disrupted kind of energy field."[16] The image of the energy field is quite in keeping with numerous reports in the Oriental mystical traditions of the past several thousand years. In his report, Rausch mentioned several significant points. One of his considerations concerned the limitations of the experimental approach in ascertaining the effectiveness of these methods in anesthesia and in pain control in general. "The experimental approach . . . does not and cannot accurately measure such factors as

need, expectancy and motivation. The urgency and quality of pain in
clinical situations varies greatly from experimentally produced pain in the
laboratory."[16]

Examinations and minor surgical procedures

We believe that there are many minor surgical procedures, as well as
other medical procedures, for which the use of ASC and imagery, either
in whole or as an adjunct to chemical methods, are of extreme importance. In these situations, it is important to remember that the motivation
of an individual is of extreme importance in his or her response. For this
reason, we feel the techniques are even more influential in traditional
medical and surgical situations than in psychological situations, since in
the latter, there are many hidden forces at work preventing alleviation of
the problem.

Following is a list of situations and procedures in which ASC and
imagery have been used, either by us or by others, as described in the
literature. The list is by no means all-inclusive.

1. Radiological procedures
   a. Radiation therapy.
   b. Arteriography, venography, cardiac catherization.
   c. Myelography.
   d. Pneumoencephalography.
   e. Procedures requiring needle use, such as IVPs.
2. Endoscopic
   a. Gastrointestinal—endoscopy, colonoscopy, sigmoidoscopy, lap-
      aroscopy.
   b. Urological.
   c. Arthroscopy.
   d. Bronchoscopy.
3. Other surgical and diagnostic uses
   a. Repair of lacerations.
   b. Fractures and dislocations.
   c. Esophageal dilitation.
   d. Urethral dilitation.
   e. Examination of patient with trauma.
   f. Minor plastic surgery procedures.
   g. Diagnostic biopsies, such as bone marrow, renal, liver, breast.
   h. Lumbar punctures.
   i. Insertion of arterial and venous catheters.
   j. Urethral catheterization.
   k. Tracheostomy.
   l. Insertion of chest tubes.

The use of ASC and imagery in these procedures does not require complex inductions and imaging. As an example of the usefulness of these methods for minor procedures and the ease with which they can be accomplished, we would like to cite the following case history.

The patient is a 64-year-old female with a long history of chronic gastroesophageal reflux and esophageal stricture requiring dilation. She has required this procedure an average of once every three months for the past four years. She would be guided through a very short relaxation involving concentration on her breathing and then utilizing all her senses, starting with the visual mode because she is highly visual. She would be directed to dissociate by mentally traveling to a scene that was very pleasant and comfortable. Previous questioning determined that this place was Las Vegas. Prior to the dilation, she would image herself in a large casino by the dollar slot machine. She would drop the dollar into the slot machine, hear it register, and hold the arm, ready to pull. When the doctor was ready to do the dilation, she would pull the lever and watch the dials spin around and then stop on the winning jackpot. She would then see lights flash, hear the sound of the coins dropping from the machine, and experience exuberance as she watched and felt the people gather around her. The time required to produce this effect has been decreased to only a few seconds: She is simply asked to close her eyes and imagine that she is in Las Vegas.

There is a corollary to this story that is worth mentioning. After approximately a year of winning these imaginary jackpots she actually went to Las Vegas and, with her first dollar, won the large jackpot. We are not suggesting that the mental practice of such an image will make one an instant millionaire, but the effectiveness of these methods in minor surgery procedures is quite apparent.

The induction of ASC in these situations can be quite brief, involving simple relaxation or focusing on one's respiratory pattern, for example. An image of significance to the individual may then be suggested. If the procedure involves a considerable period of time, the image can be reinforced either by monologue by the operator or by dialogue between the operator and the client. Specific analgesic images can be used, as outlined in Chapter 5 and 7.

More specifically, we suggest several images from Kroger and Fezler's textbook.[17] Image 4 can be utilized for the development of analgesia. Images 6 and 7, which they call Space Image and Form Image, can be utilized for time distortion and detachment, both of which are helpful during surgical procedures. They have used Image 8, Jungle Image, to elicit dissociation, which, in our opinion, is the most helpful phenomenon during minor surgical procedures. Time condensation, the subjective shortening of objective time, is accomplished by scenes they call Clock Scene (Number 11) and Bluebird Scene (Number 12).

Another image for time distortion appears here through the courtesy of Masters and Houston:[18]

> Now you are about to have an experience that will involve you in many sensory, emotional, and symbolic changes, and re-orientations in time and space as you experience the internal rhythms and cycles of nature on the planet Earth, knowing it all as it happens spontaneously to and with your mind-body system.
>
> Your mind-body, when I tell you to begin, is going to experience the seasons as they are happening within you, so that you will feel the coming and passing of the seasons as an objective occurrence, but also in the deeper and mythic meanings of this progression. These meanings will be personal for you but they will also be larger than that, and universal.
>
> Go deeper now, and be completely attentive, and when you are told to begin you will experience, first of all the springtime. New life growing and coming to be. And in the summer, the heat and the ripening, the sultry sensuousness of the summer.
>
> And in the fall, the autumn, the richness, the lightness after the heavy heat of summer, the Christmas, the differences in vitality and growth.
>
> After that, the winter, the maturity, the knowing, the ending, the cold and the dying, knowing your own dying.
>
> And after that, finally, once again spring.
>
> And, with the spring, rebirth, joyous ecstacy, hope in the sense that all life is renewing, feelings of youth and a sense of surging, certainty that life continues, freshness recurring, feeling it keenly in your body, an exhilaration of highest intensity. You will know all of this, and more, and you will know it fully.
>
> In just a moment I will tell you to begin, and you will have about five minutes of clock time, experientially all of the time you could possibly need to experience most completely what you have been told that you will experience, experiencing it in your unique way, as your own self, your own person contributes the details.
>
> Now you will begin, starting with the spring and beginning now!

Pain control

Much of what we have discussed in the anesthesia section above also has applications in control of pain, preoperatively and postoperatively. (For a more complete discourse on pain management by ASC and imagery, refer to Chapter 7.)

Postoperative care

Several studies have suggested that ASC and suggestions can be effective in reducing the postoperative hospital stay,[7] shortening postoperative rehabilitation,[19] and leading to a generally favorable postoperative convalescence.[20]

We feel that these methods are also useful in preventing and treating postoperative pain. Additionally, postoperative nausea is a very common phenomenon that we believe can be minimized by these methods. In those surgical patients in whom there is a great deal of negative metabolic deficit, the methods of ASC and imagery can be utilized to stimulate the appetite. This is particularly effective in patients with burns.[21] Learning these procedures can effectively help patients overcome the problem of insomnia, which is seen frequently in postsurgical patients as well as in hospitalized patients in general.

Another frequent problem in the postoperative patient is urinary retention, and several studies have demonstrated that ASC (in the form of hypnosis) can be useful in this problem.[22,23,24] Pulmonary infection is a quite common postoperative problem and can be minimized by these procedures by decreasing pain, increasing the effectiveness of respiration, and increasing ambulation.

Wound healing

"The response of living tissues to injury forms the foundation of all surgical practice. Indeed, from a biological viewpoint, tissue injury and its sequelae participate in the majority of general medical problems."[25] The current feeling is that individuals tend to heal wounds themselves and the best that we can do is to remove all impediments to wound healing as much as possible to stop interfering with this natural process.[25] Wound healing depends on the complex interaction of multiple systems and is beyond the scope of this discussion. However, we believe that the direction of this process, as with all processes in the body, is directly under the control of the central nervous system. There is evidence that mental processes can accelerate the process of wound healing.[26,27] Unfortunately, no good double-blind studies have been performed to substantiate this hypothesis. Personal experience and case reports, however, should at least lead us to consider these techniques for all postoperative patients, and especially for those in whom there exist severe detriments to normal wound healing.

Two of the patients that we have had experience with are a husband and wife, both paraplegic and both in their late '20s. They had severe decubitus ulcers, and on one occasion, the ulcers were deep enough to penetrate into the periosteum, causing an osteomyelitis. Long-term therapy in several rehabilitation centers failed to lead to wound healing, and in fact, several attempts at skin grafting were unsuccessful. With the addition of ASC and imagery, the wounds healed remarkably, such that in one month the healing was 75 percent complete. We feel that enough anecdotal evidence exists to warrant further studies of these methods as accelerators of wound healing.

Specific wound-healing imagery can be instituted after ASC have been taught to the patient and after the patient has practiced general imagery. Again, the imagery is limited only by the imagination of the therapist and subject. An example of specific imagery for wound healing has been adapted from the writings of Jack Schwarz, an individual who was capable of demonstrating to highly critical groups amazing power of the mind over tissue damage.[28] He has suggested going through ASC induction by means of autogenic exercises. Then the subject would visualize himself or herself in a chair, begin to merge the body feelings with the visualization, and actually become one with that visualization. The individual would then image the wounded area and slip it away from the body, subsequently enlarging the area and walking to it. The person would go inside and begin to patch the wound in any way appropriate from the inside, such as imagining that he or she was a plasterer and plastering the wound. It is important that the wound be healed from the inside outward and not just covered over. When this was completed in as intricate detail as possible, the individual would go outside and see no wound; that is, the area would be completely healed. The person would then shrink the area and put it back into place in the body and begin to feel good. This would be repeated several times a day, or at least daily, until the healing was actualized.

Bleeding

Considerable anecdotal evidence, particularly in dentistry, exists in the ability to control bleeding by means of thought processes. Unfortunately, the literature again is deficient in scientific double-blind studies. Enough evidence exists, however, to warrant the use of these procedures as an adjunct to control of bleeding, particularly preoperatively, postoperatively, and in nonsurgical situations. In one study, it was reported that bleeding was 90 percent controlled in 100 cases in which suggestions were given in the recovery room.[29] In addition to the experiences of many dentists, there are impressive reports of control of bleeding with these procedures, even in patients with hemophilia.[30,31,32]

Conclusions _____

We believe that the uses of ASC and imagery are of great value in the preparation of the patient for surgical procedures and in enhancing the response of the individual to these procedures. Additionally, ASC and imagery can be used as the sole anesthetic or in conjunction with chemical anesthesia for major procedures, or as the sole anesthetic/analgesic agent for minor examinations and surgical procedures. Postoperatively, such mental processes can decrease a patient's stay in the hospital, decrease complications, and help with wound healing.

In this chapter, we have primarily mentioned the general surgical uses of these procedures. A discussion of specific diseases and surgical procedures is unnecessary in this context. By learning the basic principles of ASC and imagery and how they can be adapted to general surgical situations, the individual will be able to apply these concepts to any specific area of expertise.

References _____

1. D. C. Sabiston, ed., *Textbook of Surgery,* 11th ed. (Philadelphia: W. B. Saunders, 1977), p. 121.

2. W. S. Kroger, *Clinical and Experimental Hypnosis,* 2d ed. (Philadelphia: J. B. Lippincott, 1977), p. 212.

3. J. Lassner, *Hypnosis and Anesthesiology: An International Symposium* (Berlin: Springer-Verlag, 1964).

4. M. M. Tinterow, "The Use of Hypnotic Anesthesia for Major Surgical Procedures," *Am Surg* 26 (1960), pp. 732–37.

5. G. Wallace, "Hypnosis in Anesthesiology," *Int J Clin Exp Hyp* 7 (1959), pp. 129–37.

6. W. S. Kroger, *Clinical and Experimental Hypnosis,* 2d ed. (Philadelphia: J. B. Lippincott, 1977), p. 213.

7. R. E. Pearson, "Response to Suggestions Given under General Anesthesia," *Am J Clin Hyp* 4 (1961), pp. 106–14.

8. D. B. Cheek, "Unconscious Perception of Meaningful Sounds during Surgical Anesthesia As Revealed under Hypnosis," *Am J Clin Hyp* 1 (1959), pp. 101–13.

9. D. B. Cheek, "Further Evidence of Persistence of Hearing under Chemoanesthesia: Detailed Case Report," *Am J Clin Hyp* 7 (1964), pp. 55–59.

10. J. R. Hilgard, E. R. Hilgard, and D. M. Newman, "Sequelae to Hypnotic Induction with Special Reference to Earlier Chemical Anesthesia," *J Nerv Ment Dis* 133 (1961), pp. 461–73.

11. J. T. Brunn, "The Capacity to Hear, to Understand, to Remember Experiences during Chemoanesthesia: A Personal Experience," *Am J Clin Hyp* 6 (1963), pp. 27–30.

12. B. J. Hartman, "Parahypnosis: Unconscious Perception under Chemoanesthesia," *J Natl Med Assoc* 61 (1969), pp. 246–47.

13. H. B. Crasilneck and K. W. Erwin, "The Effects of General Anesthesia on Post-Hypnotic Suggestion," *J Clin Exp Hyp* 6 (1958), pp. 45–49.

14. D. C. Sabiston, ed., *Textbook of Surgery,* 11th ed. (Philadelphia: W. B. Saunders, 1977), pp. 200–24.

15. H. B. Crasilneck and J. A. Hall, *Clinical Hypnosis: Principles and Applications* (New York: Grune and Stratton, 1975).

16. E. Rausch, "Cholecystectomy with Self-Hypnosis," *Am J Clin Hyp* 22 (1980), pp. 124–29.

17. W. S. Kroger and W. D. Fezler, *Hypnosis and Behavior Modification: Imagery Conditioning* (Philadelphia: J. B. Lippincott, 1976).

18. R. Masters and J. Houston, *Mind Games* (New York: Dell, 1972), pp. 76–77.

19. K. B. Bonilla, W. F. Quigley, and W. F. Bowen, "Experiences with Hypnosis in Surgical Service," *Milit Med* 126 (1961), pp. 364–70.

20. E. W. Werbel, "Use of Hypnosis in Certain Surgical Problems," *Am J Clin Hyp* 7 (1964), pp. 81–83.

21. H. B. Crasilneck, J. A. Stirman, B. J. Wilson et al., "Use of Hypnosis in the Management of Patients with Burns," *JAMA,* 158 (1955), pp. 103–6.

22. R. C. Doberneck, A. S. McFee, F. J. Bonello et al., "The Prevention of Post-Operative Urinary Retention by Hypnosis," *Am J Clin Hyp* 3 (1961), pp. 235–37.

23. W. A. Day, "Use of Hypnosis in Anorectal Surgery," *Dis Colon Rectum* 7 (1964), pp. 331–35.

24. S. U. Chisson, "Hypnosis and Post-Operative Urinary Retention," *Am J Clin Hyp* 6 (1964), pp. 366–68.

25. J. W. Madden, "Wound Healing: Biological and Clinical Features," in *Textbook of Surgery,* 11th ed., ed. D. C. Sabiston (Philadelphia: W. B. Saunders, 1977), p. 271.

26. W. F. Bowers, "Hypnosis: Useful Adjunct in Surgery," *Surg Bull* 46 (1966), pp. 8–10.

27. D. B. Cheek, "Unconscious Reactions and Surgical Risk," *West J Surg Obstet Gynec* 69 (1961), pp. 325–28.

28. E. Green and A. Green, *Beyond Biofeedback* (New York: Delacorte Press, 1977).

29. V. B. Benson, "One Hundred Cases of Post-Anesthetic Suggestion in the Recovery Room," *Am J Clin Hyp* 14 (1971), pp. 9–15.

30. J. Dufour, "Tooth Extraction under Hypnosis in a Hemophiliac," *Rev Franc Odo-Tostomat* 15 (1968), pp. 955–60.

31. O. N. Lucas, "Dental Extractions in the Hemophiliac: Control of the Emotional Factors of Hypnosis," *Am J Clin Hyp* 7 (1965), pp. 301–6.

32. M. Newman, "Hypnosis and Hemophiliacs," *J Am Dent Assoc* 88 (1974), p. 273.

Chapter 14

Obstetrics, gynecology, sexual dysfunction, and pediatrics

Obstetrics

The effectiveness of altered states of consciousness such as hypnosis in labor and delivery is well documented. However, there has been significantly less use of hypnosis in the earlier stages of gestation and in the immediate postpartum period.

In Chapters 2 and 9, we commented on the role of ASC and imagery in combating the deleterious effects of the stress response. We feel that the effects of repeated initiation of the stress response in the mother is shared by the fetus. They have a common circulation, and therefore the hormonal secretory products of the stress response are shared by these two organisms. The fetus also is in direct contact with the various vibratory modes of the mother, such as respiration, heartbeat, and muscular activity, and thereby conceivably could be influenced by changes in these parameters. It is known that the soothing and comforting effect of the mother's heartbeat carries over into the immediate postpartum period and maybe for a considerably longer period of time. Changes in these vibratory qualities induced by stress could also affect the fetus in an adverse way.

By the 8th to 12th week of fetal development, brain growth begins to surpass body growth,[1] and the fetus probably begins to functionally perceive at some level, thereby recording changes related to stress in the immediate surrounding environment. Pearce feels that learning takes place in the uterus at this time and possibly even earlier. "Whenever any two like cells are in proximity," he writes, they tend to function as a unit . . . [and] there . . . almost surely [is] a form of learning taking place."[1] Although there are no hard data to substantiate this recommendation, we feel that the regular practice of ASC, by reducing the built-up effects of the stress response in the mother, will likewise lead to a more healthy physical and emotional state in the infant. Additionally, if one extrapolates the data in earlier chapters regarding the use of imagery in programming outcomes, then the use of end-result imagery such as the image of the birth of a healthy, happy baby and the picture of comfort in the mother can lead to the realization of these images.

Labor and delivery

ASC have been determined to aid in many facets of labor and delivery. Hypnosis, for example, has been shown to decrease the length of labor,[9,10] decrease the pain associated with labor and delivery,[11,12] and improve the Apgar score in infants delivered by this method.[13] Much of the work in obstetrics has been performed via hypnosis,[2,3,4,5] but other methods employing ASC have also been found to be effective, including practices such as the Lamaze method.[6,7] Studies with the use of biofeedback also have demonstrated significant benefit, when compared to controls, with respect to shortening the duration of stage-one labor, decrease in sedation requirements, decrease in analgesics, and decrease in tranquilizers. The preceding findings were in multiparous patients. In primigravida patients, there was a significant decrease in stage-one labor but less-marked differences in the amount of medication needed.[8]

We feel that these methods, when used in labor and delivery will

1. Increase the ease and comfort associated with labor and delivery.
2. Decrease the duration of labor.
3. Decrease the medication requirements of the mother.
4. Increase the vitality and respiratory effort of the newborn infant.
5. Enable bonding between the mother and the infant to take place with a greater depth.

6. Decrease the amount of work (labor) that the mother must experience.

These methods can also be successfully used for the relief of hyperemesis gravidarum seen in earlier stages of pregnancy.[14]

Methods

We believe the individual should first be taught to enter ASC by means of a relaxation method (see Chapter 5). In pregnant women, particular attention should be directed toward breathing regulation and control. The expectant mother should establish a routine of daily practice. End-result imagery can then be used with the focus of attention being the safe delivery of a healthy child and the comfort and warmth of the child-mother bonding.

Additional imagery for pain control may be utilized as outlined in Chapter 7. We believe that the sooner these processes are instituted in the pregnancy, the more effective and beneficial they will be both for the mother and the developing fetus. In most cases, the self-learning and self-use of these techniques would be sufficient. In more complicated situations, however, the use of a therapist during labor and delivery may be necessary.

We feel that if these methods were routinely employed in labor and delivery, the experience of this facet of life would be significantly improved and the quality of result likewise would demonstrate significant improvement.

Infertility

Infertility may have a strong psychophysiologic basis. The factors contributing to this problem are well delineated in textbooks of obstetrics and gynecology. Psychosomatic factors can be countered by using ASC and imagery—to alleviate stress, which is a significant factor in infertility, and to aid in understanding the psychodynamics, and thereby lead to removal of the blocks that inhibit fertilization.

After instruction in relaxation, the single most effective imagery to be utilized in treating infertility we feel, would be end-result imagery of successful pregnancy and delivery. Later, specific process images of the sperm fertilizing the ovum would be helpful. As mentioned previously, it is not necessary that the person have an exact anatomical image of a sperm or egg—only their own fantasy and imaginal creations. The commitment to practice these images on a regular basis is essential for the desired result to come to fruition.

Gynecology _____

Psychophysiologic parameters

"The female generative tract is extremely susceptible to the physiologic expression of emotions."[15] As such, many of the statements and factors discussed in Chapter 12 are directly applicable to this section. The use of ASC and imagery as an adjunct or sole treatment of gynecological problems is extremely helpful and appropriate.

Examinations and surgery

Gynecologic practice necessarily involves examination of the female pelvic organs. In many women, this is a somewhat demeaning and possibly even fearful procedure. Additionally, the practice of gynecology requires both major and minor surgical procedures. Because of this, the factors and techniques discussed in the chapter on surgery (Chapter 13) are directly applicable to the performance of gynecologic surgery and physical examinations.

Amenorrhea

Emotions may play a significant role in the disruption of the normal menstrual cycle. The endocrine system is directly under the control of the brain and, therefore, alterations in brain function can certainly affect the delicate balance of the hormonal cycle of the female.

The relaxation and antistress results of the induction of ASC alone may be enough to correct amenorrhea. End-result imagery, such as imaging a menstrual period in all pertinent sensory modalities, may be effective. These methods may also be used to investigate the psychodynamics in women failing to respond to the simple images mentioned. We believe that many cases of abnormal bleeding can be controlled by these same simple measures.

Dysmenorrhea

Dysmenorrhea, or painful menses, is a very common problem. In this disorder, we believe that there is a significant psychosomatic overlay. Part of the overlay is related to belief systems that may have been conveyed by a woman's mother or close associates who had dysmenorrhea, creating a significant chance that the woman will have the same problem. A role in dysmenorrhea may also be played by the woman's instructions, learning, and attitudes toward sex, many of which were developed at an early age.

Even simple methods of induction of ASC, such as hypnosis with direct suggestion of symptom removal, may be extremely effective. Leckie used these methods to free 80 percent of 25 patients from this distressing symptom.[16] Although direct symptom removal may be effective, qualified therapists may use these techniques with patients who have deeper psychodynamic problems to uncover the meaning of the patient's symptoms. The techniques include hypnotic ideomotor questioning, age regression, and a hidden advisor, for example.

Since dysmenorrhea is primarily a syndrome of pain, the methods mentioned in the chapter on pain (Chapter 7) are appropriate. The instructions in altering states of consciousness are helpful in that, by reducing the overall baseline level of stress, they also reduce the stress-related symptoms.

Sexual dysfunction

During the past several years, numerous techniques have been developed to aid in the therapy of sexual dysfunctions. Most of these methods involve some form of behavior modification and include systematic desensitization, sensate focus exercises, and similar approaches.[17] While this section is not intended to be a treatise in the treatment of sexual dysfunction, we believe that the experienced therapist in sexual dysfunction will recognize the value of ASC and imagery in the rehearsal and fantasy techniques that they would normally use.[17]

In a recent review of 26 reports, Brown and Chaves concluded that case studies of the use of ASC such as hypnosis are encouraging, but that controlled studies are needed.[18] They feel that these methods may be useful in the treatment of sexual dysfunction:

1. As a diagnostic tool
2. To increase self-esteem and self-confidence.
3. As an adjunct to behavioral therapeutic techniques.
4. For direct symptom removal.
5. To facilitate the resolution of neurotic conflicts.

Menopause

The symptoms of menopause are varied and have been attributed to estrogen deficiency. However, the great variability in severity and types of symptoms and the lack of correlation between symptoms and tests of estrogen adequacy lead to the belief that many of these symptoms are psychosomatic in origin. Since estrogen replacement therapy is not without significant risk, other, less risky forms of therapy should be considered.

ASC and imagery, by decreasing the stress response, can lead to alleviation of significant menopausal symptoms. Also, many of the menopausal symptoms are due to sympathetic, vascular irritability, and these factors can be stabilized by methods outlined in Chapter 9.

Breast enlargement

One of the more recent fascinating uses of imagery has been in mammary augmentation. Two studies have demonstrated the effectiveness of imagery and hypnotic states of consciousness to increase breast size. With 22 subjects over a 12-week period, Willard noted that all of them had some increase in breast size. Eighty-five percent were aware of significant increase, and 46 percent had to increase their bra size. While 28 percent of the patients reached their goal, an interesting fact is that 42 percent realized a decrease in body weight even though breast size increased.[19] Staib and Logan also demonstrated significant increased breast size, which persisted three months after the therapy was stopped. At that time, 81 percent of the gains made were retained.[20]

These methods may not be as immediately effective as surgery, but they certainly are associated with less risk. After instruction in ASC, end-result imagery can be used as well as specific process images involving mobilizing fluid and warmth to the breasts.

Contraception

At this point, data are lacking as to the use of ASC and imagery in contraception, both in the male and female. However, since many autonomic functions play a role in pregnancy and therefore in contraception, certainly the increasing autonomic control produced by the methods of ASC and imagery could aid in contraception. There are some preliminary data that have demonstrated thermal biofeedback training on the scrotum after prior training in hand thermal biofeedback led to a marked decrease in viable sperm in tested males.[21] We feel that this would be a fascinating area for further study.

Uses of imagery with children

In the course of several years of teaching these techniques to professionals, the question is invariably asked, "Are children adequate subjects for these methods?" Rather than being merely adequate subjects, children are, we believe, the best subjects because they routinely spend a great deal of time in ASC and utilize the powers of imagery as natural phenomena.

It has been stated that imagery is the means by which children experience cognitive functions.[22,23] "The Child's preoccupation with fantasy and imagination," says Von Senden, "is vital to development."[24]

Hypnosis, which has been shown to be a type of ASC and also a group of phenomena in which imagery can be particularly effective, has been demonstrated by many authors to be particularly effective in children and, in fact, may be even more effective in children than in adults.[25,26,27] According to Mears, this is probably due to the great ability of children to engage in a world of fantasy and imagination.[28] It has been felt that children become highly susceptible to suggestion at age 7, an ability that peaks between ages 8 and 11 and then fades at about age 14. However, even children below the age of seven are amenable to those methods.

Techniques and methods

The importance of imagery in childhood is hinted by the fact that hypnotic induction techniques with children are more effective if, instead of verbal suggestion, imagery is utilized. Kroger and Fezler write: "With children, images . . . serve to catch and maintain their attention, whereas other induction, such as counting and instruction for progressive relaxation, do not involve them sufficiently."[29]

Wright has outlined principles which are important to consider in the use of these methods with children.[30] The induction of ASC needs to be more interesting and should involve a method employing fantasy and imagery, such as watching a movie or a television screen or engaging in some activity of the child's liking. Praise and immediate reward are more necessary for a child. The material and session should be presented in a friendly nonthreatening way. Rather than being abstract and general, the imagery needs to be that to which the child can relate and understand. The content and tone should be consistent, without sudden changes.

It is important to treat the child as an individual and neither talk down to nor speak over his or her head. Making a game of the situation is even more helpful and will lead to deeper rapport.

Since children frequently go in and out of ASC in their daily lives, less time should be spent in inducing ASC and more in dealing with the problem at hand. All of the basic concepts in imagery described in Chapter 4 and the techniques and principles described in Chapter 5 are applicable to this section on imagery with children. End-result imagery is effective with children, and because of their game-like quality, process images are particularly appropriate. Images that provide rather immediate rewards, such as the creation of analgesia or anesthesia or such phenomena as handwarming, are particularly effective.

Pediatric disorders

For the reader interested in pediatric disorders, we suggest the chapters on pain (Chapter 7), rehabilitation and sports (Chapter 8), wellness and learning (Chapter 9), psychotherapy (Chapter 10), habits and phobias (Chapter 11), medical and psychosomatic disorders (Chapter 12), and surgery (Chapter 13). We would particularly like to direct the reader's attention to a detailed case report in Chapter 8, to demonstrate more specifically how these methods are used with children.

Because many of the subjects that could be covered in this chapter are already outlined in previous chapters, we would like to limit our discussion here to certain problems more specific to children that are particularly amenable to therapy by the use of ASC and imagery.

Enuresis. Studies on the use of imagery methods in the therapy of enuresis have been limited to hypnosis. It has been stated that hypnosis reduces or eliminates enuresis in 80 percent of cases.[31] Before these techniques are used there should be a thorough examination and evaluation to determine if the cause is organic. Although psychological causes are usually the basis of the enuresis, a detailed investigation into the psychodynamics is necessary. We have found that using the hypnotic techniques of ideomotor questioning (asking the child in ASC by means of finger signals whether he or she really wants to have a dry bed) is helpful in assessing motivation. Having the patient commit himself or herself to a date for stopping is frequently successful. Imagery methods can be used to enable the child to awaken when sensation of bladder fullness occurs.

A positive attitude is essential. The child should not be subjected to ridicule because the bed is wet, since this only tends to worsen the problem. Rather, the emphasis could be on increasing the amount of dryness in the bed. In fact, dryness in the bed can be used as an end-result image.

Assessing a child's likes and dislikes is helpful in determining imagery for enuresis. For example, a child we treated for enuresis also had daytime incontinence. This was interfering with his ability to play soccer, an activity which, under ideomotor questioning, we discovered he truly enjoys. End-result imagery of completing a soccer game effectively and keeping dry was the single most successful image utilized.

Stuttering. Hypnosis has been demonstrated to be an effective therapy for stuttering.[32,33] We believe the antistress and antianxiety effects of ASC in and of themselves are helpful in improvement of speech patterns. Additionally, the use of imagery for rehearsal, desensitization, and successful results add to the effectiveness.

Functional megacolon. Functional megacolon is a disorder of gut motility that has a psychophysiologic basis. Since the individual has the ability to obtain conscious control over his or her internal visceral processes, the methods of ASC and imagery are directly applicable to a physiologic problem such as this. Studies have shown that these methods can be used in very young children, even as young as 3½ and possibly younger.[34]

The relaxation and antianxiety effects of ASC can help alleviate the problem. Next, end-result imagery, such as successful bowel movements and clean pants (similar to the dry bed approach to enuresis) is helpful. Process images, such as imagining the intestine as a sausage being squeezed of its contents, when practiced for a sufficient period of time, should enable the child to overcome the problem. In some cases, deep-seated emotional trauma may necessitate psychotherapy in addition to the use of these methods.

Mental retardation. Contrary to previous thought, mentally retarded children can be hypnotized,[35] and we have demonstrated that the methods of ASC and imagery are effective with such children.[36] The use of these methods as a general adjunct to the life of a mentally retarded child is effective because "by increasing motivation, [they] convince the child that he can learn more than was anticipated; thus, the child's self-concept is altered and healthier attitudes are developed."[29]

Minimal brain injury. We believe these methods, by decreasing anxiety and by increasing the attention span, creativity, and learning ability of children in general, can be an effective adjunct in the therapy of children with minimal brain injury. These children, because of their baseline irritability, require considerably more patience than do other types of patients participating in ASC and imagery techniques. The rewards for patience and perseverence, however, are substantial.

Summary

We feel that children are the subjects most apt to respond to the methods of ASC and imagery. This is partly due to the fact that children are in and out of these states a great deal of the time and also that these states serve as the basis of many cognitive operations in childhood. The health professional dealing with children in any capacity will find significant rewards for adding these methods to his or her armamentarium.

References

1. J. C. Pearce, *Magical Child* (New York: E. P. Dutton, 1977).

2. J. E. Carter, "Hypnotic Induction of Labor: A Review and Report of Cases," *Am J Clin Hyp* 5 (1963), pp. 322–25.

3. D. B. Cheek and L. M. LeCron, *Clinical Hypnotherapy* (New York: Grune and Stratton, 1968).

4. G. L. Hoffman and D. B. Kopenhauer, "Medical Hypnosis and Its Use in Obstetrics," *Am J Med Sci* 241 (1961), pp. 788–810.

5. W. S. Kroger, *Clinical and Experimental Hypnosis,* 2d ed. (Philadelphia: J. B. Lippincott, 1977), pp. 227–41.

6. P. Vellay, "Psychology of a Pregnant Woman and Painless Childbirth," *J Int Fed Gynecol Obstet* 2 (1964), pp. 16–30.

7. A. Nikolayev, "Psychoprophylactic Preparation of Pregnant Women for Childbirth and Painless Parturition in the Soviet Union," *J Int Fed Gynecol Obstet* 2 (1954), pp. 3–15.

8. A. M. Jacobson, T. P. Hackett, O. S. Sherman et al., "Raynaud Phenomenon: Treatment with Hypnotic and Operant Technique," *J Am Med Assoc* 225 (1973), pp. 739–40.

9. M. Abramson and W. T. Hero, "An Objective Evaluation of Hypnosis in Obstetrics: Preliminary Report," *Am J Obstet Gynecol* 59 (1950), pp. 1069–74.

10. A. Mellgren, "Practical Experiences with a Modified Hypnosis-Delivery," *Psychother Psychosom* 14 (1966), pp. 425–28.

11. R. V. August, "Obstetric hypnoanesthesia," *Am J Obstet Gynecol* 79 (1960), pp. 1131–38.

12. K. S. Tom, "Hypnosis in Obstetrics and Gynecology," *Obstet Gynec* 16 (1960), pp. 222–26.

13. F. Moya and S. James, "Medical Hypnosis for Obstetrics," *J Am Med Assoc* 174 (1960), pp. 80–86.

14. K. Fuchs, J. Brandes and A. Peratz, "Treatment of Hyperemises Gravidarum by Hypnosis," quoted in *Clinical Hypnosis: Principles and Applications* (New York: Grune and Stratton, 1975).

15. W. S. Kroger, *Clinical and Experimental Hypnosis,* 2d ed. (Philadelphia: J. B. Lippincott, 1977), p. 242.

16. F. H. Leckie, "Hypnotherapy and Gynecological Disorders," *Int J Clin Exp Hyp* 12 (1964), pp. 121–46.

17. W. S. Kroger and W. D. Fezler, *Hypnosis and Behavior Modification: Imagery Conditioning* (Philadelphia: J. B. Lippincott, 1976), pp. 140–49, 153–55, 165–66.

18. J. N. Brown and J. F. Chaves, "Hypnosis in the Treatment of Sexual Dysfunction," *J Sex Marital Therapy* 6 (1980), pp. 63–74.

19. R. D. Willard, "Breast Enlargement through Visual Imagery and Hypnosis," *Am J Clin Hyp* 19 (1977), pp. 195–200.

20. A. R. Staib and D. R. Logan, "Hypnotic Stimulation of Breast Growth," *Am J Clin Hyp* 19 (1977), pp. 201–8.

21. D. French, C. Leeb, and S. Fahiron, "Self-induced Scrotal Hypothermia: An Extension," *Proceed Biofeed Res Society* (abstract), 1974, p. 62.

22. H. Werner, *Comparative Psychology of Mental Development* (New York: Follett, 1948).

23. J. S. Bruner, R. R. Liver and P. M. Greenfield, *Studies in Cognitive Growth* (New York: John Wiley & Sons, 1966).

24. M. Von Senden, *Space and Sight: The Perception of Space and Shape in the Congenitally Blind Before and After Operation* (London: Methuen, 1960).

25. G. Ambrose, "Hypnosis and Treatment of Children," *Am J Clin Hyp* 11 (1968), pp. 1–5.

26. E. Hilgard, *Hypnotic Susceptibility* (New York: Harcourt Brace, 1965).

27. A. Morgan and E. Hilgard, "Age Differences in Susceptibility to Hypnosis," *Int J Clin Exp Hyp* 21 (1973), pp. 78–85.

28. A. Mears, *A System of Medical Hypnosis* (Philadelphia: W. B. Saunders, 1960).

29. W. S. Kroger and W. D. Fezler, *Hypnosis and Behavior Modification: Imagery Conditioning* (Philadelphia: J. B. Lippincott, 1976).

30. M. E. Wright, "Hypnosis and Child Therapy," *Am J Clin Hyp* 2 (1960), pp. 197–205.

31. H. B. Crasilneck and J. A. Hall, *Clinical Hypnosis: Principles and Applications* (New York: Grune and Stratton, 1975), p. 185.

32. H. McCord, "Hypnotherapy and Stuttering," *J Clin Exp Hyp* 3 (1955), pp. 210–14.

33. C. L. Rausey, "Hypnosis and Speech Pathology and Audiology," *J Speech Hear Discord* 26 (1961), pp. 258–67.

34. K. Olness, "Autohypnosis in Functional Megacolon in Children," *Am J Clin Hyp* 19 (1976), pp. 28–32.

35. H. McCord, "Hypnotizing the Mentally Retarded Child," *Brit J Med Hyp* 8 (1956–57), p. 17.

36. K. Johnson and E. R. Korn, "Hypnosis and Imagery in the Rehabilitation of a Brain-Damaged Patient," *J Ment Imagery* 4 (1980), pp. 35–39.

Chapter 15

The applications of imagery with cancer and the dying process

Since the mid 1970s, published studies and anecdotal reports from clinicians who work with people who have cancer or who have died and been revived have been increasingly indicative of personal power and choice in the determination of the quality of remaining life and, in fact, the course of progression or regression.[1,2,3,4,5,6,7,8] It has become more apparent that people have both conscious and unconscious choices in the matter of development of catastrophic disease and in the process of death, and that these choices focus on lifestyle management. Thus any therapist has a responsibility to focus on life and the quality of life, and to allow each client and family member to seek and find his or her own level of involvement. The use of altered states of consciousness and imagery circumvents many barriers, stereotyped expectations, and defenses so that the involvement becomes voluntary and compatible with the person's desires.

It is our belief that the therapist who chooses to work with people who have seemingly terminal diseases or who are dying imminently can utilize ASC and imagery quite effectively for many types of interventions at many levels. Since terminally ill people often become isolated because of fear, ignorance, resentments, and other negative feelings that may exist within the patient and/or the family, the therapist may initially use ASC to encourage continuation of interrelationships. Further work can be then directed toward controlling symptoms so that the patient can use imagery to decrease pain, increase food intake, decrease anxiety regarding procedures, decrease the ill effects of radiation, and improve general mental attitude, motivation, and relaxation. If a therapist becomes a specialist in working with terminally ill people, it may be of considerable benefit to prepare the attending staff of nurses and technicians in the use of ASC and imagery for themselves and their patients. Professionals can become more attuned to the quality of contact which the patient may require, so that in their struggle to prolong life the patient is not denied knowledge of the reality of his/her situation. The teamwork of informed, sophisticated professionals and patient can minimize de-personalization and maximize the effect of therapeutic interventions within the belief system of the patient.

It is becoming more accepted clinically that the treatment of cancer must be based in part on an understanding of the interplay between emotions and the immune system of the cancer patient. Major stressors can lead to a suppression of the immune response, which then no longer can recognize cancerous cells and stop the formation of tumor or the general condition of the cancer. Achterberg and Simonton have outlined a typical cancer patient's life history pattern, which is characterized in youth by isolation, neglect, and despair, and in adulthood by a major loss of meaning in life.[9] Goldfarb indicated that cancer patients had lost an important emotional relationship prior to the development of the neoplasm and were unable to secure any effective outlet for that psychic energy.[10] LeShan reported other characteristics: an inability to express hostile feelings, tension over the deaths of parents, and a basic emotional attitude of helplessness and hopelessness. To summarize the personality characteristics of a person with malignancy, Goldfarb listed maternal domination, immature sexual adjustment, inability to express hostility or to accept the loss of a significant other, and pre-neoplastic feelings of helplessness, hopelessness, and despair.

Meares has reported similarities between immunological reactions and allergic reactions, both of which can be influenced and modified by meditation.[11] In his work, Meares proposes that, since cancer is a state in which the immune system has gone wrong, the patient must be guided to go back to the state of affairs which was present before the system went wrong, to effect self-righting systems.[12]

Treatment of the person with cancer can also maximize the placebo response and encourage "spontaneous remission," a term which indicates a noncommitment and nonresponsibility within the person for control of health. What actually seems to occur in the reversal of cancer is an alteration in the degenerative cycle of helplessness and hopelessness, so that the person can maximize energy for self-healing. Important factors in the patient's progress or regression are the belief systems of the patient, family, and significant others, including the attending physician. Those systems can lend power to the healing process and to the positive surveillance. In the surveillance theory of cancer, the normal pysiological response of the immune system is to detect and destroy cancerous cells, but when the response is suppressed, the cancer cells multiply. Thus, in the conceptualization of treatment, the patient can be guided to image himself or herself well and to assume a stance of personal responsibility so that the mental, psychological, and physical participation in disease development and maintenance is not equated with blame.[13]

Once the cancerous or other degenerative condition brings the patient to the imminent point of dying, the therapist can apply imagery and ASC to ease the patient and family into a new stage of growth. Curent views on the dying process as proposed by Kubler-Ross[14] and Moody,[15] among others,[16,17] picture the experience of dying as follows: Death occurs, then there is a loud noise, ringing or buzzing; the person then experiences movement through a long, dark tunnel, viewing his or her body from a distance, as a spectator; there is a light that emerges and the person notes a state of emotional upheaval; the person may meet a relative long dead or a being of light who may ask for a life evaluation; the dying person then meets a barrier and must return to the living.

At present, we accept Weisman's view of an appropriate death; that is, it is relatively pain free, with minimal to nonexistent suffering and its emotional and social impoverishments are minimized.[18] The therapist can facilitate the experience of dying by integration of the patient's inner and outer roles. Each piece of information that is given to the dying person becomes substrata for images that can be directed to maximizing the appropriate death.

Guidance of a person into death is an old profession. In the *Tibetan Book of the Dead,*[19] a person is taught how to die well by preparing a state of mind that is conducive to good rebirth; i.e., to remain alert and attentive, to keep the mind clear and focused, to remain calm and lucid. The process of dying is eased by familiarization, by decreasing helplessness, by establishing answers to questions such as "Of what value am I now?,"[20] by acceptance or rejection of the reality of death, by clearing up unfinished business so as to relieve burdens.

Any therapist who begins to work with people who are dying must be clear about his or her own images of death and dying before using imagery. Such clarity assures that the therapist will recognize what imagery is appropriate and know when the client is ready to utilize imagery. Carey[21] has indicated that important to the emotional adjustment of a dying person is the ability to cope with stressors in the past and to feel a sense of having lived a meaningful life. Those adjustments can be facilitated by imagery and ASC by having the person review situations that produced stress or feelings of accomplishment in a relaxed, receptive state of mind; i.e., to give himself or herself a mental pat on the back for having survived difficulty and gained self-respect. Another transition that Carey reported is the ability to talk frankly about the meaning and consequences of the terminal illness; this viewpoint is made use of by having the patient alter his or her state of consciousness and use imagery as if spectating.

The concept of positive spectatorship is valuable also in ASC rehearsal of the death experience, such that the person can imagine the experience of ego dissolution prior to confrontation with the actual experience. The therapist can create the image of the death experience and blend in the concept of merger with a greater unity. When death images are used to prepare the patient, confusion is also alleviated because the unknown becomes known and familiar.

These same principles apply to the grieving that the family, significant others, and staff may experience once the person has received the terminal diagnosis or has actually died. Through imagery with ASC, the survivors can be guided into an internal dialogue of anticipatory grief over being "left." The imaginary dialogue can also include the person who is dying or who has died, so that the very personal, private goodbyes can be said. We emphasize the privacy of that imagery to allow for the maximum amount of honesty and, therefore, closure.

References

1. A. Meares, "Regression of Cancer after Intensive Meditation," *Med J of Australia* 2 (1976), p. 184.

2. C. Goldfarb, J. Driesen, and D. Cole, "Psychophysiologic Aspects of Malignancy," *Am J Psychiatry*, June 1967, pp. 1545-52.

3. A. Meares, "Atavistic Regression As a Factor in the Remission of Cancer," *Med J of Australia* 2 (1977), pp. 132-33.

4. B. Butler, "The Use of Hypnosis in the Care of the Cancer Patient," *Cancer* 1, no. 54, pp. 1-14.

5. O. C. Simonton and S. M. Simonton, "Belief Systems and the Management of Emotional Aspects of Malignancy," *J of Transpersonal Psychol* 7, no. 1 (1975), pp. 1975.

6. J. Achterberg, S. M. Simonton and O. C. Simonton, "Psychology of the Exceptional Cancer Patient: A Description of Patients Who Outlive Predicted Life Expectancies," in *Psychotherapy: Theory, Research and Practice,* June 1976.

7. K. R. Pelletier, *Mind as Healer, Mind as Slayer* (New York: Dell, 1977).

8. J. Achterberg, S. M. Simonton and O. C. Simonton, eds., *Stress, Psychological Factors, and Cancer* (New Medicine Press, 1976).

9. Achterberg, Simonton, and Simonton, "Psychology of the Exceptional Cancer Patient."

10. C. Goldfarb, J. Driesen, and D. Cole, "Psychophysiologic Aspects of Malignancy," *Am J Psychiatry* 123 (June 1967), p. 1546.

11. A. Meares, "Regression of Cancer after Intensive Meditation," *Med J of Australia* 2 (1976), p. 184.

12. A. Meares, "Atavistic Regression As a Factor in the Remission of Cancer," *Med J of Australia* 2 (1977), p. 132.

13. O. C. Simonton and S. M. Simonton, "Belief Systems in the Management of Emotional Aspects of Malignancy." *J of Transpersonal Psychol, 7, no. 1 (1975), p. 36.

14. E. Kubler-Ross, *On Death and Dying* (New York: Macmillan Publishing, 1969).

    _____ , *Death: The Final Stage of Growth.* (Englewood, N.J.: Prentice-Hall, 1975).

15. R. A. Moody, *Life After Life and Reflections on Life after Life* (Mockingbird Books, 1975 and 1977).

16. R. Fulton, ed., *Death and Dying: Challenge and Change* (Reading, Mass.: Addison-Wesley Publishing, 1978).

17. K. R. Pelletier, *Toward a Science of Consciousness* (New York: Dell, 1978).

18. R. Fulton, *Death and Dying*, p. 193.

19. *Tibetan Book of the Dead.*

20. E. Kubler-Ross, *Death: The Final Stage of Growth* (Englewood, N.J.: Prentice-Hall, 1975), p. 81.

21. Ibid.

Index

This book has been set VIP in 10 point Times Roman, leaded 2 points. Section numbers and titles are set in 24 point Times Roman Bold; chapter numbers and titles are set in 20 point Times Roman Bold italic. The size of the type page is 27 by 46 picas.